The Daughter *of* Auschwitz

Tova Friedman was born in 1938, just one year before the outbreak of the Second World War. She was one of thousands of Jewish children living in the Polish town of Tomaszów Mazowiecki at the time. By the war's end, only five children from Tomaszów were still alive. Tova is one of the youngest survivors of Auschwitz and a campaigner against anti-Semitism. She was the director of a non-profit social service agency for twenty-five years. She is a therapist, and lives in Highland Park in New Jersey, US.

Malcolm Brabant is an award-winning British former BBC war correspondent, who witnessed genocide in Bosnia. He is now a Foreign Correspondent for America's PBS Newshour, with several accolades to his name. He met Tova at the 75th anniversary of the liberation of Birkenau, and they became firm friends. He lives in Brighton.

The
Daughter
of
Auschwitz

Tova Friedman
and
Malcolm Brabant

QUERCUS

First published in Great Britain in 2022 by

QUERCUS

Quercus Editions Ltd
Carmelite House
50 Victoria Embankment
London EC4Y 0DZ

An Hachette UK company

A CIP catalogue record for this book is available from the British Library

HB ISBN 978 1 52942 346 4
TPB ISBN 978 1 52942 347 1
Ebook ISBN 978 1 52942 348 8

Every effort has been made to contact copyright holders. However, the publishers will be glad to rectify in future editions
any inadvertent omissions brought to their attention.

Kind permission has been granted to use the English translation of the poem 'The Little Smuggler' by Henryka Łazowertówna,
published in *Children During the Holocaust* (United States Holocaust Memorial Museum, 2011). The poem was originally written
in Polish in 1942, in an edition by Borwicz.

Plate section: p.2 (top) a Jewish man cutting the beard of another, from the United States Holocaust Memorial Museum,
courtesy of Instytut Pamięci Narodowej; (bottom left) Saint Wenceslas Church, courtesy of the Jerzy Pawlik Collection;
p.4 (top left) Tova Friedman's Aunt Helen, courtesy of Pearl Belkowitz private collection; p.7 (top right) Tova Friedman
speaking at Calvin University, courtesy of the January Series, Calvin University; p.7 (bottom) Tova Friedman at Delaware
Valley Regional High School, courtesy of Rick Epstein; p.8 (bottom left) Tova and Maier Friedman, courtesy of Lynette Seader;
(bottom right) Tova Friedman attending the 75th anniversary of the liberation of Auschwitz, courtesy of Shahar Azran.

10 9 8 7 6 5 4 3 2

Typeset by CC Book Production
Printed and bound in Great Britain by Clays Ltd, Elcograf S.p.A.

Papers used by Quercus are from well-managed forests and other responsible sources.

To my amazing parents, Reizel and Machel,
who saved us all.

And to my children and grandchildren
who will always remember.

PRAISE FOR *THE DAUGHTER OF AUSCHWITZ*

'Every so often a book arrives that demands to be read. This is such a book. It should be compulsory reading for those who know little of one of humanity's greatest crimes and the awe-inspiring bravery of those like Tova Friedman who survived to tell their story. But also for those who think of the Holocaust as ancient history. It is not. It is an eternal reminder that evil needs only ignorance to flourish. That is the true value of this remarkable book.'

John Humphrys

'Tova Friedman's vividly written and compelling story serves as proof that after suffering unimaginable cruelty and trauma, it is still possible to forge a life. This unforgettable book not only ensures we remember the horrors of the Holocaust, but can see the dangers of anti-Semitism and other forms of racism today.'

Lindsey Hilsum

'I read this book with gratitude and urgency. Gratitude for the courage Tova Friedman has shown in deciding to share her story. We are all the beneficiaries of such powerful witness. The urgency comes from the knowledge that as time marches on such vivid voices are becoming increasingly rare. Read this book, cherish the lessons. It is a book rooted in the terrible events of another time, but the truths it reveals are eternal.'   **Fergal Keane**

'An unforgettable and deeply moving story. Malcolm Brabant brilliantly evokes the world of the ghetto and of Auschwitz through the eyes of Tova Friedman, a small child who survived the brutality of the Holocaust.'   **Jeremy Bowen**

FOREWORD

On driving away from my morning with Tova, the closing lines of Shakespeare's *King Lear* came to mind:

> The oldest hath borne most; we that are young
> Shall never see so much, nor live so long.

Elie Wiesel would, I'm sure, allow us to use his phrase when we cite Tova Friedman as a heroine of truth and memory.

Sir Ben Kingsley, February 2022

PROLOGUE

My name is Tova Friedman. I'm one of the youngest survivors of the Nazi extermination camp known as Auschwitz-Birkenau. For much of my adult life, I've been speaking about the Holocaust to ensure people never forget.

I was born Tola Grossman in Gdynia, Poland, in 1938, a year before the Second World War began. After living through every stage of the Nazis' attempt to wipe out the Jewish people, I eventually moved to America, married Maier Friedman and later began calling myself Tova.

No matter how much I and the last few remaining survivors share our stories, it seems that people are forgetting. Personally, I was horrified to learn about the levels of ignorance revealed in a survey of young Americans that was commissioned by the Conference on Jewish Material Claims Against Germany and published in September 2020.

Two thirds of the people who were interviewed had no idea

how many Jews died in the Holocaust. Almost half couldn't name a single concentration camp or ghetto. Twenty-three per cent believed the Holocaust was a myth or had been exaggerated. Seventeen per cent said it was acceptable to hold Neo-Nazi views. A similar survey in Europe in 2018 showed that a third of all Europeans knew just as little or hadn't even heard of the Holocaust. It also showed that 20 per cent thought that Jewish people had too much influence in the worlds of business and finance.

Those astonishing, alarming numbers point to just one thing: anti-Semitism, or hatred of the Jews, is on the rise again in the United States and across Europe. I find it very hard to believe, after everything we endured in the ghettos and the extermination camps during the Second World War, that the insidious attitudes of the 1920s and 1930s are resurfacing. The Holocaust, the worst crime in the history of mankind, happened fewer than eighty years ago, and it's fading from memory already? That, quite frankly, is appalling.

I'm now eighty-three years old, and with this book, I am trying to immortalize what happened, to ensure that those who died are not forgotten. Nor the methods that were used to exterminate them.

Many people wonder whether the world we inhabit now is similar to Europe of the 1930s, when Nazism and Fascism were on the rise in the run-up to the Second World War. Back then, anti-Semitism was the official state policy of Adolf Hitler's Germany. It's true that no government in the world today has such a doctrine enshrined in law and supported by the population at large. Nevertheless, we all know countries where discrimination is prevalent and perhaps even tolerated.

Hatred is one of the fastest-growing phenomena today. Hate of every kind, especially towards minorities. Wherever you are in the world, I implore you, do not repeat the history to which I was subjected.

Remember, the Holocaust began fewer than twenty years after Adolf Hitler wrote *Mein Kampf*, his masterplan for eradicating the Jews. In the age of warp-speed internet, change can happen much faster than it did eighty years ago. We need to be constantly vigilant and brave enough to speak out.

On that note, just as we were putting the finishing touches to this book, President Vladimir Putin ordered Russian troops to invade neighbouring Ukraine, imperilling world peace in the process. The images were so familiar to me. Terrorized children and adults, destruction of homes and families, war crimes, millions of people displaced, hunger, bomb shelters and communal graves. And I hope that after nearly eight decades of reflection on man's inhumanity during the Holocaust, Ukraine reminds us of the importance of helping those affected by the ravages of war.

As you read on, I want you to taste and feel and smell what it was like to live as a child during the Holocaust. I want you to take a walk in my shoes and in the footsteps of my family, even though, in the worst of times, we didn't have shoes. I want you to understand the dilemmas that faced us and the impossible choices we had to make. I hope you get angry. Because if you are angry, there's a chance you'll share your outrage, and that increases the chances of preventing another genocide.

I come from a long tradition of oral history. I consider myself more of a narrator and storyteller than a writer, which is why my friend Malcolm Brabant has been helping me. He has a way with words and images.

We met in Poland in January 2020, as the world commemorated the seventy-fifth anniversary of the liberation of Auschwitz, which took place on 27 January 1945.

Malcolm has been a war reporter. He witnessed ethnic cleansing close at hand in Bosnia-Herzegovina in the 1990s. He knows the stench of genocide. He's had some narrow escapes and painful experiences that are different to mine. What we have in common is that we are both survivors.

He has delved into the Nazi occupation of Poland to try to place my childhood in the right context.

As we worked together to revive the sounds, smells and tastes of the Holocaust, I found that hidden memories came flooding back. Sometimes they kept me awake all night. Everything that happened to me and the people around me is buried somewhere deep in the recesses of my subconscious. As a practising therapist I must accept the possibility that age and time have blurred my worst memories. The human brain and body are extraordinary instruments, and they have survival mechanisms that we may never fully comprehend.

Some details of my story may not precisely align with other accounts of the Holocaust. After the war, my mother talked to me incessantly about what happened to us, to make sure I didn't forget. The conversations I recall in this book are not verbatim. The content, tone and nature, however, are an honest representation of what was said at the time. We all have different memories and versions of the truth. This is my truth.

I don't believe I suffer from survivor's guilt, which is one component of what psychiatrists call 'survivor's syndrome'. Those who experience this condition punish themselves for surviving, even though they are blameless. I don't think the 6 million Jews who died in the Holocaust would want me to feel guilty. Instead, I have chosen to embrace a new term – 'survivor's growth' – through which I actively use my experiences to build a meaningful life in honour of those who died in the Holocaust. I will remember them.

I have channelled the trauma into what I call 'undoing Hitler's plan'. He wanted to stamp out our faith by murdering our children. I have spent most of my adult life doing the opposite by ensuring my own family is steeped in our culture. My eight grandchildren are testament to our continuity.

In this memoir, I refer to this genocide as the Holocaust, however the Hebrew term for catastrophe, Shoah, is more accurate in expressing this uniquely Jewish tragedy.

Auschwitz imprinted itself in my DNA. Almost everything I have done in my post-war life, every decision I have made, has been shaped by my experiences during the Holocaust.

I am a survivor. That comes with a survivor's obligation – to represent 1.5 million Jewish children murdered by the Nazis. They cannot speak. So, above all, I must speak on their behalf.

Tova Friedman, Highland Park, New Jersey, April 2022

CHAPTER ONE

RUNNING FOR OUR LIVES

Auschwitz II, aka Birkenau extermination camp,
German-occupied Southern Poland, 25 January 1945

Age six

I didn't know what to do. None of the other children in my barrack knew what to do. The noise outside was horrifying. I had never heard anything like it before. So much shooting. Volleys and single shots. A pistol and a rifle made different sounds. I'd seen and heard both in action up close. Rifles cracked and pistols popped. The result was the same. People fell down and bled. Sometimes they cried out. Sometimes it happened too fast for them to make a sound. Like when they were popped in the back of the head or neck. Other times, they just rattled and rasped and gurgled. That was the worst. The gurgling. My ears hated it. I wanted the gurgling to stop. For them and for me.

Somewhere outside the barrack, there were cracks and pops and rata tata, rata tata tata. The fast sounds were machine guns. I'd seen them in action as well. I knew the damage they caused. And they terrified me.

Glass rattled in the window frames that ran the length of each wall, about 10 to 15 feet above my head in the eaves. Normally the glass shook from the wind. This was different. It was like a storm without lightning. What sounded like thunder rumbled in the distance. Although the wooden walls muffled the din outside, it seemed as if all the people in all the barracks were moaning or screaming at once. All the dogs in the camp were growling and barking with more malice than usual. Those dogs. Those fearsome, wicked dogs.

I could hear the German guards yelling at the tops of their voices. I despised their guttural language. I was gripped with fear whenever the Germans opened their mouths.

I never heard German spoken softly. It was always harsh, alien and, more often than not, accompanied by violence. Formed in the back of their throats, so many words burst forth, snarling and spitting and hissing. Like the high-voltage barbed-wire fence that kept us caged in and sometimes electrocuted any of us who had managed to die on their own terms, not in a manner dictated by the Nazis. Many prisoners were shot before they reached the wire.

The German voices seemed angrier than usual. Was this what the end of the world sounded like? The war was closer than it had ever been. For once, a war with soldiers fighting each other. Not the war that I had witnessed, where well-fed brutes in grey and black uniforms trampled starving women and the elderly to the ground and then shot them in the back or in the head. Where children were dispatched to gas chambers and flew out of chimneys in tiny, charred flakes.

I couldn't tell what lay behind the tension seeping through the timber-planked walls. I glanced up at the long windows. Viewed from an acute angle, through the slits of glass above, the sky seemed strange. Of course, it was gloomy because it was deep winter. But it seemed darker than it should have been. Was that smoke in the air? Were those particles dropping to the ground? They were not the usual ones. These seemed bigger. Was there fire outside? Were flames getting closer? All it would take was one spark and our barrack would be a funeral pyre. I had knots in my empty stomach. I felt more trapped than ever.

I did what I habitually did when I needed solace. I climbed onto the wall of red bricks that ran the length of the barrack. The bricks were about 2 feet above the ground. They acted as a divider between rows of three-decker bunks on either side and absorbed heat from an oven in the centre of the room. Although the fire was dying out, there was a little warmth still in the bricks. I sat on my haunches, wiggling my toes on them to extract the maximum amount of comfort.

There were so many children in my block, I couldn't count them. Forty, fifty, sixty, maybe. The oldest were nearly teenagers.

I was one of the youngest and smallest. We all had smudged, dirty faces and sunken eyes, ringed black from sleeplessness and starvation. We were mostly clad in rags that hung from our bones. Some of the children wore striped uniforms.

None of us knew what was going on. There hadn't been the morning *Appell* – roll call. The numbers on my left forearm suddenly felt itchy. For the first time since they were carved into my flesh, they had been ignored. A-27633. The identity imposed on me by the Nazis. I hadn't heard it being called out. Our routine had been broken. Something strange was definitely taking place.

We hadn't been fed and were ravenous. We should have lined up for a crust of dry bread and a bowl of lukewarm gruel containing, if we were lucky, traces of indeterminate vegetables. Hunger pangs punched us all in the gut.

How long had we been left like this? I had no means of measuring time, apart from watching daylight lifting the shadows inside the barrack and then watching them return. It couldn't be long before the sun, wherever that was, would sink beneath the level of the windows, and we'd soon be in total darkness again.

Coughing, sniffing and whimpering rippled around the bunks. Despite the arctic temperature, the block reeked of urine-soaked blankets and of faeces from overflowing bedpans. Some children were mewling or trying to suppress their tears. Crying was contagious. It made us all miserable. Once you started, you felt even sadder than usual. You began thinking about how dreadful life was and then you couldn't stop. I didn't succumb. I never cried. Although I felt like sobbing, I set my jaw and rose above it.

Mama taught me never to cry, no matter how frail or scared I felt. For someone so young, I'm proud to say, I had a strong will.

'Where has the *Blokälteste* gone?'

'I haven't seen her today.'

'I haven't seen her since yesterday.'

'She's not here. Let's go outside.'

'No, we mustn't go outside.'

'If she catches us, she'll beat us, and she'll report us to the Germans.'

The *Blokälteste* was the woman in charge, or block elder, who carried out the Germans' orders. Like us, she was Jewish. The Germans rewarded her with extra food and a space of her own. She had quite an appetite. I thought she was sturdy. But then, to a child, everyone was big. In return for carrying out the Nazis' dirty work, the block elder could stretch out and sleep in peace without someone else stealing the blanket or jabbing her in the back with their knees or elbows.

Although the block elder used fear to control us, her presence provided a sense of *Ordnung muss sein* ('There must be order'), as the Germans never tired of saying. I don't mind admitting I was afraid of the woman. But without her there was chaos. And, worst of all, no food.

Normally, all the barracks were locked and bolted. The block elder must have been in such a hurry to leave, whenever that was, that she hadn't bothered to count us or secure the door. I was tempted to sneak outside, but the noise was too scary. None of the children dared cross the threshold. It was as if a force field was restraining us. We had been conditioned to obey commands and couldn't move without them.

Suddenly, the door opened. We all jumped.

In walked a woman I didn't recognize. She looked terrible. Her features were distorted by malnutrition. Her face was little more than a skull covered in parchment-thin skin. Her eyes had retreated into their sockets. But her body was puffy. Starvation did that to a person. It made their flesh swell. Tufts of dark brown hair sprouted from beneath a piece of cloth fashioned into a scarf in a futile attempt to seal in some warmth.

The woman looked at me.

'Tola!' she exclaimed. 'There you are, my child!'

Relief swept over her face. Her taut cheek muscles relaxed, and her eyes sparkled. The voice was weak but familiar. So were her sad green eyes, as well as her faint smile. I stood up on the bricks, confused. She looked more like a scarecrow than a human being. She sounded like my mama, but was it really her?

And what was she doing in my barrack? She was supposed to be in the women's section. I had been taken away from her five months earlier in the high summer after I fell sick. I had heard her voice close by when we walked to the gas chamber and when we walked back again. But I hadn't seen her. In fact, I hadn't seen Mama's face for so long that I had forgotten what she looked like. I had become accustomed to not having a mother or father. I had forgotten that I had anybody on this earth. I thought I was all alone. But now maybe I wasn't? I was confused. The woman noticed my hesitation.

'Tola, it's me. Mama,' she said, with a bigger smile.

I was incredulous.

Is that really my mama? I wondered.

I jumped down from the bricks and ran up to her. I felt a smile spread across my face from ear to ear. It was the first real happiness I had experienced in months.

She crouched down, held my face and looked me straight in the eyes. Then she wrapped her arms around me and kissed me. I hugged her back as tightly as I could. She smelled like my mama. It truly was my beautiful mama. Prisoner A-27791. My mama.

'Listen to me, Tola. They are rounding up people to walk to Germany. All the way to Germany, hundreds of miles away,' said Mama. 'Look at me. I'm going to be shot. I'm going to die. I can't walk. Look at my feet.' She pointed downwards.

Mama wasn't wearing shoes. Her feet were swathed in rags. They looked as though they had been bandaged in a hurry. The undersides were saturated, and moisture was leeching upwards. Chafed red from the cold, Mama's calves and ankles were swollen, a sure sign of starvation. The camp was full of scarecrows and skeletons.

'Maybe you will make it. You might survive the march. But this is not a world for children. I don't want you to survive alone.

So let's try to hide. There's a chance we can survive together. And if we die, we'll die here together. Will you come with me?'

'Yes, Mama. Yes, I will,' I replied.

Ever since I was born, I had inhabited a world where being Jewish meant you were destined to die. It was perfectly normal to be asked to die. All Jewish children died. And I always did what Mama said. Mama always told me the truth. I trusted Mama. I didn't trust anyone else. Mama told me the truth because knowing the truth could save my life. That's what Mama said. And she repeated it. In the ghetto. In the labour camp. In the cattle car. And before we were separated in the concentration camp.

Although she had spoken of dying together, Mama lifted my spirits by saying we had a chance of living, if I followed her instructions. As always, she was being truthful. Other parents might have tried to hide the truth in such circumstances. Not my mama. She believed that information was power, and it could save my life.

For months I had been alone. There had been no one to protect me. I always thought I would die alone. Whatever death was. But now I had someone who cared for me. I would do whatever Mama asked. A wave of relief washed over me as I realized I was no longer alone.

Mama said nothing. She took me by the hand and led me out of the barrack block.

We were hit by the smell of burning. The sound of wood

crackling. Spitting. Was it a huge log fire? More than anything, I was desperate for any kind of warmth to unfreeze my body. But then Mama squeezed my hand and I forgot about the cold. The sky was full of smoke. The fire was close. It was loud and made me nervous. Woodsmoke mixed with other smells. Something oily. The black stuff they put on roads and roofs. And there was something else. The rotten smell of garbage being burned. Tons of it.

Mama's head jerked left and right and back again, as she looked for potential trouble. Hand in hand, we walked briskly through the snow in silence. She seemed to know where she was going. I knew I had to be as quiet as possible. Making a noise could get you killed. Mama didn't need to say anything. Her urgency transmitted itself to me. I was electrified by the adventure. My hunger pangs vanished. Mama's love made me feel safe and secure. The rags on her feet squelched with every step. I didn't register the snow seeping through my thin white lace-up shoes straight to my sockless feet. I only felt the warmth of Mama's hand and her love coursing through my very being.

I couldn't quite believe what my eyes were seeing. For the first time ever, there were no SS troops or their German stooges blocking our path. Briefly, as we crossed gaps between the buildings, I caught glimpses in the distance of soldiers in greatcoats, corralling prisoners and preparing for the march to Germany. The Nazis seemed to be cursing and screaming orders.

I was almost exactly a year older than the war. I had never known freedom. My survival depended on my ability to judge the mood of my captors. Despite their brutality, I knew that ordinarily, the Germans were terrifyingly composed. This morning they had been verging on hysteria and fired point blank at wretches who were too slow to obey.

I didn't wince in the face of murder. I had witnessed violent death for as long as I could recall. I had learned to suppress my emotions. What scared me were the German Shepherds and their savage, frothing jaws. Straining at the leashes of their handlers, those awful dogs were bigger than I was. When Mama and I had arrived at the platform and got down from the cattle car back in the summer, I had seen the dogs chasing people along the rail tracks in the direction of the chimneys and the smoke.

I never looked in the eyes of the SS, the *Schutzstaffel*, Hitler's elite military corps, which contained the Third Reich's most fanatical Nazis. I had managed to avoid their fury for more than half a year. Mama had taught me well: 'Whenever you pass a German, always look down or look away. Never catch their gaze. Never ever look them in the eye. They hate it. It makes them angry, and they'll lash out. They might even kill you.'

I saw their black riding breeches; the smart, black highly polished boots – those SS jackboots that came up to the knees. I saw their swagger sticks, the daggers hanging from their belts, their death's-head symbols and trigger fingers. I looked as far as their shoulders and their epaulettes. I might have seen an Iron Cross on a chest or around a neck. I thought this was the uniform worn by all the non-Jewish men on earth. But I never looked at their faces. I had, however, stared into the eyes of the dogs. And they stared right back. They slobbered and drooled and snarled and growled and flexed the sinews in their necks. The dogs wanted to sink their teeth into my flesh and rip me to pieces.

Mama gripped my hand and made sure we stayed close to the low wooden buildings. We were on the north-western side of the extermination camp, better known as Birkenau, which was formally part of the Auschwitz complex. On our right, we had cover from buildings that comprised the male infirmary. On our left, were row upon row of barrack blocks separating them from the camp's entrance gate – the Gate of Death – where prisoners were gathering for the exodus. As stealthily as she could, Mama shepherded me southwards. We headed towards the railway line which had brought us to Birkenau six months earlier.

Truck engines throbbed in the distance, some setting off, others idling. Commands shouted into bullhorns competed for attention. Once or twice, Mama pulled me into the lee of a building, and we crouched as low as we could get. We were desperate to be invisible. Although we were some distance from the watchtowers on the perimeter fence, I knew that if the guards spotted us, they would open fire or alert soldiers below. And if we were caught, we would be forced into the line. Surrounded by the men and their dogs. Unable to escape the march that Mama said would kill her.

Where possible, we ducked into shadows and rode our luck. The density of the barracks helped to shield us. But more than anything, we were helped by the Germans' panic. The Russians were coming. They weren't far away. The vengeful Russians. The Nazis were in such a hurry to flee that they didn't notice that prisoners A-27791 and A-27633, the girl with the white lace-up shoes, were making a break for it.

An adrenaline rush heightened my senses. My ears and nose told me almost as much as my eyes. What was missing was the stench that had hung over the camp ever since we had arrived. That sickening, lingering aroma. The sulphurous, bad-egg *shtinkt* – the stink of burning hair blended with roasting flesh that flew up the nostrils, fastening itself, limpet like, to nerve endings and memory. For once, I didn't have that dreadful nauseating taste in my mouth.

Today was much noisier than yesterday when I had been outside by myself for a few minutes. I had been intrigued by the silence from the other children's hut, two buildings down the row from ours. It was eerily quiet, and so I'd peeked inside, despite the risk of upsetting the block elder in charge. But I wasn't challenged. The building was empty. The children had simply disappeared.

As I clung to Mama's hand, I found I couldn't ignore the cold any more. I wished I had some mittens. I had seen a pair of gloves attached to a string by a girl's coat in the barrack next door. My fingers were freezing. I really needed some respite from the cold. Scavenging was the norm. It was an essential part of survival in this place. It wasn't the same as stealing. But I hadn't taken the gloves. As soon as I could speak and understand, I had been taught to be honest and kind. The girl to whom they belonged might need them if she returned; although I knew in my heart she wasn't coming back. Still, I didn't want to benefit from her death. And so, I'd left the gloves hanging there.

After ten minutes or so, we reached the building Mama had been seeking. She pulled me inside. The block was a women's infirmary, although there was precious little medical equipment to be seen. It was a staging post between life and death. Scores of beds were occupied by the dead and the dying. In their haste, the Germans had abandoned them. The room reverberated with moans and women sobbing.

Mama went from bed to bed, shaking the outlines of the blankets. Sometimes a woman twitched. Where there were signs of life, Mama moved on. I couldn't work out what she was doing, and I was too scared to ask. Mama checked every bed, putting the back of her hand on corpses.

'That one is cold,' Mama said, resuming her search.

And I finally understood what Mama was seeking. She reached beneath a blanket and touched another body. This one didn't move. But it was still warm. The woman had only just expired.

'Tola, listen to me,' said Mama. 'You have to do everything I tell you. If you don't, there's a risk you'll be killed.'

'Yes, Mama.'

'Take off your shoes and climb into bed.'

I unlaced the white lace-ups as quickly as I could. The bed was higher than the bunk I normally slept in, and I needed help to get onto the frame.

'Get under this blanket, cover yourself and lie down facing the floor. You're going to lie next to the woman and I'm going to cover you so that nothing is visible. Not your feet or your head. You must lie here very quietly. Not a word out of you. No matter what happens, no matter what you hear. Do you hear me? I will be the only person who's going to uncover you, nobody else.'

She leaned in closer.

'You must breathe towards the ground. You stay there and do not move. Do not move. You stay there until I come to get you. Do you understand?'

'All right, Mama.'

Mama's word was the law. Ignoring her could be fatal.

My bed companion must have been about twenty years old. She was not unlike hundreds of corpses I had seen. Bags of con-torted, jagged bones held together by skin. Skulls with mouths locked in silent screams. The dead woman was pretty. And definitely younger than Mama.

'Put your arms around her,' Mama commanded.

She manoeuvred my head beneath the corpse's armpit and entwined our legs. Then she pulled up the blanket, so the dead woman's head was just showing.

'I'm leaving now, Tola,' she said. 'I have to go and hide as well. But I won't be far away. I will come back and get you. No matter what you hear, do not move until I return. Under any circumstances. Do you promise?'

'Yes, Mama. I promise.'

I did exactly as Mama said. I barely moved. I wasn't afraid of the corpse. Why should I be? The pretty woman was dead and couldn't hurt me. She was a friend who might save my life. My protector. So I followed Mama's instructions, hugged the dead woman and waited.

At first the corpse was warm. I was grateful for that. Feeling returned to my feet after tramping through the snow. But slowly, slowly, the corpse became cooler. I lay there listening, taking shallow breaths and waiting. I wondered why the pretty woman had died. I presumed it was hunger.

I was extraordinarily calm. A strange kind of peace came over me. I relaxed and began to visualize a doll with a green face. Not a complete doll. Just a head. I'd seen it sticking out of the mud as we ran. I didn't know whether the head and body had become separated, or whether the body was still attached to the head beneath the mud. I'd wanted to pick the head up. But we hadn't time to stop.

The head had friendly eyes and a kind mouth. I wanted that doll's head. I didn't have any toys here in the camp. I didn't want to play. I didn't know what playing was. Life was just about surviving. But I wanted the doll's head to talk to and to keep me company. What pretty eyes she'd had.

My eyes began to feel heavy. I felt safe. Mama was nearby. The adrenaline from our adventure out in the open had subsided.

Then I heard the boots.

CHAPTER TWO

BEYOND THE TABLECLOTH

Jewish ghetto, Tomaszów Mazowiecki,
German-occupied Central Poland, 1941
Age two and three

My domain extended all the way under the kitchen table. The boundaries were defined by the ragged borders of a cheap cloth, draped over the piece of furniture that was the beating heart of life in our overcrowded home in the ghetto. Beyond the tablecloth was the world of adults – and their lopsided war between Nazi persecutors and oppressed Jews. When in residence in my personal realm, I rarely saw the grown-ups' faces – from my perspective, the outside universe only existed from the knees down. But I heard them talking, and I made it my business to work out which voice was coming from which pair of legs.

I heard snatches of conversations. And key words repeated

23

over and over again, with a mixture of fear, anger and venom. Words that stuck in my mind.

'Gestapo.'

'SS.'

'*Aktion.*'

'Rations.'

'Margarine.'

'Hitler.'

'Dropped dead in the street.'

'Starvation.'

'Palestine.'

'*Judenrat.*'

'Ghetto.'

'Kropfitsch.'

'Another one.'

'That poor child.'

'Back of the head.'

'Those poor parents.'

There was never any good news outside the tablecloth. Life was a litany of catastrophes, of people disappearing, massacres and the constant struggle to find food.

Not to mention the shooting and the screams outside the window.

When the news was particularly bad, they whispered. They tried to keep me from hearing. I knew it was really bad when there was a deep intake of breath and the sound of a hand clasped over a mouth to prevent a cry from escaping. My ears were my early-warning system. I recognized how lightly or purposefully people walked. I could tell when a new set of shoes or boots entered the apartment. Sometimes they were friendly. But when I heard heavy boots, I knew trouble was imminent.

Beneath the table was my sanctuary. There I stayed and talked to my doll.

'Are you hungry, *bubale?*' I inquired.

'I'm starving. You must be, too. But don't worry, Mama's in the kitchen and she's cooking potato-skin soup.

'Here it is. Eat it up. Be a good girl, *bubale*. Tasty, isn't it? Mmmmmm. Lovely. Come on now. Eat your soup, *bubale*. It's good for you.

'I'm sorry there's no bread today. Please don't cry.'

Occasionally, I would surface above the tablecloth and go to perch on the knee of my father, Machel, or I'd nestle in the lap of my mother, Reizel. Whenever Uncle James came to visit in the early days of the ghetto, when it was easier to move around, I sat on his knee and twiddled his bushy eyebrows. But usually I stayed under the table because I didn't have a chair. There wasn't sufficient space in the four-room apartment and there wasn't enough furniture to go around.

We weren't the only family living in flat number five, 24 Krzyżowa Street, Tomaszów Mazowiecki. Jews were forced to share cramped accommodation. In many apartments, instead of five or six people, there were maybe twenty. In others, the numbers might have been as high as sixty or seventy. One bathroom had to service maybe thirty to forty people. I had to eat and sleep under the table because there was so little space. Some people slept on the floor. My parents squeezed together in a single bed. I joined them in the middle of the night if I woke up scared.

If you were lucky, you lived together with friends or extended family. If not, you were compelled to cohabit with strangers you couldn't bear. I have no firm memory of how many people were there or who they were. The situation was so fluid that the apartment was a constant revolving door of refugees. One day a whole set of familiar faces would vanish. Their disappearance would be accompanied by urgent whispers coming from beyond the tablecloth. It didn't take long before they were replaced by others. Perhaps by even more people. The atmosphere inside the apartment would change. It was not always an improvement. I could sense it under the table.

We were stuffed like mice in there.

The Nazis created the Tomaszów Mazowiecki ghetto in December 1940. Jews were banned from the main part of Tomaszów Mazowiecki, an industrial town in Central Poland, 70 miles south-west of the capital, Warsaw. They were required to identify themselves as Jews by wearing a white armband adorned with a blue star of David. Failure to comply was punishable by death.

The Germans severed the electricity supply as one of their first strictures. Depriving us of a key component of modern life was another snip of the scissors cutting us slowly and painfully to death. There was no sewage system either. We were ordered to hang curtains or screens at windows that overlooked Aryan neighbourhoods. The sense of isolation and segregation from the outside world was reinforced with every new restriction. Not only were we no longer supposed to look at our Polish neighbours, we were also denied sunlight as we were pushed back towards the Dark Ages. The Poles were ordered to block windows that over-looked the ghetto, so they wouldn't see what was happening and inform the outside world. Mind you, significant numbers of Poles in Tomaszów were anti-Semites. Some of them might have taken pleasure from our suffering. At least the curtains denied them that.

Initially, my mother, father and I lodged with my grand-parents in Kościuszko Square, which, before the war, was a relatively smart address in the heart of the town's commercial district. At first, the ghetto had three sections and people could move between them, although they were banned from leaving the outer confines without a permit. Twelve months later, the Germans forced Jews from two of the ghetto's districts into the third much smaller section. This had a perimeter they could seal off far more easily. The sense of claustrophobia intensified. We were kicked out of our home in Kościuszko Square and were more than grateful when another family that we already knew took us in at 24 Krzyżowa Street.

During the three and a half years I lived behind the ghetto walls – if 'lived' is the right word – I rarely breathed fresh air. I spent almost all my time inside, for the simple reason that it was too dangerous to be outside. My air smelled of boiling potato skins. Not even boiled cabbage.

By 1941, more than 15,300 Jews were squeezed into the ghetto. The pre-war community was swollen by over 3,500 refugees from neighbouring *shtetls* or small towns. The ghetto was horrendously overcrowded. Conditions were unhygienic.

Apartments were breeding grounds for disease. In the latter half of that year, a typhus epidemic ravaged the ghetto. So many of the community's doctors had been murdered that any surviving medics struggled to contain the outbreak. The Germans transferred 600 Jews from Tomaszów Mazowiecki to other ghettos in nearby towns to try to reduce the spread of infection. Those people were effectively exiled from Tomaszów and warned not to come back. Thirty-three Jews defied the order, made their way back to Tomaszów and were executed.

Sometimes, when I came out from under the table, I'd look out of the window and see lines of steel-helmeted Germans marching with rifles sloping on their shoulders. Their stout knee-length boots struck the cobblestones in unison, creating a sound that radiated strength and irresistible superhuman force. The vibrations travelled up through our building and into my stomach. And then I would duck back down beneath the table-cloth.

In my child's mind, I regarded the table as my safe haven, although in reality, it was a cell. A prison within a prison. No matter our age, we were all inmates. And the walls of our prison were constantly closing in. Jews were eliminated at every stage. All the time, the Germans shoehorned more prisoners inside, squeezing every one of us, physically and psychologically, to the limits of human endurance. And beyond.

In towns across Poland and all the territories the Nazis conquered, Jews were forced into ghettos that were prisons in all but name. Ghettos were the first stage of the Nazis' masterplan to eradicate the Jewish race. The best known is the Warsaw Ghetto, a sprawling city within a city where 420,000 Jews were incarcerated and starved behind high walls and razor wire. A quarter of a million of them were rounded up in the ghetto in the summer of 1942 and gassed. The Warsaw Ghetto is synonymous with courage and resistance because of the uprising in the spring of 1943, when 700 under-equipped Jewish fighters held crack German troops at bay for almost a month. But Warsaw was not the only city where such a place existed.

I was two and a quarter when my parents and I entered the ghetto of Tomaszów Mazowiecki. We didn't have a choice. Resistance was futile. You didn't argue when guns were trained upon you by the most brutal military machine the world had ever seen.

Still, when I was nearly three and a half, I displayed my own innate spirit of resistance. It was in January of 1941, when the

Germans instigated what they called a fur *Aktion*. They ordered ghetto inhabitants to hand over fur coats so they could be sent to Germany to clothe people on their home front. It was part of a systematic effort to strip us of our valuables. Earlier, they had scoured the ghetto demanding people surrender their jewellery.

Our apartment was raided by thugs in uniform. Mama didn't possess a fur. But I did. It was a beautiful white fur coat with a hood and white neck ties with fur balls at the end. I was so proud of that coat. It was my favourite possession; and it was so warm. Although I hardly ever got to wear it because I rarely went outside, in a time of utter deprivation, it made me feel special.

The instant one of the German soldiers went to the closet and took the coat off a peg, I became incandescent with rage. I flew at him. I started punching and kicking him. He was a big man, a giant compared to me. But no one was going to steal my prized coat. I had no fear. I just wanted to fight. Mama was shocked. She tried to pull me away. But I wasn't listening to her. I tried to bite the soldier's knees and lunged at him. He kicked me away with his heavy boots and then walked away with my most treasured possession. I could have been killed. People were shot for much less.

I recognize that little girl in me today. She was fearless. What other child would do such a thing? I like to think I am still the same feisty creature. The memory of that coat stayed with me. I bought one almost exactly like it for my granddaughter decades later.

The episode with the coat demonstrates clearly that when a

child reaches the age of three, they are blossoming into a sentient human being, capable of feeling and understanding sensations, and of processing information as their cognitive abilities begin to fly, although most lack the vocabulary to articulate what they are seeing. That period should be a time of wonder at the simple joys the world has to offer. Marvelling at the aerial dance of a butterfly. Recognizing the love of a mother and father and reciprocating. Seeing smiling faces, feeling safe and secure. Falling asleep with a full stomach in a warm bed. Waking up the next morning, excited about exploring another day ripe with promise.

Within the ghetto of Tomaszów Mazowiecki, the only certainty was my parents' unconditional love. And I knew that I loved them back with all my heart. Beyond them, however, there was nothing but the abyss. Colour drained from our ever-withering universe. We inhabited a monochrome world that was always in the shadows. We were mentally shackled together in a collective state of depression. Nothing ever offered a shaft of light or hope. There was no cure. The cavalry wasn't ever going to ride in to rescue us. The only release was death.

Every new day brought a different form of terror. I remember soldiers coming for my widowed maternal grandmother Tema and her brother, whose name I don't recall. They ordered them to go downstairs, and they shot them in the street. Two dead Jews out of 6 million. Their ages were a death sentence. The

Nazis had no use for old people. Anybody over the age of fifty was regarded as ancient by the Germans. I never saw a person with white hair until I came to America. To the Nazis, older people were useless as *Zwangsarbeiter* (slave labourers) and an unnecessary burden. There was nothing extraordinary about the summary executions of Tema and her brother. Their killers displayed not a flicker of hesitation. The Germans snuffed out my relatives' lives, and those of others, as casually as a pest controller might exterminate rodents. Because that is what we were to them. Vermin. I can't begin to tell you how much it hurts me to use that word.

What I still find hard to comprehend all these years later is the absence of conscience and the casual manner in which the murders of harmless civilians were committed, as if this was just another bodily function.

My father put his hand over my eyes and dragged me away from the window. His first instinct was to protect my innocence – because once seen, murders like that could never be unseen and would be forever imprinted in the mind.

I remember the sound of the guns that cut them down, along with the peal of shell casings cascading onto the sidewalk. The screams I heard were so visceral that if I conjure up the memory, I find that they are still ringing in my ears. A chorus of wails seemed to travel all the way from the centre of the earth up to the heavens.

But I didn't hear Mama cry. She manifested shock in a manner unlike other people. She didn't allow herself that initial explosion of grief. When my father took his hand from my eyes, I saw her. Mama was silent. It was as if all the air had been punched out of her lungs. She was incapable of making a sound. She took all the tears and torment, plunged them deep inside her and never let them out.

A little piece of my mama was murdered that day. With every new corpse, the Germans were killing us all from the inside. I still feel the mourning cloud that descended on our household and the overwhelming sense of impotence. We, as a people, could do nothing to stop these murders, nor the next. There was no retribution. No eye for an eye. They were killing us with impunity.

I lived with the constant fear that my parents would be butchered in front of my very eyes, or that they would disappear and never come back. From the moment I awoke, I was scared that it would be my turn to be killed next. I went to sleep fretting that I wouldn't wake up in the morning.

All the while, I was crippled by hunger. When the ghetto was established in 1940, the Germans introduced food rationing. We were supposed to live on just six pounds of bread and seven ounces of sugar per person per month. For most adults, that might have lasted for a week, no more. At first, the Germans prohibited us from getting meat from the butchers. Then they restricted access to bread. Bakers' opening hours were limited. Mothers got out of bed in the middle of the night to queue for a loaf. They risked being shot if caught in the streets before curfew was lifted. Sometimes they would come back empty handed. Sometimes they didn't come back at all. As the months passed, food supplies diminished. A soup kitchen was set up to keep the neediest from starving to death.

I remember having difficulty walking. I was a slow developer, probably because my body was deprived of vitamins at a time when it needed to be nurtured, to grow, to be healthy. I didn't really walk well until the age of four because of malnutrition. Being stuck under the table for such long periods also probably hindered the development of my bones and muscles. I must have been desperate for calcium, essential for bone density and strength. When I got out from under the table, I would walk around the apartment licking the walls. I must have been intuitively trying to extract calcium from the chalk in the paint. Mama tried to curb this habit.

'You've been licking the walls,' she said.

'No, I haven't,' I replied.

'Yes, you have. Don't lie to me. I can see the tongue marks. The wall is wet.'

She would smack me. It didn't really hurt. And at the first opportunity, as soon as her back was turned or she left the room, I'd start licking again.

We were subjected to an ever-worsening famine. The most

desperate parents sent their children beyond the ghetto perimeters to forage for food, despite the threat of a death sentence the Nazis imposed without even the most rudimentary trial.

> Through walls, through holes, through sentry points,
> Through wires, through rubble, through fences:
> Hungry, daring, stubborn
> I flee, dart like a cat.
> At noon, at night, in dawning hours,
> In blizzards, in the heat,
> A hundred times I risk my life,
> I risk my childish neck.

No one described the children's courage better than the Polish–Jewish poet Henryka Łazowertówna in this historic work, 'The Little Smuggler', written in 1942 in the Warsaw Ghetto where she lived and died. The poem is specifically about child smugglers in Warsaw, but it honours every one of them in every ghetto in every town occupied by the Nazis, including Tomaszów Mazowiecki.

> Under my arm a burlap sack,
> On my back a tattered rag;
> Running on my swift young legs
> With fear ever in my heart.
> Yet everything must be suffered;
> And all must be endured,

So that tomorrow you can all
Eat your fill of bread.

Some parents may have told their children to ask for help from sympathetic former Polish neighbours. Others gave them money or valuables to barter with Poles outside the wire. Some of these young couriers also carried letters, to try to get word to the outside world about the nature of our suffering. Their size meant there was less chance of them being spotted. But if they were caught, that household had one less mouth to feed.

Through walls, through holes, through brickwork,
At night, at dawn, at day,
Hungry, daring, cunning,
Quiet as a shadow I move.

And if the hand of sudden fate
Seizes me at some point in this game,
It's only the common snare of life.
Mama, don't wait for me.
I won't return to you,
Your far-off voice won't reach.

An Austrian called Johann Kropfitsch used to wait near a secret entrance to the ghetto and shoot children as they returned with their bounty. Their bodies were taken to the Jewish cemetery and unceremoniously buried in unmarked graves. All their parents heard was a distant shot in the night. And their child vanished.

At thirty-nine years old, Kropfitsch, was old enough to avoid military service, but young enough to be a Nazi policeman. He developed a passion for his nocturnal 'hunting' expeditions. Kropfitsch prided himself on being some kind of gamekeeper. As if children were badgers or foxes that needed to be culled. What type of sick individual does such a thing? Despite a lifetime of exposure to all manner of human frailties, I struggle to understand how such depravity is possible. Kropfitsch was a serial killer responsible for the slaughter of scores of children. A photograph of him in his Nazi uniform reveals a man with cold, psychopathic eyes. After the war he was hanged as a war criminal. What a pity he only died once. He deserved to be killed a thousand times over.

In the ghetto there were no smiling faces. Especially among the men in field grey with knives in their belts and a gun always close at hand. On the rare occasions I ventured over the threshold of the ghetto with my parents, these men looked at me as if they wanted to kill me. Others, the ones in the sharp black uniforms, with the sinister peaked caps and the red band on their arms with the white circle and swastika in the middle, wanted to kill me even more. Me. An innocent child. All because I was born Jewish. Before the war, Jews comprised about 30 per cent of Tomaszów Mazowiecki's population. But out of the 13,000

Jews resident in 1939, just 200 were still breathing at the end of the war in 1945. Only five were children. It is extraordinary that I was among them.

Reizel gave birth to me almost exactly a year before war broke out. At the time, she and Machel were living in Gdynia, a city close to Danzig, a beautiful, international free port on the Baltic Sea coast in Northern Poland. Danzig was predominantly populated by people with an ethnic German background. You'll know the city today by its Polish name, Gdansk. Its shipyards were the birthplace of the Solidarity trades-union movement led by Lech Wałęsa in the 1980s and whose *Solidarność* anti-Communist rebellion led, ultimately, to the collapse of the Soviet bloc.

My father first went there in 1932 as a delegate to a conference on Zionism. He was just twenty-two years old. Representing his hometown of Tomaszów Mazowiecki was a great honour. I have a photograph of him taken just before he headed off to the conference. In it, he has a full head of wavy hair and he's very much a confident young man about town. His face is a combination of innocence, youthful optimism and determination. His soft eyes betray a sensitive, artistic personality. How soon those eyes would become accustomed to horror.

Papa was a highly intelligent man and an idealist. Along with other Zionists, he believed that the diaspora — Jewish people scattered around the world — should move to the land of their ancestors, then called Palestine. He was a follower of Theodor Herzl, a charismatic Austrian Jewish journalist, playwright and lawyer, considered the founder of modern Zionism and author of a trailblazing manifesto called *The Jewish State.*

'We want to lay the foundation stone,' Herzl declared, 'for the house which will become the refuge of the Jewish nation.'

At the turn of the twentieth century, Herzl believed that anti-Semitism in Europe was so virulent that it was impossible for Jewish people to live alongside or assimilate with the Gentiles of other nations. He argued that the only solution for Jews was to create their own state and emigrate from Europe.

'If you will it, it is no dream,' Herzl wrote.

By the 1930s, the Zionists' goal became more urgent. Hitler's rise, accompanied by surging anti-Semitism across Europe, accelerated the need for a Jewish haven. But the Zionists failed to convince the world's major powers to permit the establishment of a Jewish state. They were thwarted by concerns about a backlash from Arab nationalists, who opposed Jewish immigration. Great Britain was the principal impediment to the dream of a Jewish state. Following the break-up of the Ottoman Empire at the end of the First World War, Britain was given an international mandate to govern Palestine. British opposition to Jewish immigration intensified as the Second World War approached.

British self-interest outweighed concern for endangered European Jews. The Suez Canal, sandwiched between Palestine and Egypt, was a key artery for ships carrying British imported goods. Britain didn't want any trouble on the Palestinian flank of the canal. And the last thing it needed was to intervene in possible clashes between Zionists and Arabs.

In 1939, the British government laid down a new policy which limited Jewish migration to 75,000 people over five years. That amounted to 15,000 a year. Thereafter, any further immigrants would have to be approved by the Arab majority.

With millions of European Jews at risk from the Nazis, the Zionist movement was outraged at British intransigence. My father was among those who were dismayed and angry at what was regarded as a betrayal of the Jewish people.

But back in 1932, when his political principles were developing, my father was full of the optimism of youth. As a delegate to the Zionist conference, Papa was intoxicated both by the debate about Israel and by Danzig. It was springtime and the city was in full bloom.

'I felt that I was at the centre of a bouquet of beautiful flowers,' he once told me. 'Even the air was perfumed.'

This was his first adventure away from provincial Tomaszów Mazowiecki, and he was entranced by Danzig's relative grandeur, with its wide, sweeping boulevards, as well as its quaint harbour, lined with brightly painted fifteenth-century timber buildings.

The desire to spread his wings was energized by promenades next to the Baltic Sea, past fine, sandy beaches, and observing the busy traffic of pleasure boats and cargo vessels heading to all corners of the world. He was also drawn to Danzig by the

Great Synagogue, with its vaulted ceilings and large dome. It was one of the most distinctive buildings in the city, but while the architecture may have been aesthetically pleasing, it was the spiritual power within that fostered his sense of belonging.

When the conference ended, Papa was reluctant to leave Danzig. He resolved to return, to make it his home and to improve his knowledge of German, which was the city's official language. How could he have known that his linguistic skills would become so useful, so soon, for all the wrong reasons?

Papa could quite easily have remained in Danzig, but he was drawn back to Tomaszów Mazowiecki for one very good reason: a beautiful young woman who worked in a bridal store, embroidering gowns. Her name was Reizel Pinkusewicz, and she was two years younger than my father. Reizel shared Machel's vision of exploring the world beyond the confines of provincial Poland. She was studying Esperanto, the fledgling international language, so that she could communicate with people everywhere.

Mama was born in a village just outside Tomaszów called Paradyż. How profoundly ironic a name for a place that in 1939 became a living hell. For 200 years, the region was something of an idyll for the Jewish community. Jewish children enjoyed a high level of private education from good schools. The town had a thriving textile industry. Factories made silk, carpets and all manner of clothing fabrics. Our family had a presence in Tomaszów for over two centuries.

Mama came from deeply religious orthodox Hasidic Jewish

stock. Some members of the Pinkusewicz family were devout scholars. They came from a rabbinical dynasty stretching back 200 years. They disapproved of my father, who was far more liberal in his outlook. For a start, he was clean shaven. Within the Jewish community a beard was a sign of profound religious faith, as was a hat or head covering. Papa rarely wore a hat, another thing that was unacceptable to the Pinkusewicz family.

A tailor by trade, in his soul, Papa was an actor and singer who loved to dance at every opportunity. He adored the theatre and never missed a show when travelling performers came to town. The Pinkusewicz elders regarded the theatre as frivolous. They believed a man should study the scriptures and holy matters. In their view, people who sang secular songs on stage were immodest. They didn't approve of theatre and even less so cinema, where performance was filmed close up and, once projected on screen, was larger than life itself.

In 1936, Papa secured a small part alongside the former silent-movie star Molly Picon in *Yiddle With My Fiddle*, critically acclaimed as one of the greatest Yiddish films of all time. In truth, he was an extra and participated in a dance scene. The film was shot on location in Warsaw and in *shtetls* in the Polish countryside. Molly starred as Yiddle, a woman who masquerades as a man to land a gig as a fiddle player in a travelling band, playing klezmer music, the popular Yiddish genre of the time. Life becomes complicated and comical when she falls in love with one of her fellow musicians.

Full of energetic songs and dancing, the images in this road movie reveal a genuine slice of Jewish life in pre-Holocaust Poland. At a time of fascism and endemic anti-Semitism, it provided Central Europe's Jewish communities with a resounding sense of identity and solidarity. Now, gathering dust in film archives and institutes, *Yiddle With My Fiddle* stands as an epitaph to a culture that the Nazis attempted to eradicate.

My father travelled a long way to Warsaw just to be in Molly's presence. If you blink, you might miss him. Still, although he only had a small cameo, I'm proud that he is part of this historic work.

Given the opposition of the Pinkusewicz family, Papa held back from approaching Mama. Fortunately for him, the attraction was mutual, although she also hesitated over making the first move. The impasse was finally broken when she joined the Zionist organization together with a few of her girlfriends. Machel and Reizel started talking, and then they began meeting in secret. They took long walks, avoiding familiar streets and people.

Papa had a fine tenor voice and when he was courting my mother, he used to serenade her with a popular Yiddish song called 'Reizel'. It was written by Mordechai Gebirtig, an influential inter-war poet and self-taught musician who tapped out compositions on a piano with one finger. Gebirtig was shot dead by the Germans in the Krakow ghetto in 1942.

THE DAUGHTER OF AUSCHWITZ

In a street,
In the attic of a little house,
Lives my dear Reizel.
I pass under her window every evening,
Whistle and call out,
Reizel come, come, come.

Gebirtig's lyrics almost exactly mirrored the nature of my parents' relationship and my grandparents' displeasure. In the song, Reizel replies:

I'll ask you,
Don't whistle anymore.
'You hear – he's whistling again' – says Mother.
She's pious, and it upsets her.
Whistling is not for Jewish boys.
Simply give a sign in Yiddish.
One, two, three.

In the summer of 2021, as I looked at old photographs and books to remind myself of my past, I listened to that song for the first time in maybe fifty years. There's a charming live recording on YouTube. I sat at home in Highland Park and wept. I'm no longer the girl who couldn't cry.

I never heard my father singing to my mother. The eternal darkness that engulfed our apartment in the ghetto prohibited

44

the simplest acts of pleasure. Singing such flippant popular songs would have felt almost immoral. Consequently, for my father, music also died in the Holocaust.

In Reizel's orthodox family, it wasn't customary for a girl of marriageable age to choose her own partner. Within the Pinkusewicz circle, it was unheard of. In their world, marriages were organized by a *schadchanit* or matchmaker – a woman who knew the family background of both parties and almost everything about them. The theory was that if a couple were well matched, they would learn to love each other. Reizel, however, wasn't prepared to tolerate such anachronistic tyranny and made it abundantly clear that she would rather remain single than succumb to an arranged marriage.

If her father had been alive, perhaps he might have been able to ban the wedding. But Mama overruled her widowed mother and married for love. My parents' nuptials took place on 23 August 1936. As both families had limited means, it was a modest affair. And despite their initial objections, my father was accepted into the Pinkusewicz family with open arms after the wedding.

Six months later, the newlyweds shocked both sides of the family by moving 500 miles north, from Tomaszów Mazowiecki to Danzig. No one ever moved away from family and friends. But Papa's resolve to go back had not subsided. He wanted to open his own clothes store, but he also harboured dreams of joining a Yiddish theatre that was starting in Danzig.

In keeping with her independent spirit, Mama rebelled against the orthodox Jewish convention of a married woman wearing a wig as a sign of modesty. Mama knew her refusal to conform to orthodox principles caused hurt and possibly an element of shame for some of her relatives. So although Machel was welcomed after the wedding, her desire to choose love over her family's faith created a fault line for which she felt entirely responsible. Moving to Danzig made things worse. Seeds of guilt had been sown. And they grew.

The early days of my parents' marriage in Danzig were complex and conflicted. The young couple were overjoyed to be in each other's company. Papa was a talented tailor and his clothing store flourished. But with Danzig's local authority in the grip of the Nazi party, anti-Semitism was rampant. In 1937, about twelve thousand Jews resided in Danzig. Within a year, half had decided it was too dangerous and abandoned the city, driven out after a pogrom in October 1937 in which sixty Jewish homes and businesses were damaged by anti-Semitic thugs. They had been inflamed by a speech by Albert Forster, the Nazi head of the city state, who labelled Jews as *Untermenschen* – sub humans.

In 1938, Forster tightened the screws of repression. Some Jewish businesses were seized, and the deeds transferred to Gentiles. Jews were also banned from cinemas and theatres.

46

They were barred from public baths and swimming pools and denied the right to become lawyers, doctors or any other type of professional.

Persecution reached its zenith on *Kristallnacht* (the Night of Broken Glass), on 9 November 1938, when I was just two months old. The name refers to the shards of glass that littered the streets of Germany, Austria and some parts of Czechoslovakia, after Nazis rioted and destroyed synagogues, Jewish businesses, homes, schools and cemeteries. The official Jewish death toll was recorded as ninety-one, but the true number of victims ran to several hundred.

Kristallnacht was a turning point in Hitler's grand scheme to eradicate the Jews. The acquiescence of the German population at large, and the lack of any significant objections gave the Nazis the confidence to ratchet up anti-Semitism and institutionalize it as German government policy.

The destruction on *Kristallnacht* was most severe in Berlin and Vienna. The Nazis in Danzig also went on the rampage. They intended to burn down the Great Synagogue. But the building was defended by a ring of Jewish First World War veterans who had fought in the trenches on the German side.

Being a Jew in Danzig was now extremely precarious, but my parents continued to stick it out. Then, in late August 1939, with my first birthday looming, Mama was anxious to return to Tomaszów Mazowiecki to mark the occasion. Papa's parents, Emanuel and Pearl, hadn't seen me since my birth. Nor had Mama's family. She wanted to show me off and try to heal divisions. Mama kept pushing Papa to leave and they argued.

'Who is going to look after the store while we're away?' Papa complained.

Mama was insistent. She had a premonition. Something told her we had to leave immediately. Her arguments were so persuasive that Papa relented. His younger brother, whose name I can't recall, had also moved to Gdynia, and Papa convinced him to hold the fort while we took a series of trains south.

As a major port, Danzig was a key strategic target for Hitler's armed forces on 1 September 1939, the day their *Blitzkrieg* began. Squadrons of Stuka dive-bombers attacked a flotilla of Polish warships in Danzig Bay. The aircraft roared over Gdynia's waterfront, one of them scoring a direct hit on Papa's clothing store. My poor uncle was killed. He was one of the first civilian casualties of the Second World War. It could so easily have been us.

The German army, the *Wehrmacht*, swept through Poland at such a pace that it had reached Tomaszów Mazowiecki by 6 September 1939, just three days after the conflict escalated into a world war. My parents' hometown was attacked on land and from the sky. We were living with Mama's mother and her family at the time.

Tanks from two German Panzer units bombarded a lightly armed Polish infantry division while Stukas terrorized civilians. The Stukas were fitted with sirens called Jericho Trumpets, which screamed as they plunged into vertical dives. The sirens' wail intensified as the planes accelerated and amplified the panic of those in the line of fire. Just as they did in the battle for Old Testament Jericho, the trumpets shattered the psychological defences of their victims. Bombs fell near my grandparents' home with some fatalities, but we all escaped injury.

The battle for Tomaszów Mazowiecki was brief and one-sided. The Polish defenders fought with courage, destroying twenty-one German tanks and killing 100 enemy troops. But they were quickly overwhelmed. After 770 men were killed, and more than 1,000 wounded, the Polish division retreated, abandoning Tomaszów Mazowiecki's civilians to their fate.

One of the Germans' first acts was to demand from Jewish leaders 1 million zlotys in hard cash from the local bank. That's the equivalent today of $5 million. When the men failed to raise the money in time, they were gunned down.

Within a week of occupying Tomaszów, the Germans inflicted another taste of the future. At first, the soldiers abused Jews by hacking off the beards of the religiously devout, often tearing at flesh in the process. They used knives or bayonets to lop off the side curls that traditionally dangled in front of the men's ears. They were shredding the self-esteem of our most venerated people and undermining the fabric of our civic society.

Sidling up to German soldiers, clusters of Aryan Poles looked on with approval as Jews were humiliated. The Nazis ascended to power in Germany by legitimizing the muscle of the mob and appealing to thug mentality. Immediately after the invasion, they likewise encouraged anti-Semitic Poles to give vent to their most base instincts. Other Poles watched and concluded that adopting German attitudes offered them the best chance of survival within the growing boundaries of Hitler's Third Reich. And they joined in.

Seven days after seizing control of Tomaszów, the Germans rounded up 1,000 inhabitants, targeting the intelligentsia and professional classes. Three hundred of them were Jews. Rabbis, lawyers, teachers, doctors – the very fibre of our society. They neutralized the brightest minds who might possibly have been a threat. It was a form of decapitation. Cutting off the head to get rid of the brains, so lessening the chances of rebellion. As far as the Germans were concerned, the only Jew with a purpose was one with a skill or strength to work for the Nazi war machine. They were lining us up for slave labour.

Ninety Jews were imprisoned at Buchenwald near Weimar, 170 miles south-west of Berlin. Buchenwald was one of Germany's first concentration camps and a test bed for Hitler's Final Solution. Of the 300 Jews arrested in Tomaszów Mazowiecki on that day, 13 September 1939, only thirteen survived the Holocaust.

The Germans were just getting started. A month later, on 16 October, they burned down the Great Synagogue of Tomaszów Mazowiecki. Then, another month later, they razed the town's two remaining places of Jewish worship. Jewish businesses were ordered to display the star of David. Many families were evicted from their homes to make way for the Germans who would rule over us.

The early days of occupation set the tone for my childhood. The events of 1939 moulded my life, just as they did for every Jew on earth. So did the ensuing liquidation of the Jewish ghetto. I'm not claiming that my experiences are the worst of the Second World War. But the scenes I witnessed were some of the most depraved in the history of humankind. Because I was a child, and it was so long ago, I don't remember the specific dates or details of all that took place in front of my eyes. Names from the past that were once familiar have faded from my memory. Although their faces have not.

Still, everything I do, every decision I make today, is forged by the forces that surrounded me in my formative years. I believe in God. According to our Torah, the scriptures that guide us, we understand that God taught humanity the difference between good and evil. We believe that God gave us all free will. One of the consequences of free will is that humans can choose to follow a dark path.

No child should see what I have seen. No child should be starved or tortured or treated like a subhuman. My childhood was stolen from me as soon as I learned to communicate. Perhaps the innate innocence of youth enabled me to live a full and relatively happy life. But I took my experiences and used them as fuel to move forwards. Children the world over are resilient and, given a fair wind, can rebound from the darkest of experiences.

Adults are less fortunate. In my experience, they suffer far more, because they understand more. I know that because of what happened to my beautiful, wonderful, brilliant mama whose light was extinguished prematurely. To this day, I cherish her memory, not least for her courage and the wisdom she imparted.

I lost my innocence in the Jewish ghetto in Tomaszów Mazowiecki, the moment I looked beyond the tablecloth.

Throughout the early years of my childhood, evil was riding on my shoulder every step of the way. As far as I'm concerned, the common post-war German excuse of 'I was just following orders' has no validity. So many chose the dark side. If you take anything from my story, it would be to turn towards the light.

CHAPTER THREE

AND THEN THEY CAME FOR ME

Jewish ghetto, Tomaszów Mazowiecki,
German-occupied Central Poland, 1942

Age four

One of the maxims of the Holocaust was that first they came for the intellectuals. In reality, they kept coming back just in case they missed some. The SS guards took their time getting to the front door of one of the brightest people in my family. But, just as inevitably as death itself, they eventually turned up in the spring of 1942, and took away Uncle James (he of the bushy eyebrows), married to my wonderful Aunt Helen, my father's sister.

Uncle James was a German Jew. He was a lawyer with a fine mind, and I idolized him. Sitting on his lap and playing with his eyebrows is one of my sharpest first memories. Uncle James had thought that he might be useful to our jailers. He hoped his language skills might save him, securing him work

53

as an interpreter. Poor Uncle James. Like so many Jews, he was deluded. To the Nazis, all Jews were expendable. They didn't need translators. They weren't having conversations that required Polish, Yiddish or Hebrew interpretations. They were issuing orders in a language understood by every race on earth: violence.

Even now, eighty years later, I don't know precisely how Uncle James' life ended. But having read various historical accounts, I suspect he was shot outside his home. I just hope his death was instant and painless. I know that his wife, Helen, wasn't there at the time. She was younger than him, with an enchanting elfin face and a beautiful smile. Helen was about eighteen years old, and like everyone else of her age, she was a forced labourer, possibly in a textiles factory hitched to the German war effort. It was a small mercy that Helen was absent when they came for her husband. She would have done anything for her family. She might have been killed there and then. But her time would come and not in a manner or place that one might imagine.

I remember my father coming back and telling me in the gentlest way possible, 'I'm afraid you won't be seeing your Uncle James again. He's gone and he won't be coming back.'

I was really upset. I loved Uncle James very much. He was such a handsome man. His murder was part of my ghetto education. Although I was only three and a half, I was learning that people just disappeared. You had to get used to it, along with the numbness that accompanied the feeling of helplessness.

Uncle James' murder aligns with a series of raids on 27 and 28 April 1942 by the German Security Police. They conducted an *Intelligentsia Aktion* and rounded up lawyers, doctors, members of the Jewish police and the *Judenrat*, the Jewish council or administration that nominally ran the ghetto, but which had to acquiesce to German demands. Many of the victims were shot for 'trying to escape', as they were arrested. Over the course of those two days, 200 people were murdered.

Mama didn't cry when Uncle James was killed. As ever, she hid her tears behind an invisible veil. With each new murder, a memorial stone was cemented on top of her spirit. Uncle James' was laid next to those of her mother and uncle. The cenotaph being constructed inside her mind grew with every passing day. It weighed her down. She was slowly drowning.

As spring turned to summer in 1942, the Germans once again tightened the screws on the ghetto in Tomaszów Mazowiecki. I know this because every European Jewish community eradicated in the Shoah has a *Yizkor*, a book of remembrance. Containing photographs of and tributes to the dead, and written mostly in Yiddish and Hebrew, the *Yizkor* books were a post-war attempt by survivors to reconstruct and honour the history the Germans tried to wipe out. Included are descriptions of individual tragedies, acts of heroism and revelations about the names of tormentors and criminals.

Ever since I've lived in Highland Park, the black leather-bound *Yizkor* book of Tomaszów Mazowiecki has been in my collection. For decades, it sat untouched in my bookcase. But in the summer of 2021, I took it from the shelf once more and braced myself.

Yiddish was the language of my childhood. I stopped speaking it when my father died, but lately, I have been studying the language again. I found that I was able to read the *Yizkor* book with ease. It was as if I was reliving my early life and it was mesmerizing.

My father wrote seventeen pages of the Tomaszów *Yizkor* book. There, he portrays the destruction of the ghetto and the accompanying slaughter. So graphic are his descriptions that his contribution to the *Yizkor* book has become a cornerstone of the history of the Tomaszów Mazowiecki ghetto.

My father knew what was going on, because he was a member of the *Ordnungsdienst*, the Jewish Order Service or police force. The Germans had ordered the *Judenrat* to establish a police force in late 1940. Their role was to maintain order, to guard the internal border of the ghetto and to stop people escaping. It was also part of the Nazi strategy of sowing division among the Jewish population. Baruch Szoeps, the first chairman of the *Judenrat*, was beaten to death by the Gestapo for refusing to cooperate with the Germans. His successor, Lejbusz Warsager, determined it would be wiser to comply.

In ghettos throughout Poland, Jewish councils reluctantly concluded that if they acceded to some of the German demands, they would have a greater chance of saving their people. The councillors might have managed to preserve some lives, although as history sadly demonstrates, all they did was delay the inevitable genocide. The Nazis had no intention of responding with mercy to the *Judenrat*'s gestures. But how could anyone have imagined that people from a cultured, modern, intelligent country like Germany were planning to exterminate another race? Germany, the birthplace of composer Johann Sebastian Bach, of writer Johann Wolfgang von Goethe. It was simply unthinkable.

Members of the Tomaszów Mazowiecki *Judenrat* were highly selective about which men they chose to be police officers. Some councillors instructed their sons to join. They also sought out men from 'good' families. The *Judenrat* was determined to exclude types who might be either violent or corruptible. According to a *Judenrat* wages ledger, discovered by archivists in Tomaszów Mazowiecki, my father was paid 25 Polish zlotys a month. The salary was effectively worthless at a time when food and other staples were difficult to find because the Germans controlled the supply chain.

In the black market for Poles, people paid 15 zlotys for a loaf of bread weighing 2.25 pounds. But in Jewish ghettos, the black-market rate more than doubled to 32 zlotys. Bear in mind that as part of the Nazi campaign to wipe us out, Jews only obtained a third of the rations that Poles were getting, and so black-market prices for Jews were twice as high.

As the ledger suggests, there was no financial incentive for joining the police – the only real motivation for the Jews was to obtain information. In the ghetto, information might make the difference between life and death. Mama told me that my father was trusted, presumably by the *Judenrat*, to get intelligence that might help save his friends and neighbours, and that he could be relied upon to soften German orders. So when he was recruited, together with his friend Aaron Greenspan and several others on 1 February 1942, as life in the ghetto was becoming increasingly perilous, he must have seen it as a way to protect Mama and me. As far as I'm concerned, my father was a hero.

There has long been a casual misconception that the Jews went like sheep to the slaughter – that they were passive and didn't fight back. That is simplistic and inaccurate. The Jews were certainly overwhelmed, but there was a spirit of resistance across occupied Europe, especially in Poland, Lithuania, Belarus and Ukraine. Underground movements sprang up across the Nazi empire. There were uprisings in one hundred Jewish ghettos. That's one in every four. The participants weren't naive enough to believe they could defeat the Germans, but where they could be, they were disruptive.

By watering down the Germans' orders, by being kind and humane in the face of unbelievable sadism and by picking up information he thought might help save some people, my father, in his own small way, was a rebel who hid in plain sight. This is the conclusion I reached after re-examining his contribution to the *Yizkor* book: 'In the summer of 1942, there was a spate of rumours that strange things were going on in the towns and neighbouring townlets.' He continues:

No one knew what this was all about. Information and communication with the area was totally absent.

We were cut off from the outside world. Any sort of travel to a nearby town or village was strictly forbidden. Mail, all correspondence, and the sending of telegrams ceased immediately after the closing of the ghetto in 1941. The only persons able to go outside the town and into the villages and nearby townlets, were holders of the 'green armband'. These were collectors of rags, and leather merchants, who bought these materials from the local peasants and supplied them to the factories sequestered by the Germans. These 'green armbands' brought news of deportations, removal of Jews from many townlets that were now *Judenrein* – 'cleansed of Jews' – and continuous transports of deported Jews.

But to where?

No one knew. There were rumours that the deportees were sent to labour camps in Germany. The words 'concentration camps' were also heard. If people ventured the supposition that the Jews were being taken to their deaths, not only did people turn a deaf ear to them, but they were also branded as madmen. Was it possible that young and healthy people without handicaps would be sent to their deaths?

During prayers in the synagogues, at the time of the High Holy Days, a feeling reigned that something terrible was about to happen. Something compared to which, life in the ghetto was child's play.

Sure enough, something terrible did happen when I was about four years old. I can place it back to that time because the table in 24 Krzyżowa Street was still my reference point. When I was four, my shoulders reached the tabletop and I no longer had to stand on tiptoes to see what was on it.

The apartment door opened. My father entered and slumped into a chair. Tears were streaming down his cheeks. I remember it as if it happened today. I remember where I was standing and where my father was sitting and where my mother was. Mama was to the left of me and Papa was to the right.

'I took them to the truck. I had to help them climb up,' he said. 'The truck was full. Full of old people. They were sitting right at the back next to the tailgate.'

My father was talking about his parents, Emanuel and Pearl.

'We just looked at each other. I saw the look in their eyes. They knew where they were going. I couldn't save them. There was nothing I could do.'

The Germans must have taken sadistic pleasure in forcing a Jewish policeman to lead his own parents to their death. Two or three days earlier, my father and other men of his generation had been ordered to dig a mass grave for their parents. Papa knew what was coming and was powerless to prevent it. Having repeatedly considered this crime over the years, I have tried to comfort myself with the knowledge that he was able to help them in a small way at the end, just by being there.

But how traumatic must it have been for my father to know that he was unable to save them? If he had tried to thwart the Germans, he undoubtedly would have been killed, and Mama and I would have been more vulnerable than we already were. He was caught between the hammer and the anvil. He was damned whatever he did. Every day presented him with new insoluble moral dilemmas.

In the ghettos and the camps, Jews like my father were compelled to make impossible choices several times a day, every day, every week, every month, every year. As a Jew in occupied Europe, there were no good decisions. There were only bad and worse ones. All you could do was make a less bad decision. Make the wrong one and you were dead, and your family would probably join you shortly afterwards. Anyone who has ever faced imminent annihilation knows that you do what you must to survive.

I'm convinced my father didn't have a choice about becoming a policeman. There was no guarantee that those who enlisted would be safe. The Germans killed some officers within the force, and the *Judenrat* was obliged to maintain the numbers. It appears he was selected as a replacement officer. I don't think he would have volunteered. He would only have enlisted if asked to do so by Jewish community leaders who were keen to maintain the best possible standards under the most impossible circumstances. It was a position he detested, because, despite his good intentions, he was required to perform duties that were abhorrent. Jewish police officers had to enforce the orders of their Nazi controllers or put themselves and their families at risk. Plain and simple, it was blackmail.

Honourable policemen like my father strove, wherever possible, to mitigate German orders, or to send people discreet warnings that gave them a chance to save their lives, or at least choose the least bad option. I believe that he did his best to ease the suffering of the Jews of Tomaszów Mazowiecki. Mama was his conscience, and she helped him navigate that terrible moral maze.

That day, when my father told us about his parents, not only was Mama internally grieving the murder of family and friends, but her grief was exacerbated by the pain borne by my father, the man she married for love. At the table, Mama tried in vain to console my father, while silently putting two more bricks in her invisible memorial wall.

It was hard for me to imagine not seeing my grandparents again, but I had to come to terms with it almost straight away. Today, I struggle to picture their faces. They have faded over the years. The abiding image that keeps coming to me is of my grandfather with a yellow measuring tape around his neck in his tailor's store in Tomaszów Mazowiecki.

But what I do clearly remember are my father's tears. I recall his sense of resignation. He talked very quietly. He wasn't surprised that they were taken away to be shot. They lived with the expectation that we would all be killed. My father was numb. The way he and Mama accepted death is very frightening to me today. It shows just how surreal life and death were in the ghetto.

My grandparents were taken to the woods on the outskirts of the town. I have no proof of what happened to them, but I imagine they would have done their best to follow a traditional Jewish ritual when death is imminent. When we know we are about to die, we recite a prayer called 'Shema Yisrael'.

'Listen Israel, the Lord is our God, the Lord alone and you shall love the Lord your God with all your heart, with all your being, and all your might.'

I wonder if they had time to make their peace in that way, as did other Jews heading for the gas chambers in Birkenau. I can picture what happened to them. After struggling to climb down from the truck, along with other Jews condemned to death, they would have heard guttural German voices ordering them to walk towards the pit dug by their son and others. Pearl and Emanuel didn't speak German; they must have been completely confused. I suspect their last moments were spent agonizing over what the Nazis might do to the rest of their family.

I doubt they would have stared at the muzzles pointing at them. So many were shot in the back. One would have heard the bullets that killed the other, a fraction of a second before he or she fell, too. Sometimes, after a massacre, the ground would heave as those buried alive tried in vain to dig themselves out. More than anything, I hope they weren't still breathing when the earth was heaped upon them. I pray the soil didn't move after the shovels were tossed into the back of the truck that had been their hearse, and the slave labourers were driven away to perform that task again another day.

All the while, life was getting harder in the ghetto. Every household was stricken with hunger. Old people collapsed and died in the streets. Children who were allowed out of their homes begged for food on the sidewalks. A soup kitchen set up by community leaders had long ceased operating. A good-hearted young man called David Goldman, who'd prepared meals specifically for children, contracted typhus and passed away. The cramped, unhygienic living conditions meant typhus ripped through the ghetto like wildfire.

And things were about to get worse. For two years, we had lived in darkness after sunset. But on 23 October, the ghetto was suddenly brightly illuminated by streetlights which hadn't operated since 1940. All the lights on the perimeter of our prison were turned on. People were dazzled by the glare and their broken spirits darkened further. If I think back hard enough, I can recall looking out of the window after dusk and thinking the street was brighter than in daytime. The lights made us realize that we had nowhere to hide.

Nazi volunteers from Ukraine materialized, dressed in black uniforms, and carrying sub-machine guns. They were joined by men from Poland and Lithuania.

'They were all wearing steel helmets and armed for battle. Sounds of firing were soon heard and first victims fell,' recalls my father in the *Yizkor* book. 'In the light, the angels of death who surrounded the ghetto had a better view of the living targets they would fire at and could thus relish the horrors they would inflict on the ghetto.'

Reading such descriptions in the *Yizkor* book helped to rekindle memories buried deep inside me. I always had a vague recollection of hearing shooting, feeling terrified and watching the traumatized faces of the people with whom I lived. It was painful to relive those terrible days. At the same time, thanks to my father's witness testimony, written after the war, I was able to put that part of my childhood into context and in a historical timeline.

Six days after the ghetto was floodlit, Jewish anxieties reached fever pitch. Ghetto inhabitants were convinced there were going to be deportations to death camps. In a swirling fog of rumour and counter rumour, they gathered outside the headquarters of the *Judenrat*, demanding answers. The crowd's agitation was a source of potential trouble for Hans Pichler, the regional commander of the *Schutzpolizei*, the Nazi Reich police. He wanted to calm the mood and calculated that using his troops would not have the desired effect. So he passed the problem to the *Judenrat* – in other words, Jewish community leaders – giving them the unenviable task of implementing German decrees.

My father takes up the story in the *Yizkor* book:

> In the evening, the Gestapo, led by Meister Pichler, made their appearance. Pichler told the Jewish police and the sanitation workers to calm the crowd, saying that 'everything was quite all right' and assuring it that all the people in the ghetto would remain and none would be deported.

I presume my father was one of the policemen commanded to get the crowd under control on that day, 29 October 1942. If so, he would have had to pass on the Gestapo edict that anyone caught spreading false rumours about deportations would be shot. The crowd had little alternative but to disperse. It goes without saying that the assurances were a lie.

Then my father writes, 'But later that evening a group of Jewish policemen and with them, German and Ukrainian police armed with sub-machine guns, appeared at the station, where hundreds of Jewish men, women, children and even tiny babies born that day or the day before were already assembled.'

It's important to emphasize that the Jewish police didn't have guns. They had truncheons for crowd control. The Germans didn't arm the Jewish police in case they turned on their tormentors and opened fire. As I sat reading the *Yizkor* book, I could sense the pain my father went through as the noose tightened around the ghetto.

Throughout that day, hundreds of Jews from neighbouring towns and villages were funnelled at gunpoint into a barbed-wire stockade, hastily erected in a field next to the station, about a mile north-east of the ghetto.

The crowd became increasingly agitated as the hours went by. Day turned into night and, all the while, more Jews were pushed into the field, taunted and prodded with rifle butts. The Gestapo berated the Jewish policemen. Here again, I'm sure my father is talking about orders he received himself: '*Mach mal ordnung mit dem Juden-Gesindel*' ('Get that Jewish rabble under control').

It's obvious the Germans wanted the Jewish policemen to use violence against their own people. But I'm certain that when those like my father failed to carry out the Germans' demands, the Gestapo piled into the stockade and began lashing out. Because my father wrote that the Gestapo 'hurled themselves into the crowd to impose order on the babies and their mothers, who were waiting for the train to take them somewhere or other . . .'

My father doesn't identify the train's destination. Perhaps at that stage, he genuinely didn't know, because I think it's highly unlikely the Germans would have revealed that the train was heading to Treblinka.

Treblinka is a name that makes me shudder to this day. It's a name the world needs to remember, even though it no longer exists. The Germans destroyed the camp in 1943 to try to hide evidence of their war crimes. All that stands in its place is a giant Neolithic-style stone memorial, surrounded by a sea of sharp rocks, shaped like sharks' teeth, pointing towards the sky. At the foot of the centrepiece is a stone, chiselled into the form of a burned book, inscribed with the words, 'Never Again'.

Treblinka was hidden in a forest, 50 miles north-east of Warsaw. It contained six gas chambers and was one of six extermination camps built by the Nazis with the sole intention of eradicating Poland's 2 million Jews. With characteristic German efficiency, the Nazis improved the rail connections to Treblinka from the Warsaw Ghetto and Central Poland, where I lived, to accelerate the mass murder of Jews.

That means that somewhere in an office within the Third Reich, there was a master statistician with a warped mind, who calculated the extra number of railway tracks and points and signals required to ensure the death trains ran like clockwork. Psychopaths alone were incapable of implementing the Holocaust. And they were dependent on an army of complicit drones, as well as highly educated professionals to lubricate the mundane logistics of industrial slaughter. I wonder what happened to that little man with his pencil sharpener, his pristine blue-squared maths books and his multiplication tables? Did he survive the war? Did he end up in the dock at the Nuremberg trials? Or did he manage to slip away and reinvent himself as a railway administrator after the armistice? The statistician may not have pulled a trigger or popped a Zyklon B canister down a gas-chamber chute, but he surely was a war criminal.

The last major deportation from Warsaw to Treblinka took place on Monday 21 September 1942. Just another day for most of the world, but for us it was Yom Kippur, the Day of Atonement and the holiest day in the Jewish calendar. We believe it's the day when God decides each person's fate, and on it, we ask for forgiveness for sins we have committed during the previous year.

The timing of that train journey could not have been more sadistic. The Jews' fate was decided by the Nazis. All hope was extinguished.

Then they came for us.

My father describes the night before the first of Tomaszów Mazowiecki's Jews boarded the trains to Treblinka:

> All night long these wretched people waited for the train, under strict orders not to move from their places. Jews kept arriving, on foot or in carts – all of them goaded on by the Germans or Ukrainians with truncheons or rifle butts. These vented their rage, too, on the Jewish police, who were trying their best to lessen

the suffering of the internees by giving them water or being asked to find the parents of children gone astray in the turmoil.

I know this was my father's own personal experience. He was beaten with rifle butts for trying to be kind. I remember seeing him coming home that night with dried blood caked on his face and my mother trying to clean him up. The next day he was obliged to go out again. He writes:

At dawn on Friday 30 October, most of the Jews were crammed into railway wagons. Families were torn apart. Increasing numbers of Jews expelled from their townlets began to arrive.

The station area was, however, too small to absorb all the arrivals, so some of them were sent into town, to be deported together with the Jews of Tomaszów to their unknown destination.

Some of those were shot to death. The others were crammed into empty factory halls. Local Jews wanted to give them food and water but were prevented from doing so by the Ukrainians.

On 30 October, the cattle trains from Tomaszów Mazowiecki transported over 7,500 Jewish people to Treblinka. They were all gassed and then cremated on open pyres.

The apocalypse alighted upon the ghetto the next day, our Sabbath. We awoke to a dawn chorus of rifle butts smashing front doors open.

They had come for me. A four-year-old.

We were heading for *selektion*.

Selection.

A word as chilling as Treblinka.

Its meaning?

Life or death.

CHAPTER FOUR

CALIGULA'S THUMB

Jewish ghetto, Tomaszów Mazowiecki,
German-occupied Central Poland, 31 October 1942
Age four

Just in case we didn't get the message the first time, it was repeated in Polish and Yiddish. The soldiers were bellowing into bullhorns. They were screaming the commands that every Jew dreaded.

'*Alle Juden raus. Alle Juden raus.*'

The words were full of venom. The guards knew just how brutally the day was going to play out. They had their orders. No matter how many times they had killed before, they were psyching themselves up to spill even more blood. They were creating confusion and panic, breaking down our resistance to make it easier to herd us wherever they wanted.

Mama had time to put a coat on me to protect me against

the cold. We stumbled into the courtyard, through an archway and into the street. We were surrounded by guards in different-coloured uniforms shouting orders at us from all directions. Their eyes bulged with hatred and the exertion of yelling. Some leaned backwards, pulling on the choke collars of their attack dogs to rein them in. The dogs breathed in our collective fear. Their slobbering, slavering jaws wanted to know what terror tasted like. They were itching to feast on it. Their claws drummed the cobblestones in frustration. Those awful, terrible dogs. Snarling, growling, baying. Merciless.

Down on the cobbles of Krzyżowa Street, I felt smaller than ever before. The soldiers all towered above me. Through half-closed eyes, I scanned our tormentors. I tried not to twist my head, to avoid attracting attention from the wall of helmeted skulls, baring their teeth, like a pack of wolves, contorting their faces as they spat out their bile.

I didn't know what kind of weapons the soldiers were carrying. I only knew that they looked more dangerous than the rifles that cracked and the pistols that popped. All the while, the soldiers swivelled their guns from side to side in a sweeping motion. I was afraid they would open fire at any moment. It felt as though the guns kept coming back to point directly at me. It was terrifying for a four-year-old. And now, having reread my father's contribution to the *Yizkor* book, I understand what I was witnessing: 'All of the Jews of the ghetto were ousted from their houses into the courtyards, where the Jewish police, and

Gestapo, Ukrainians and Blue Police armed with sub-machine guns as if going into battle, were waiting for them.'

I now know that the Blue Police my father refers to were Polish police officers, or 'murderers in uniform', as they've been labelled by historian Jan Grabowski, a professor of Holocaust studies at the University of Ottawa.

The only officers who didn't have guns were the Jewish policemen, like my father. 'From the houses more and more Jews arrived, guarded by Jewish policemen. These Jews had been given severe warnings by Commandant Pichler,' he writes.

Pichler's Reich police unit comprised former soldiers who were members of the Nazi party and affiliated to the SS. They were as brutal as any fanatical Jew-hating stormtrooper.

What seems obvious to me from my father's testimony is that the Jewish policemen were told by Pichler there would be dire consequences if they disobeyed orders to help round up their fellow Jews. Because then my father writes: 'And therefore, a Jewish policeman had to escort his own family, lest they be killed on the spot.' It must have been so heartbreaking for him.

Holding their weapons at waist height, the soldiers aimed at us and ordered us to line up. They were organizing us as if we were about to march in a parade. We had to stand still and not move a muscle. I kept quiet and was conscious of the bustle of ill-shod shuffling feet, nervous snatched conversations and all of us breathing heavily with fear and exertion. Suddenly, I was shaken by the jarring rasp of guns being fired.

'Shots rang out nearby, the first victims fell and there were many wounded, crying for help,' writes my father. He goes on:

> The Jews threw down their rucksacks and bundles and lined up in rows of five, to form twenty or twenty-five rows, and thus under armed guard, marched towards the former hospital in Wieczność Street, leaving behind them the dead and the wounded, who fell on the way, unable to keep up with the forced pace.

We filed down Krzyżowa Street and turned right when we reached the bottom. Other children were whimpering. I knew better than to cry. Mama had taught me well. Some were carried in their parents' arms and had a clear view of the carnage. I was surrounded by people taller than me, but through the gaps, I saw corpses on the ground. Blood trickling along the flagstones. I heard people wailing as they passed bodies they recognized. My father picks up the story:

> Children unable to find their parents cried for them, others were torn from their fathers' grasp. The adjacent streets resounded with screams and sobs. The marchers stumbled on the corpses of their loved ones, and the German and Ukrainian murderers rained blows on their heads with the butts of their machine guns.

I trembled as I walked with my mother, gripping her hand. I was always terrified of being separated from Mama. She was my protector-in-chief. I can't precisely remember where my father was. But now I realize he must have been close by, on the outside of the marching column. I wished he was next to me, holding my other hand. The experience was terrifying for Mama and me. It must also have been excruciating for my father. Being separated from us, knowing that we were being subjected to the vicious whims of the Gestapo, that he could do nothing. He was there, hating being forced to submit to the Germans, but doing his utmost to try to save us, while at the same time, bearing witness. I can tell from the language he uses that he must have been crying the whole time he was writing.

> The street filled with blood. And more victims were left behind. Husbands were torn from their wives, children searched for their parents. Blood, screams and tears, and still the march went on. The marchers reached the hospital courtyard and lined up again in rows of five. There were now twenty rows left.

The hospital courtyard was called the *Umschlagplatz* – literally a place for the transhipment or transfer of cargo. A sinister euphemism if ever there was one. From here, hundreds of Jews were marched to the railway station. I don't remember seeing the hospital, but I distinctly remember marching to a churchyard.

Here, again, is my father's eye-witness account: 'Not far from the hospital courtyard, in Wieczność Street, where the small church was situated, a painstaking inspection took place, as the Gestapo soldiers again and again perused the documents permitting the Jews to remain in the ghetto and work for the Germans.'

This was another part of the dreaded selection process. By now, my father was with us, to make sure, as he wrote earlier, we weren't killed on the spot. We lined up by the church, behind a brick wall that was taller than me, waiting to go through a black wrought-iron double gate. But first we had to go through *Selektion*.

How ironic that the Godless Gestapo chose a church as the location to deliver judgment. Saint Wenceslas was a small, rustic, whitewashed wooden Catholic church, with a steep, sloping roof and an onion-shaped steeple above the nave where the altar would have been. On either side of the church lay symmetrical paths.

Barring the way was a uniformed officer, sitting at a table, checking people's papers to determine whether they were qualified to work and worth preserving. For the time being. My father was in the lead. Mama stood behind him, clutching me in her arms. I wrapped mine around her neck. I distinctly recall the electric tension in the air as we got closer to the selection officer. Mama was terrified. Her chest was heaving, and I could feel her heart thumping. Two other children were clinging to the back of her skirt. They were my cousins. One was four years old, the same as me. The other was five. They were the daughters of my aunt, my mother's sister. She motioned them to join Mama just before she was led off by the Gestapo. As she was being hustled away, my aunt begged Mama to save her girls. We were all standing behind another family.

'*Papiere!*' the Nazi snarled.

The man in the queue in front of us handed over his documents. The officer leafed through a cluster of identity cards imprinted with an array of Third Reich stamps and said, 'You only have documents for four. Why do I see six people?'

'I'm taking my younger sister and her son,' the man replied. 'They're strong and they're going to work.'

'But you only have papers for four people, so why are you taking six?' the officer persisted.

The man became distressed and tried to appeal to the gate-keeper's sense of reason. There was desperation in his voice as he pleaded.

'But Herr Oberleutnant, you're looking for people to work, aren't you? Please, sir, let us through. *Bitte.*'

'Do you take me for a fool? *Lügner!*' ('Liar!') growled the Gestapo officer. He raised his thumb and snarled as he rotated his wrist to the left.

'*Links.*' ('Left.')

Left meant death. *Rechts*, or right, meant life.

The man gasped as he registered the enormity of the sentence that had just been passed. But he composed himself and led the five members of his family through the gate and took the path to his left. I watched them walk beside the church, along the stone path, beyond a small clump of trees. There, they sat on the ground, huddled together in the cold along with the rest of the Damned – Jews heading towards the cattle car train, and as we now know, onwards to the Treblinka extermination camp;

The Gestapo officer watched the family over his shoulder, then he peered up at us. From my vantage point in Mama's arms, I looked down on the uniformed man, swaddled in his thick greatcoat, comfortable and warm, while we all shivered from fear and the chill in the Polish air. I couldn't see his eyes. But as he tilted his head to look at my parents, I had a perfect view of the insignia on his hat. What a strange-looking bird, I thought. I had seen it before, but never so close. There was a grinning death's-head silver skull and crossbones next to the shiny peak of his cap, above which was the *Reichsadler*, Nazi Germany's Imperial Eagle.

Hitler had appropriated the heraldic emblem of the Ancient Roman Empire. His territorial conquests mirrored many Roman ones. But he garnished his Imperial Eagle with a swastika, debasing Rome's civilizing legacy.

The Gestapo officer sitting at the table before us was a modern Barbarian, immaculate in Nazi tailoring. He emulated Caligula, the despotic first-century Roman emperor, who used his thumb to dictate the fates of defeated gladiators. How many other uniformed Caligulas were sitting at tables outside *shtetls* and ghettos across Central Europe, deciding with the wave of a finger who could walk right through the gate of life to become a slave labourer and who would trudge left, towards cattle cars transporting them directly to the inferno?

'*Wie viele?*' ('How many?')

My father didn't say anything. Mama also hesitated for a moment, then she drew a breath. 'Three,' she said, as she reached behind her and pushed her nieces away.

'*Rechts,*' replied the officer, with a twist of his thumb.

My father led the way. Mama put me down.

'Take Papa's hand,' she said.

I did as Mama told me and immediately felt a sense of security from the big, warm hand wrapped around mine. We walked through the iron gate and took the path to the officer's right, towards a small cemetery. Together, Mama, Papa and I walked into the churchyard.

I looked back and saw my two little cousins standing alone, until someone took them away. They were never seen again.

The Gestapo officer hadn't even glanced at my parents' papers. It was an abominable illustration of how we could only make bad or worse choices. How could my mother possibly have known that the Nazi wouldn't examine the documents? Why hadn't he checked them? Normally, they were so fastidious.

Mama had had to make a lightning-fast decision. She'd had no time to consider all the options. Every calculation was based on instinct. Above all else, from the start of the Holocaust, through to the very end, Mama's pre-eminent consideration was my survival. As was my father's. Thanks to them, I was one of the handful of Jewish children from Tomaszów Mazowiecki to survive the Shoah.

At the age of four, I had no understanding of the significance of the exchange between my parents and the Nazi. Years later, however, when I was old enough to understand, Mama broke down in tears and told me about the Gestapo officer sitting at that table.

'He didn't even open the papers. I killed my sister's children. I forced them to let go of me. How can I forget their faces? I killed them.'

It was a pivotal moment in Mama's life from which she never recovered. Until her dying day, she was tormented by hypothetical 'what-if' questions. What if she had said we were a group of five instead of three? Would they still be alive? But on that day, there was no time to dwell on the death sentence imposed on my cousins. Her immediate priority was to ensure that we lived through the next few dangerous hours.

CHAPTER FIVE

THE CHURCHYARD

Jewish ghetto, Tomaszów Mazowiecki,
German-occupied Central Poland, 31 October 1942
Age four

We had passed through the first selection process, but were far from safe.

In the graveyard, Mama must have felt so alone. Having ensured that we made it past the officer, my father was obliged to leave us and return to the deportation of the Jews from Tomaszów Mazowiecki. People were marched to the railway station. Their shoes and possessions were taken away and they were crammed into cattle wagons.

My father writes that by the end of that day, some six thousand Jews had been expelled from the ghetto. In just one day, the Nazis transported almost half the Jews of our town on their last journey.

We were just one component of Operation Reinhard, the sick brainchild of Heinrich Himmler, chief of the SS and one of the principal architects of the Holocaust. Operation Reinhard was designed to achieve the physical annihilation of every Jew who lived in occupied Poland. Ultimately, it was responsible for the murder of approximately 2 million children, women and men, most of them Polish Jews.

The logistics for Operation Reinhard were devised with chilling clarity. Those who were too old, sick or frail were meant to be shot while still in the ghetto or on their way to the station. These murders were committed because the smooth operation of the extermination camps relied on victims being able to walk from the platform to the gas chambers on their own. Those who couldn't do that were killed immediately. *Ordnung muss sein* – there must be order. German efficiency and thoroughness at its most despicable.

That first selection, where my cousins, their parents and most of my mother's family were taken away, was not the last. The Germans continued to reduce the numbers of people they considered would be useful workers. In the *Yizkor* book my father talks of at least two further selections. The first was on that Sabbath, 31 October. Papa writes that even those with working papers were detained for a while in a factory, before some of them were sent back to the hospital courtyard, one of several staging posts before the gas chamber.

Somehow, Mama and I, just a four-year-old child, survived

that process. Time has blurred my memory, and I have no recollection of being in the factory. So my father's testimony in the
Yizkor book is the most accurate guide to what happened. He
paints images I could not begin to convey. 'Next day there was
a lull in the killings,' he wites, then goes on:

> The murderers were doubtless tired after a night of
> bloodshed. Perhaps some went to church to pray for
> succour for their handiwork? More certain it is that
> they went to the inn to get drunk and harbour strength
> for the next day. Yet the vigil around the barbed-wire
> fences was intensified to prevent escape.

Here, I'm fairly sure my father is making a reference to
himself. One of the main duties of a Jewish policeman was to
guard the perimeter of the ghetto, to prevent internees from
fleeing. The Nazis used the policemen to distance themselves
from their victims and to make their own lives easier. If, indeed,
my father was obliged to act as a sentinel by the barbed-wire
fence enclosing the ghetto's remaining Jews, I can only imagine
the mental anguish he endured. Every second must have been
an ethical and moral minefield. How did he manage to resolve
the quandary that being a policeman probably enabled his
immediate family to survive, while simultaneously meaning he
was obliged to escort his friends, neighbours and other family
towards their deaths.

'The tension and the horror into which those remaining in the ghetto were plunged on that day defy description,' writes my father. 'Nevertheless – they still hoped the spirit of evil would abate and that they would be allowed to stay alive.'

But any such hopes were crushed on Tuesday, 2 November 1942, when the events of the previous Sabbath were repeated with 'even greater cruelty and energy'. As my father writes:

> Screaming like wild beasts and with murder in their eyes, the Germans began to root all the Jews from their houses into the morning cold of incipient winter. Feeble old people, men, women and children were all lined up in rows. Horrible was the sight of children aged four to five years, separated from their parents, as they faced their murderers. Thus did Jewish children march to the hospital courtyard on their way to annihilation.

It was then that there was another selection:

> The Germans inspected the already authorized work permits of Jews, and then decided who would remain in the ghetto and who would be deported. Once more, wives were separated from husbands and children from their parents. Each group stood alone, and woe betide anyone who tried to cross over to another group. A

blow on the head from a rifle butt removed all desire
to try again.

As I was so young at the time, I can't remember the exact
sequence of events. I can't be sure whether what happened to me
in the churchyard took place on 31 October or on 2 November,
but whenever it was, it is imprinted in my memory.

We were ordered to kneel and I kneeled close to Mama. After a
while, I was able to shift and sit on her lap. She bent over me and
whispered words of encouragement in that kind, gentle voice.

'Tola. We will be all right, just as long as you don't cry out
or move. Stay as still as you can.'

In the churchyard, the air was filled with shooting and
screams of terror and pain. A massacre was taking place all around
us. Mama bent down lower and clutched me even tighter. My
face was almost touching the ground. I could feel Mama's weight
on my back. Although she was thin, she was still heavy for me.
I couldn't see what was going on. My ears were ringing. The
soldiers must have been shooting with those frightening new
guns I'd seen as we'd marched through the streets. They fired
bullets much faster than rifles. Mama's body jerked and twitched
involuntarily with every burst. Haunting cries accompanied the
metallic churning of the guns. The chemical smell from the
muzzles hung in the air and filled my nose.

All the while, through her fear, Mama kept trying to reassure
me. She did her utmost to be my physical and psychological

shield. Her fragile body was all that stood between me and a hail of Nazi bullets. The Germans were capricious. The slightest irritation and German trigger fingers were liable to twitch and squeeze. Mama was making herself small and insignificant. I felt her anxiety as she sought to avoid drawing attention to herself and, therefore, to me. I took comfort from nestling in her lap. Her touch always made me feel safe.

I could still feel her heart thumping. I can remember the sensation as if it were yesterday. Her body was quivering from fear and the distress of knowing her sister and nieces were going to die, if they were not already dead. She didn't make a sound, despite no doubt screaming inside from the pain of her snap decision. Her sister would have watched as Mama removed her children's hands from her skirt. Mama resisted crying out loud, but I felt her tears tumbling onto my face.

Whenever those dreadful days resurface in my mind, my reverence for my mother is rekindled. The image I hold and cherish is not just of my own mother defending me, but one of a universal mother fulfilling the primal covenant to safeguard her child, no matter what the cost. From the moment of creation, a woman carries her children in her soul, as well as her womb, and would sacrifice herself willingly to ensure that life continues for them.

Hitler tried to eradicate the Jews by exterminating their children. So my mother was not just trying to preserve her own family by saving me. She fought for my survival as an act of defiance on behalf of her people. When faced with complete annihilation, just one child could offer the Jewish race a life-line. As she sheltered in the graveyard next to St Wenceslas Church, Mama could never have imagined that by the end of the Holocaust, 150 members of her family would have perished, and that the only person left to tell her story would be me.

Every day of my life I honour her. I see my mother, Reizel, much like the Old Testament matriarch Rachel, who protected and wept for her children and became a universal icon of motherhood. As the symbolic mother of a nation, Rachel wept for the children of Israel when they were sent into exile; Mama's tears that fell on me in the graveyard were as powerful as hers.

Back then, I was relieved that my mama was protecting me. That relief, I recall, along with the sounds of genocide. Greased gun bolts sliding rounds into chambers. Guttural insults and curses before murder was committed. And fading away in the distance, the rhythmic panting of a steam engine slowly heading north.

Why wasn't I shot? At the time I thought it was a miracle I survived the carnage. The shooting seemed to go on for ever. I attempted to shut out the noise and willed the gunfire to cease. And then it did. The ringing slackened. That muffled sense of being deafened subsided. The silence was chilling. My ears took a while to acclimatize to the hush, although the churchyard wasn't completely quiet. I heard moaning and weeping and people trying to suppress groans. I still couldn't see anything, but I could sense agony rippling among the survivors.

After a moment, I felt my mother relax and she lifted herself up a little. I was no longer crushed.

'They've stopped shooting, Tola. You can stop feeling afraid,' Mama whispered. 'They aren't going to shoot any more. They've killed enough people.'

How did she know that? But she was right. The massacre was over.

The pain of having been fixed in one position was now aggravated by hunger pangs. I could barely feel my legs when, eventually, we were ordered to stand up. I looked around and caught the faint, strangely metallic smell of blood. There were bodies everywhere. So many dead, locked in unnatural poses. Among them were children I recognized. But I do recall that Mama and I were in a daze as we were marched back under guard to the ghetto, in the blackness of mid-autumn, past even more corpses.

Not far away, my father witnessed the courage of my mother's niece. Her name was Pesska Pinkusewicz. Pesska was allowed to stay behind in the ghetto because she was in possession of an authorized work permit. But she ran to a Gestapo soldier and told him that she wanted to stay with her parents and the rest of her family. My father wrote that the Gestapo soldier cautioned Pesska that her request meant 'an ascent to heaven through the chimney'.

But Pesska ignored his warning and tearfully repeated her entreaty, despite knowing that the German was telling her the truth. My father must have been close by when the soldier opened the gate because he overheard the German shouting to Pesska, 'Go, go stupid goose'.

'Her tear-dimmed eyes are radiant,' writes my father. 'She embraces her mother and father and cries out: "Let us be in heaven, but together!"'

That particular German was honest about the Jews' fate, but those in charge of the ghetto engaged in subterfuge to make it easier to herd people onto the trains. Horse-drawn carts headed to the station loaded with baggage the deportees were told they could take with them – a measure designed to fool them into thinking they were bound for a work camp and to rob them of their belongings.

My father wrote next:

Among the marchers was Bracha, the baker, and in her arms, her daughter. She felt that her strength was failing and whispered something to the Jewish policeman escorting her (whom she knew from days past). He took the child from her and placed her on the cart.

Marching beside Bracha was Regina Pakin of the Stern family . . .

Regina was carrying her three-year-old daughter, Marilka. The little girl too knew the policeman and she said to him; 'Put me on the cart as well. I'm so tired.' The policeman then put Marilka on the cart, but at once, a guard struck him on the head with his machine gun and blood gushed over his whole body.

I'm positive my father is talking about himself here, because I distinctly recall him coming back to our apartment covered in blood. He was lucky to escape with his life.

The German cocked his gun, but at that moment was called away by another soldier. The policeman, with the last of his strength and with blood seeping over his clothes, continued to escort the cart to the station.

Thus did the Jews of Tomaszów march, none knowing to where, their hands grasping a family member, their eyes glaring hatefully at their murderers. They were surrounded by armed guards. The faces of their Polish townsmen were contented. And yet it seemed that they still did not believe the calamity that was about to befall them. Even those who were exhausted physically and mentally showed no sign of their anguish.

My father describes how, in a 'blood orgy', the Germans and Ukrainians forced up to 120 Jews into each cattle wagon. There was no water or any other provision for human needs:

When it appeared impossible to pack more Jews into a wagon, they were 'assisted' with indescribable violence and cruelty by blows to the head of whips and rifle butts, until the last one had been crammed inside. The wagons were then bolted tight, and a soldier placed on the roof, his weapon at the ready lest anyone try to escape.

Such were the scenes of horror at Tomaszów station that day; families wrenched apart, children and parents searching frantically for one another. The Ukrainian butchers did not for a moment cease to belabour their victims. Nor did the Jewish policemen at the station escape their attention. They too were beaten mercilessly, rifle butts crushing their skulls, whereafter they were thrown into the wagons to share the final sufferings of their fellow Jews.

By the end of that day, about eight thousand more Jews had been placed in cattle cars and sent to their deaths. Hundreds more were slaughtered on the spot. Over the course of those three days, some fifteen thousand Jews were transported to the Treblinka gas chambers. The precise death toll has never been confirmed. Most records of that time simply state that hundreds were murdered during the liquidation of the Tomaszów Mazowiecki ghetto.

Sitting at home in New Jersey reading the *Yizkor* book

brought occupied Poland back to life and my heart bled for my father, who consigned to memory everything he had witnessed. He recorded the last known words of Rabbi Gedaliahu Shochet, one of the most devout people in the ghetto. The rabbi was hiding his salt and pepper beard behind a scarf, for fear the Germans would unsheathe their bayonets and cut it off, along with the skin beneath it.

> Rabbi Gedaliahu stood in the hospital courtyard and saw how the satanic Germans mercilessly thrust the ailing onto the trucks, while others fell from their bullets. And the Germans, their faces inflamed with alcohol, ran along the rows, and beat the heads of their victims with their rifle butts. And the blood flowed and flowed.

My father describes how, as his congregation was being exterminated all around him, the rabbi threw off his 'kerchief' and covered his head with it, as he would at prayer in the synagogue. 'Suddenly,' my father writes, 'he lifted his head to the skies and cried, "and thou, Lord of the Universe, sitting on high, see all this and art silent?"'

How striking that a rabbi should turn on his God and condemn Him. It's not surprising that his faith was shaken to its core. The brutality of the Holocaust led some of us to conclude that God did not exist because He did not intervene. But in the charnel house of Tomaszów Mazowiecki, another rabbi, Emanuel Grossman, maintained that humans were to blame because God gave them the power of individual choice. Grossman had the same name as my paternal grandfather, although I'm not sure if he was connected to us by blood.

Reading the *Yizkor* book in Yiddish is a more powerful experience for me than the English version, translated by Morris Gradel, a gifted linguist who died in 2010. The Yiddish is more precise, and I hear the cadence of the words that were used at the time, reconnecting me to the agony of 2 November 1942, when my father heard Rabbi Grossman's final pleas, as described below.

My father writes that as Rabbi Grossman walked with his family to the station, his 'usual self-confidence had faltered, although his face showed no signs of the struggle that was going on inside him':

> He believed that our enemies would perish, but now his hopes had collapsed. But neither did he show his despair. He exhorted his children, 'Go my children, save your lives, but remember always to remain Jews and tell the world what the German murderers did to us'.

I don't know whether the rabbi's children survived. I doubt it. But my father took his words to heart and did his duty by bearing witness and relating in graphic detail the nature of the Nazis' crimes in Tomaszów Mazowiecki.

My father is no longer here to tell that story. But I am. He passed the baton to me. I am speaking on behalf of Rabbi Emanuel Grossman and his family. Now I'm passing the baton to my own children and grandchildren.

The same day, after the deportation, the remaining Jews were ordered to assemble, according to my father's notes. I don't remember being there. But reading through my father's account, it seems clear that the crowd of survivors from the ghetto must have included Mama and me. We were allowed to live because the Nazis deemed that we were still of some use to them. After forcing us to watch genocide taking place, the Germans compounded our distress by compelling us to clean up the massacre they had perpetrated. At gunpoint, we were forced to sanitize the scene of the crime to comply with the Nazi dictum: leave no witnesses, leave no traces.

'There were clearly distinguishable bloodstains in the houses – the blood of aged and ailing Jews, who had been unable or unwilling to leave their beds and who were shot on the spot,' writes my father in the *Yizkor* book. 'On the tables were plates with soup the Jews did not have time to eat, glasses of tea they had not drunk.'

As a four-year-old, I couldn't process the images that passed in front of my eyes. There's no doubt that I was traumatized by the brutality of the sights I witnessed. But my heart aches for my father. I believe his torment was more profound. He saw the same war crimes as I did, and many more at closer quarters, but he understood much better than I could the magnitude of what had taken place. He had hoped that his position would allow

96

him to save more of his family and friends. But instead, he had to stand by, helpless, as they were slaughtered in front of him. 'Again, there were heart-rending scenes,' he recalls:

> The remaining Jews, fooled, robbed and despondent, looked vainly about for other members of their family, and did not know what had happened to them.
>
> The Germans, who had declared that they would not split families, had deceived them in the cruellest fashion. After an evening of horror, the remaining Jews felt like branches torn from a tree full of life. A dreadful feeling of loneliness overwhelmed them.
>
> How could they get through the coming night? How could they face the morning sun? Some of them were older, but most of them young. But in a trice, they had grown up. Now they were all orphans. All lonely and desolate.

According to the archives of the Jewish council, my father stopped being paid as a policeman from that day forward. But he and other members of the Jewish Order Service were compelled to dispose of the remains of those killed during the liquidation of the main ghetto. In all, about two hundred and fifty corpses lay contorted in apartments, on cobbles and in the churchyard. The Jewish policemen were under constant German military escort, as they removed the bodies of friends, relatives, neighbours and strangers alike, and buried them without ceremony in the Jewish cemetery of Tomaszów Mazowiecki.

Their skeletons lie there still. Entwined. Somewhere, beneath the mulch. Trampled underfoot. They have no headstones. But they are remembered. If you go there, look down and think of them. Maybe say a prayer that it should never happen again.

CHAPTER SIX

THE BLOCK

The small ghetto, Tomaszów Mazowiecki,
German-occupied Central Poland, winter 1942

Age four

Our world had shrunk. The surviving Jews of Tomaszów
Mazowiecki were confined to four streets: Wachodnia, Pierkarska,
Handlova and Jerozolimska. We were now prisoners in the small
ghetto that was known as the Block. There were about nine
hundred or so of us, including Mama, Papa and me. A barbed-
wire fence sealed us in and separated us from the buildings that
comprised the old, larger ghetto. We were guarded by Germans,
Ukrainians and Poles. From their shoulders dangled the sub-
machine guns that had irrigated the ground by St Wenceslas
Church with the blood of our people.

The northern end of Jerozolimska was the only official way
in and out. It was the portal to the outside world. As we all

99

now knew, from there, it was a 2-mile walk to the rail tracks, and extinction.

'I guess there's no way they would let us go back into our buildings.'

I overheard Mama whispering to Papa, as we were marched back under guard to our new quarters.

'We can't go back to the old buildings. I guess they're going to kill us a different way,' she said.

The sound of steam engines and shunting cars in the middle distance provoked looks of concern among the adults. But for the time being, the normal railway schedule was restored. The trains weren't for us. An eerie silence descended on the ghetto's four streets. The wall of sound made by 15,000 people had blown away over the horizon in the direction of Treblinka. A sense of shock and collective depression descended over those still breathing.

Over the coming days and weeks, it became clear that those souls would never return. Our guards didn't tell us about their fate. News filtered through because some Jewish craftsmen, such as carpenters and painters, were allowed to work outside the barbed wire, escorted to and fro by policemen.

What my father writes in the *Yizkor* book is important:

From time to time, a Polish railway worker, briefly coming across Jews outside the ghetto, would tell them that the deported Jews had first been taken to

Malinka, (a nearby town) and from there directly to annihilation!

And when their hearers returned to the ghetto and reported what they had been told by the Pole, no one wanted to believe them. They said it was just a joke by some anti-Semitic Pole. After all, such things were incredible for any sane person. Was it possible? How could such a thought occur? To burn living beings?!! To burn old people, women, and children? No! No! No! Impossible!

The Germans were masters of deception. They wanted surviving Jews to believe that the deportees were still alive. In their final hours before being murdered, some were coerced into writing letters or postcards to relatives saying that they were happy and healthy, labouring in some distant corner of the Third Reich.

My father recalled that people in the Block heard a rumour that a woman on the last train to Treblinka had written a letter saying she was working on a farm in Germany and her children were with her. No one could confirm the rumour, but they wanted to believe in it. The hope it provided was sufficient to keep us all in a state of denial. The survivors refused to believe the implications of the slaughter they had witnessed with their own eyes. It was beyond their comprehension that the Nazis intended to keep murdering us until the Jewish race was extinct

Looking back, I realize that most of those in the Block were suffering from 'the delusion of reprieve' – a condition identified by Viktor Frankl, an eminent Jewish neurologist and psychiatrist from Vienna, in his book *Man's Search for Meaning*, written after he'd survived three years in concentration camps, including Auschwitz.

Frankl writes, 'The condemned man, immediately before his execution, gets the illusion that he might be reprieved at the very last minute. We too, clung to shreds of hope and believed to the last moment that it would not be so bad.'

In the *Yizkor* book, my father records something similar: '. . . the Jews fooled themselves and grew accustomed to their daily routine, guarding in their hearts the hope of better times to come.'

For Mama and me, that daily routine involved going to the *Sammlungstelle*. The literal translation is 'collection point'. What a misleading euphemism for a repository of all the personal arte-facts, photographs, pictures, books and heirlooms of an entire community that had disappeared. Fifteen thousand personal histories stretching back centuries were contained within. Their ties and hats and sweaters and socks and shoes and suits and shirts and skirts each diffused a lingering intensely individual perfume. It was the job of those left behind to categorize and sort the possessions of the murdered Jews, dumped in undulating hillocks on the floor of a disused factory, pack the items into crates and dispatch them to Germany. The owners' bodies had gone. Their belongings soon followed. Before long, it was as if those people and their families had never existed.

The Nazis were obsessive about not wasting any useful material. As we now know, even bodies weren't sacrosanct to the Third Reich. Not only did they humiliate us while we were breathing, but they subjected our remains to the ultimate indignity after they slaughtered us. The manner in which they disposed of Jewish bodies defiled every precept of our religious traditions. Jews are obliged to bury a body as close to the moment of death as possible. This compassionate obligation applies to executed criminals, to the fallen on a battlefield, to every human being. To be denied burial is a grievous insult. No doubt that is one of the reasons why, in the extermination camps, the Nazis desecrated the victims of the gas chambers. Our hair was used for stuffing mattresses. Our gold teeth were extracted and melted down for jewellery. The rapacious German war machine demanded that no resource be wasted. Mercifully, at the *Sammlungstelle* we were required to process possessions and not human remains.

While we performed our duties, the Germans who weren't guarding us, pillaged the empty homes within the former larger ghetto. They tore down walls and jemmied ceilings in a voracious treasure hunt for jewellery, gold coins or other valuables secreted by the deportees. As they ransacked what they presumed were empty houses and apartments they found people who were too old, frail or sick to move, or had been missed during the first raid. These poor Jews were murdered in their beds. Once cleared of any salvageable items the properties were torched. Reading my father's eye-witness account was heart-rending:

The shattered windows gave the houses the appearance of blind people with gouged eyes. The stillness of death hovered over the houses – yet cried unto the heavens. Silence. Silence and death permeated the air, but amid the silence there still was heard the weeping of a little child, torn suddenly from its bed. The parents' beds also held secrets; they were still warm, the pillows moist with the tears of mothers who cried into them in order not to add to the grief and the anguish of the family.

The guards didn't oblige me to accompany Mama to the *Sammlungstelle*, but I stayed by her side all day long, every day, as together we sifted through the possessions. I was too scared to remain in our room by myself. One day, as she was separating boys' garments from girls', an article of clothing caught my eye.

'I like that sweater,' I whispered to Mama.

I kept my voice low, so as not to attract the attention of the guards watching over us with guns at the ready. The sweater was white and adorned with small white and pink mock pearls.

Mama took it out of my hands, folded it and placed it on a table on top of a pile of other similar pieces of clothing. She looked at me with those intense green eyes and raised her eyebrows. No words were needed. I knew better than to protest. Mama didn't speak until we were back in our room in the Block.

'Tola, that sweater you wanted once belonged to a four-year-old girl like you. She is no longer here. And soon, all these clothes will be gone as well.'

I didn't need any further explanation. From then on, I never coveted another piece of clothing. As she toiled alongside other ghetto survivors, my mother nurtured in me the idea that I should learn to be satisfied with less.

The *Sammlungstelle* was a petri dish where my strong will and sense of self-discipline grew roots and flourished. My young mind grasped the concept that having less was just a fact. In our lopsided war, a child's ability to handle deprivation was invaluable. Ultimately, in my case, it might have made the difference between survival and death.

However, that brief conversation with my mother was not just a lesson about materialism and possessions; it delivered a much more profound message about our very existence. Every hour of every day, the Germans chiselled away at our self-esteem and our very being. They sought to demoralize us and break our spirits. Every action they performed was aimed at coercing us into a state of acquiescence, whereby we accepted their definition of us as subhuman. My mother taught me that it was important to honour our dead. In the absence of memorial stones we could at least treat their possessions with dignity and respect. She was infusing me with the principle that even in the bleakest of times, we must not lose our own humanity, sensitivity and sense of self-worth. My mother was encouraging me to be a *mensch* – a person of integrity and honour. It was a lesson I took to heart.

Thereafter, even when a beautiful pair of red boots surfaced from beneath a heap, I managed to resist. Despite imagining myself wearing them, I put the boots onto a pile of children's shoes. I helped organize the clothes. If I found a skirt, I put it on the mountain of girls' clothes. The same with shoes and boys' clothes. I spent seven months of my life as a four-year-old slave labourer. Had peace existed, I might have been at kindergarten. But what was peace? I had known only war. I was getting an education in the most extraordinary school of life, and death.

I couldn't fail to understand the significance of the articles that surrounded us. They were evidence of a terrible war crime. But no investigators would ever come. Would the perpetrators ever be brought to justice? Would we be next to be killed? All these questions hung in the courtyard while the women worked in silence. It wasn't always possible for them to suppress their emotions, however. Occasionally, someone would cry out as she recognized a garment that belonged to her mother or a child. Yet, she carried on sorting. To stop would have tempted execution. We were trapped and grief had no avenue of escape. Our life of drudgery continued for a seven-month stretch.

Some years ago – I can't remember precisely when, but sometime in the last decade – I received a cheque in the post from the German government in Berlin. It was for $2,000, and it was a reparation for my time as a *Zwangsarbeiter* – slave labourer. The figure was derisory. An insult. There isn't a big enough cheque in the world to compensate for what I endured, or the sights I witnessed in the ghetto.

As a four-year-old, my horizons were limited to the Block and the *Sammlungstelle.* I was not aware of the changes that occurred in our society after the deportation. But my father saw everything. Thanks to his testimony, it seems obvious that our persecutors relaxed a little after their murderous exertions of late October and early November 1942. Food suddenly became more plentiful. For those who came into contact with Poles outside the barbed wire, it became possible to barter clothes or household goods for food.

It was then that I encountered eggs for the first time. Their taste and texture were a revelation. What a change a fried egg made from potato-skin soup. It was heaven. The yolk was my favourite part. For a treat, my mother would sometimes mix sugar with milk and an egg yolk, whipping up a mixture that was also an excellent balm for a sore throat. It's known in Yiddish as *gogl mogl*. Italians have something similar called *zabaglione*. Eggs had a transformative power in that they made life immeasurably better and raised my morale. And I didn't just savour the yolk as it rolled over my taste buds. I took pleasure from watching my mother preparing the egg, anticipating the wholesome flavour. After I had consumed the last morsel, I relished the lingering taste in my mouth and the glow of warmth in my stomach. Eggs elevated my appreciation of food. For a starving child, potato-skin soup was fuel to fight the process of the body devouring itself, but eggs represented love, then – and they still do today. Because my mother prepared my eggs with love. And I felt it. When you are denied sustenance for such a long time, food assumes an almost spiritual significance.

Nowadays, I have a special relationship with food. It is sacred to me, and I never take it for granted. Eggs remain my go-to comfort food. If I'm feeling unhappy, I'll treat myself to a fried egg, sunny side up.

While having access to better food made a difference to our physical wellbeing in late 1942, psychological stresses remained oppressive in the extreme. It was still forbidden to leave the Block without authorization. As a deterrent, the Germans decreed that if anyone escaped, another inmate would be shot dead. In that climate, the 900 survivors of Tomaszów Mazowiecki discovered a new unity of purpose and recognized that solidarity was essential. Class and wealth barriers that previously separated us broke down and there was shared anger that we had been abandoned by the world. Many turned to alcohol to ease their pain. Some contemplated suicide but decided against it because our extinction was, according to my father, 'the aim of the Nazi butchers'.

'Therefore,' my father writes, 'despite all the suffering and lamentation, the wish of the murderers should not be fulfilled! No surrender, no bowing to their wishes! And maybe, maybe we will yet succeed in seeing our loved ones alive and our murderers dead!'

Was this wishful thinking or was it a real declaration of intent? Whatever the real meaning behind my father's words, our community was clearly at the end of its tether and couldn't take much more. 'Morals, integrity, the sanctity of family life began to disintegrate,' Papa writes.

> Lonely men sought the company of lonely women, and the women sought the company of the men. Shame and modesty disappeared. If life and the world were licentious, then long live licentiousness! Who knew what tomorrow would bring? While you live, live life to the full! After, all, you did not know if you would be alive tomorrow!

By previous Jewish behavioural standards, it certainly appears that a cloud of immorality engulfed a significant number of ghetto inhabitants. But how could anyone be blamed for seeking a tender caress when our existence hung by the most delicate of threads.

Not everyone surrendered their old values, though. Religiously observant Jews refused to succumb to the outbreak of permissiveness. They didn't want to shame their ancestors, as they saw it, and they clung to the hope that as there were so few Jews left who were productive workers, the Germans would leave the ghetto alone. And they did. Until the bells rang out the end of 1942 and welcomed in 1943.

CHAPTER SEVEN

BURIED ALIVE

The small ghetto, Tomaszów Mazowiecki,
German-occupied Central Poland, 1943
Age four

Germans and Poles celebrated the arrival of 1943 by getting rip-roaring drunk. And, at first glance, it seemed that we might indeed have a happy new year.

Pasted onto walls throughout the ghetto were large posters apparently offering hope of escape from captivity. What a change that made. Normally, posters were used to communicate new German rules and regulations, with a warning that summary execution was the punishment for disobedience. Now the Germans were dangling the prospect of paradise before the surviving Jews of Tomaszów Mazowiecki. The posters offered the chance to be transferred to the Holy Land. Anyone with relatives in Palestine who wished to participate were urged to register.

My father recalls that the news provoked an impassioned debate among the survivors. 'Tempers flared and arguments broke out,' he writes.

Some thought it was yet another example of German deceit and cautioned against it. Others believed that the promise of settling in Palestine was entirely feasible, as part of a prisoner exchange being negotiated between the Germans and the British, who, at the time, were responsible for administering the Holy Land.

As so often happened in the ghetto, wishful thinking prevailed. Sceptical voices were shouted down and people began registering in droves. The demand increased when the Germans said that qualification for travel would be extended, not just to those with relatives in Palestine, but to those with friends and acquaintances there, too.

'After a day or two, the Germans announced that the list was full and so the Jews began to bribe them with jewels and gold and *protektsia* (protection money) if only they could be on the list,' writes my father in the *Yizkor* book. 'The "fortunate ones", who were registered, at once began to pack, ready for the journey to Palestine.'

Somehow, my father managed to attach our names to the list. As a family, we were elated. For the first time in years, my parents exuded a real sense of optimism. At last, there was a chance to escape mass murder, humiliation and hunger and move to a place that Mama and Papa regarded as Utopia. Palestine represented the pinnacle of their dreams. The melancholy air hanging over our room in the Block evaporated. I fed off my parents' happiness. I didn't know what Palestine was, or where – but I understood that it epitomized safety. When my parents were happy, I was happy. But the mood quickly flipped to one of despair and panic.

I am not too sure if my father was still a policeman at this stage. According to surviving *Judenrat* records, his last salary was paid before the deportations to Treblinka. But regardless of whether he was on the police payroll any longer, his intelligence-gathering skills remained as acute as ever. He detected that the Palestine *Aktion* was a German ruse. Those who had registered had been deceived. Instead, they were destined to be shipped to another labour camp or possibly worse. Our family and all the others were in imminent danger.

My father barged into our room looking terrible.

'I've managed to get us off the list,' he told my mother, in tears and out of breath. 'But it was really hard.'

Then he dashed out of the door again, saying he had to warn other people to try to remove their names as well. Somebody was clearly profiting from the panic sweeping through the Block. Carefully reading his account in the *Yizkor* book, I now understand that he had to bribe someone, with whatever little money he had left. As he writes, 'The middlemen who had previously been bribed to include people in the list now demanded new bribes to take *them* off it and replace them with other names.'

Reality kicked in at dawn on 5 January 1943. The ghetto was

encircled by Ukrainian and German troops. My father remembers several hundred Jews being loaded onto carts and trucks. The Germans maintained the charade that they were all being taken to Palestine.

According to the *Encyclopaedia of Camps and Ghettos*, 1933-1945 published by the US Holocaust Memorial Museum, some sixty-seven Jews from Tomaszów Mazowiecki made it to Palestine. They were first transported to Vienna, then to Turkey and on to the Holy Land after being exchanged for German prisoners of war. Sadly, the majority didn't get more than 7 miles down the road to the small town of Ujazd. There, in the shadow of a ghostly, ruined seventeenth-century castle, several dozen Jews were gunned down. The remainder were transported to the gas chambers of Treblinka.

Without doubt, our little family had been fortunate to escape with our lives, as had those my father managed to alert. He was crestfallen that he hadn't been able to warn more people. From that moment onwards, however, my father was powerless to subvert the Nazis' inexorable progress towards the final liquidation of the ghetto.

Mama and I continued our daily routine of sorting, stacking and packing clothes in the *Sammlungstelle*. Added to the piles now were the belongings of the victims of the Palestine deception.

The monotony was disrupted early one March morning when

we were roused with the familiar cries that filled everyone with dread.

'*Alle Juden, raus.*'

We were ordered to line up along Pierkarska, one of the four streets of the Block. A basket was placed in front of us, and a Gestapo officer addressed us brusquely. The basket was to be filled with jewellery and any other valuables we still possessed. It wasn't a request.

You could almost touch the air of unease that rippled through the crowd. The Germans knew that people were reluctant to surrender possessions that might be useful in the future, to barter for food, or life itself.

Suddenly, soldiers pulled four men out of the line at random and shot them. This had the desired effect. On the Germans' command, the remaining Jews returned to their homes and dug out any small remaining valuables from their hiding places. The basket soon filled up. Of course, people prized life above material goods. But the loss of money, jewels, gold or silver was debilitating. It removed the possibility of buying a path to safety whenever the spectre of sudden death next loomed. The cloud of depression that hung over the Block darkened.

However, the mood lifted marginally by the time Purim came around a few weeks later. Traditionally, one of the most joyous festivals in the Jewish calendar, Purim commemorates the survival of Jews in the fifth century BC, when their Persian rulers intended to wipe them out. Some describe Purim as the

Jewish equivalent of carnival, when we are supposed to celebrate family, unity, togetherness and triumph over adversity. At that stage of the German occupation, three and a half years in, and especially after the previous six months, the idea of overcoming our oppressors was in the realm of fantasy. Still, the festival gave us a much-needed lift. As my father writes: 'March 20th, 1943. Today is Purim Eve, a warm, sunny day. Even the work of collecting and sorting Jewish belongings proceeds in a lighter spirit.'

There would be 'a tinge of festivity', he continues, following the traditional reading of the sacred scroll of Esther (a Jew who became Queen of Persia and is celebrated as a heroine in Judaism). The scroll tells of how a plot to destroy the Jews (hatched by Haman, a vizier, or high official of the Persian court) was foiled by Esther, together with one of her cousins.

'Anyway, that evening, all would be forgotten,' writes my father. 'The survivors in the ghetto would gather in fellowship, eat a little, drink a glass or two, maybe even sing, and maybe for an hour or so the burden of their tragedy would be finished.'

But at five o'clock that evening, a truck drove up to the ghetto gate and a German police officer yelled, '*Aufmachen ihr dreckige Juden-schwein*'. ('Open up, you filthy Jewish pigs.')

Meister Pichler strode into the ghetto and presented the Jewish policemen with a list of names. He told them that all of those on the roll had to assemble immediately as they were to be sent to a labour camp. The most important person on the list was Doctor Efraim Mordkowicz, a genuine hero of the ghetto who had performed miracles through the occupation. Despite a paucity of medical supplies, and the murder of so many colleagues, he had worked tirelessly to heal the sick and alleviate the suffering of his fellow Jews, especially during the typhus epidemic.

Dr Mordkowicz duly arrived at the assembly point, with his nine-year-old daughter, Krisza, who was clinging to him with one hand, while clutching a bundle of belongings in the other. He turned to the Police Chief Hans Pichler and asked him where they were going. My blood ran cold as I read my father's description in the *Yizkor* book:

> Pichler burst out sarcastically, 'You are being sent to a place of rest'. Little Krisza asks tearfully, 'Why do we have to be sent just today?' for she had invited her friends [to celebrate Purim] that very evening. 'Perhaps we could postpone our journey to tomorrow?' Pichler placed his hand on her head, and she sensed it was the hand of a murderer and, wrenching herself free of him, clung tearfully to her father. Meanwhile, everyone on the list had arrived and they were loaded onto the truck with their baggage. There were twenty-one of them.

Among their number were the ghetto's remaining physicians, patients from the makeshift hospital, several Jewish policemen and the last surviving members of Tomaszów Mazowiecki's intelligentsia.

The procession proceeded to the cemetery. Helped by blows from rifle butts, the victims jumped from the truck, which had stopped beside an open grave (to avoid attention this had been dug by Poles). At once, Pichler ordered the unfortunate Jews to take off their clothes. Terrible cries then rang through the cemetery. Two women, Yazda Rejgrodska and her sister, refused and one of them began to struggle with the murderers. The two women now started to run, screaming, towards the fence. Krisza also burst into tears and began to make for the fence.

Just then, Johann Kropfitsch, the notorious Austrian policeman who had killed so many children, appeared: 'Kropfitsch, who was known for his sadistic trait of firing at the heads of small children, put a bullet into the head of little Krisza and thus staunched her tears. The other butchers began firing at the Jews standing on the edge of the grave.'

Pichler and two other Nazis ran after the two sisters, opened fire with pistols and killed them. My father witnessed the Germans' reaction: '*Die verfluchten Hunde haben die Kleider verseucht.*' ('The cursed dogs have soiled their dresses.')

'Polish workmen filled in the graves,' recalls my father. 'Afterwards, they said that the earth on top of the graves went on heaving for some time after the murders.'

I am one of the last living links to Dr Mordkowicz and his

daughter, Krisza, who was five years older than me, and the nineteen other people murdered that day. Just a few hours after some of them were buried alive, trying to claw their way back to the surface, I was at work alongside my mother in the *Sammlungstelle*, sorting through the clothes as usual. Among those we handled were two bloodstained dresses, smudged with mud from the Jewish cemetery. We recognized them.

That massacre has gone down in Tomaszów Mazowiecki folklore as the Nazis' Purim *Aktion*. It was a reminder, as if we needed one, of the arbitrary nature of the German occupation.

For weeks, life followed a monotonous routine, then it was punctuated by a spasm of sadistic violence. Tension mounted a month later, in the middle of April when, 70 miles away, the Jewish rebels inside the Warsaw Ghetto began their heroic battle against elite German forces. The soldiers guarding us were afraid that rebellion might spread to other ghettos. They had nothing to worry about in Tomaszów Mazowiecki. We were hemmed into four streets and completely surrounded. Our rooms had been searched multiple times. The Germans must have known we had no weapons. What were we going to attack them with? Nevertheless, they still opened fire if anyone was brave enough to venture past the barbed wire.

All the while, in the *Sammlungstelle*, we were working steadily through the clothes. The mountains of possessions had shrunk.

Soon there would be nothing left. Those garments were the very reason for our continued existence. The chattels of the dead were keeping us alive. What would happen when the warehouse was empty, and our work was at an end? What would become of us?

By May 1943, there was no need for everyone to turn up for work. That spelled danger for those who were unproductive and no longer slaving on behalf of the Third Reich. There was a sense that something new was on the horizon. Experience taught us that a change in our circumstances was never benevolent.

The grim mood was exacerbated by the stench of rotting waste. In the unseasonable heat, flies swarmed around the piles of garbage. Beyond the barbed wire, to the horizon, the world was rich with colour as nature put on its summer clothes. Its beauty was a feast for the eyes. Yet at the same time, it accentuated the depth of our despair.

By this stage, there were about seven hundred people left in the ghetto. The numbers were whittled away when small groups were dispatched to the Bliżyn slave-labour camp 50 miles to the south-east.

On 30 May, there was an announcement that another selection was due to take place. The very word *Selektion* induced a sense of profound anxiety. We knew by now that it usually meant a death sentence. The Gestapo declared that thirty-six people would be chosen to be left behind. Those names were read out. All three of us were on the list. Mama, Papa and I. I was too young to realize the significance at the time, but it was a terrifying moment for my parents and the other thirty-three people. They were afraid they would be shot immediately or taken to the graveyard and executed there.

The rest of the ghetto, some six hundred and fifty people, went back to pack a few essential belongings.

'Mothers tore children from deep sleep, dressed them hurriedly and drenched them with hot tears,' writes my father. 'They knew that leaving that place meant their future was even more uncertain. People ran to their families, to friends, and helped each other to pack, and held on to each other as if saying goodbye.'

A whistle pierced the air, ordering everyone in the ghetto to gather at the *Appellplatz* – the assembly point. Apprehension rippled through the ranks of people standing five deep. Then the names of the thirty-six were read aloud again and we stepped aside. The Germans ordered the remaining 650 people to start marching towards the railway station.

'Why are you leaving us behind?' the people around me shouted, as the column of Jews passed through the ghetto gates for the last time. 'It was such a scream, that it penetrated the air like a knife, a scream that reached the heavens, a scream straight from the mothers' hearts,' writes my father. 'It was bone chilling.'

Pichler grinned and ordered our group to follow him to the *Sammlungstelle.* We were pushed into a building and locked inside. The door was guarded by helmeted guards with machine guns. The Germans took pleasure in terrorizing us.

'All those inside expected at any moment that they would be led to the cemetery and shot,' writes my father.

I can't remember how long we were locked in the warehouse, but I do recall that there was shooting not very far away. I now realize what that was. The Germans went from apartment to apartment, from room to room, in the four streets of the Block, killing anyone who was still hiding or was too sick to move. Some of those who were murdered that day had stayed because they couldn't face the prospect of being herded into a cattle car to extinction and chose to die in familiar surroundings.

After the guns stopped firing, the guards opened the door and we realized we'd been spared. They had locked us up because they wanted us to think that we were next and also because they didn't want any witnesses.

Many Jews reading this will be nodding sagely to themselves right now and thinking: I know why they survived – *gematria*.

Gematria is a Jewish form of numerology whereby each Hebrew letter has a numerical value. As such, certain words are believed to possess mystical power. A key word here is *chai*, meaning 'life'. *Chai*'s numerical value is eighteen – hence it's a Jewish tradition to present gifts of, say, eighteen dollars, or multiples of eighteen, as a good omen for life. Thirty-six – twice eighteen – is a particularly auspicious number. It represents two lives.

Perhaps it was a coincidence that thirty-six people were chosen from the ghetto that day, or perhaps a higher power was involved. Who knows? Either way, those of us in that warehouse all got a second chance at life.

As one of the handful of children to escape the slaughter in my hometown, there is no denying that I am incredibly fortunate. However, what followed was anything but a privilege.

The Gestapo commanded us to clean up the four streets of the Block. Inside and out. We had to erase all evidence that a war crime had taken place. Most important of all was that no traces of flesh or blood should be visible. We had to make it appear that the Jews had left in an orderly fashion – that no harm had been done to them – just in case the Red Cross, or another supposedly neutral organization, started asking difficult questions. But then I doubt the Germans would have allowed the International Red Cross access to the ghettos. It was more likely that the properties were being prepared to be taken over by Poles or Germans as part of Hitler's plan to ensure the population of the Third Reich was entirely Aryan.

The tasks I had to perform as I approached my fifth birthday were things no child should ever have to do, and I could not avert my eyes or hide away. The images I saw over the ensuing weeks haunt me to this day and have kept me awake at night as I have dug into my memories for this book. For nearly eighty years now, I've had one particular recurring nightmare, where I am walking among dead bodies. That dream always shakes me awake, after which further sleep is impossible, as my mind is propelled back to Tomaszów Mazowiecki.

We couldn't transport the murder victims to the Jewish cemetery and give them eternal rest in sacred ground. We buried them close to the buildings where they had been murdered. My father dug the graves, and then we manhandled the bodies from the beds and floors where they'd been killed, downstairs, along the cobbles and into a shallow pit.

I helped as best I could. I lifted an arm, or a head or a foot, as my mother and father struggled to manoeuvre the corpses into their rudimentary tombs. Lodged in the back of my mind is the stench of death in the early summer heat, and the look of agony on the corpses' faces. But what I clung to, amid all this depravity, was my parents' humanity, as they treated the dead with the dignity they warranted.

For the first time in almost four years of mass murder, my father managed to say *Kaddish* – the traditional prayer of mourning for the dead – under the noses of the guards with their machine guns at the ready. It was another act of defiance.

'Exalted and hallowed be His great Name,' intoned my father.

'Amen,' responded my mother in a whisper.

'Throughout the world which He has created according to His Will. May He establish His kingship, bring forth His redemption and hasten the coming of His Messiah.'

'Amen.'

'In your lifetime and in your days and in the lifetime of the entire House of Israel, speedily and soon, and say, amen.'

'Amen. May His great name be blessed for ever and to all eternity, blessed,' whispered my mother.

'May His great name be blessed for ever and to all eternity. Blessed and praised, glorified, exalted and extolled, honoured, adored and lauded be the name of the Holy One, blessed be He.'

'Amen.'

'Beyond all the blessings, hymns, praises and consolations that are uttered in the world; and say, amen.'

'Amen.'

'May there be abundant peace from heaven, and a good life for us and for all Israel; and say, Amen.'

'Amen.'

'He who makes peace in His heavens, may He make peace for us and for all Israel; and say, Amen.'

'Amen.'

My parents said the prayer as they shovelled earth over the bodies, the guards unaware that an important Jewish tradition was being upheld. I'm sure my mother and father were thinking of their parents and other murdered family members as they incanted those ancient words. Perhaps they had recited *Kaddish* in the privacy of our crowded rooms, first in the big ghetto, and then in the Block. I'm not sure. But I had never heard the prayer before. And this despite the fact that I am descended, through my mother's side, from a long line of Hasidic theological scholars; I had no idea what my parents were saying or doing (although I recognized its poignancy), which shows you how difficult it was to practise our faith under occupation. I find it extraordinary that my first conscious experience of a Jewish religious ritual should be in the aftermath of a war crime, in the presence, not of a rabbi, but of Nazi soldiers, who could have killed us without a second thought. Looking back, it amazes me that anyone could praise God at a time like that.

When the burials were over, we moved inside the houses. We washed away bloodstains. We picked up bone fragments. We tidied up kitchens. We swept floors. We disinfected bathrooms. We made beds. We smoothed out pillows. Everything had to be perfect. We had to leave no trace, on pain of death. I never left my parents' side, helping in whichever way I could.

It took us three months to sanitize the scene of the Nazis' crime. We finished in the first week of September, three days shy of my fifth birthday.

'We've outlived our usefulness,' I overheard my mother whispering to my father. 'There's nothing left for us to do. Now we're doomed. They are surely going to kill us now.'

Four years after entering Tomaszów Mazowiecki, in September 1939, the Germans had fulfilled the declared intention of Hitler's National Socialist movement. They had ethnically cleansed the Jews completely. A vibrant, highly cultured community that had been in existence for over 200 years was now extinct.

The Germans had a phrase for this.

Tomaszów Mazowiecki was now *Judenrein*. Jew pure. Cleansed of Jews.

Only 200 Jews from Tomaszów Mazowiecki survived the Holocaust. After the war, some returned to their former homes to try to find lost relatives. But the memories of what happened there were so dark that they settled elsewhere.

However, there is still a Jewish presence in the town today. In the overgrown Jewish cemetery, where so many of my relatives lie and in the gardens of the Block – in those four streets: Wachodnia, Pierkarska, Handlova and Jerozolimska. It's a place that I despise because of what happened there. But for me, that tiny corner of the world will always be sacred ground.

CHAPTER EIGHT

THE YELLOW DEATH CAMP

Starachowice labour camp, German-occupied Central Poland,
autumn 1943–summer 1944

Age five

The rap on the door – a rifle butt, accompanied by a string of instructions in German – demanded our full attention.

'You're moving out. You can take one suitcase each. Be at the *Appellplatz* in five minutes. Hurry up.'

The soldiers had come for us again. We'd been expecting them. But the moment still delivered an electric shock. We all twitched, as if we'd been tasered. After four years of occupation, we had precious few possessions. Still, my parents hurled clothes and other key belongings into the cases as fast as they could.

We walked out of the door without a backward glance and headed towards the assembly point. The other remaining survivors from Tomaszów Mazowiecki stumbled into the street looking apprehensive. Was this it? Was this the end?

Further along, I could see a German army flatbed truck with a canvas cover, belching out black exhaust fumes as the engine idled. The tailgate was down. As we walked briskly along the cobbles I peered up at my father, who exchanged anxious glances with my mother.

I had never been on a truck, but I had seen them from the window. I glanced back at my mother. Her face gave her away. They'd seen this scenario unfold many times since the ghetto was formed, and only rarely had deportees reached the destination mentioned by the Germans. The Nazis were mendacious. Even when they were sending people to their deaths, they always made it appear that the Jews were going to a better place. By offering a thimbleful of hope, the Germans were able to proceed with their industrial slaughter with comparably little fuss. Hope was an accomplice to murder.

My mother climbed into the back of the truck first. My father handed up the suitcases. And then he lifted me into my mother's arms. There wasn't a lot of space beneath the canvas. The bench seats were occupied by other ghetto survivors and soldiers equipped for battle. We had to sit on the floor on our suitcases. Other soldiers who were guarding us raised the tailgate. Nobody said anything as the chain bolts locked the back of the truck into place. My parents just looked at each other and tried to avoid catching the eyes of the Germans.

This was the first time that I'd been on the other side of the barbed wire. Curiosity overwhelmed me as we bumped along the road. I now know that we were heading into the sun. We were driving south-east. From my perch on the suitcase, huddled next to my mama, I could barely see over the top of the tailgate, but it was interesting for me to look at the view, as the town of Tomaszów Mazowiecki disappeared behind us. There were peasants harvesting in fields, loading straw onto horse-drawn carts. Back then, I didn't understand what they were doing or that this was what normal life looked like. Such were the limits of a child's experience inside the ghetto.

After we had driven for a short time, I sensed that my fellow passengers exhaled a collective sigh of relief. I didn't know then why the tension eased. But now I do. We had driven beyond the Jewish cemetery. And we hadn't stopped. Perhaps this time the Germans were telling the truth. Perhaps we would survive this day. And wake up the next. Maybe we were really going to the stated destination. Starachowice.

We bounced up and down on our suitcases in solemn silence. My fellow passengers were in mourning. They were leaving behind childhood homes, murdered parents, spouses, children and friends, some of whom had no known graves, although their bodies lay close to the tombs of generations of ancestors in the Jewish cemetery. Would they ever return, to place stones on the graves, as Jews do, to signify that their dead are not forgotten? We were being exiled from our history. A people which loses its past, faces a desolate future.

I was fortunate. I still had my mother and father. I snuggled up close to Mama, seeking comfort from her scent and the familiar outline of her body. A sense of security and the hypnotic rumbling of the wheels lulled me to sleep. Once, I was jolted awake, and she fed me a piece of bread.

After two or three hours, travelling at a sedate pace, our journey came to an end. From the back of the truck, I saw soldiers closing security gates behind us, and as we drove deeper into the camp, the panorama of our new prison revealed itself. It was surrounded by tall, barbed-wire fences, just like those that had encircled the ghetto in Tomaszów Mazowiecki. But tall watch towers in strategic positions around the perimeter made it significantly different. I noticed those immediately. The lookout points on top were equipped with bigger guns than I'd ever seen before. And in their crows' nests, the guards kept their eyes trained on us as we rattled along.

'You see those towers and those guns, Tola?' my mother whispered. 'From there the guards can always observe you. You must always behave in a way that you won't be shot.'

'Yes, Mama.'

The truck came to a halt in the middle of an open square.

After dismounting, everyone from the truck was scattered around this new, sinister labour camp. A guard with a machine gun directed us to our accommodation. After three years living in squalid, overcrowded rooms, we had no idea what to expect. We had become accustomed to our conditions constantly deteriorating. So it came as a pleasant surprise to discover that we had been allocated a room all to ourselves.

Even more astonishing was the realization that, for the first time in my life, I had my own bunk. We were in the family barrack. Apparently, Jews were provided with reasonable quarters because they were the best factory workers – more productive than Gentile Polish civilians who were forced to work there as well. We were also informed that the quality of our food would improve.

What was this extraordinary place? Why were conditions here better than in Tomaszów Mazowiecki, just 70 miles away?

Within the city of Starachowice were four labour camps providing workers for a sprawling armaments and industrial complex. It was a critical component of Nazi Germany's war machine, supplying a third of all the munitions for every branch of the German military. There was an enormous steel plant, connected to a wide array of production lines manufacturing shell casings for artillery and bombs, stick grenades and bullets of various calibres. The air was badly polluted from the furnaces and chemical works that were an integral part of the weapons industry. Smog from the chimneys was accompanied by the low-frequency grinding of heavy machinery. The war might have been a long way from Starachowice, but it was far from peaceful there. The engine room of German aggression never slept. There was no escape from its all-pervasive hum.

The most critical factor for my family now was that my mother and father were useful. They may have been slave labourers, but their ability to work afforded us a protective shield, albeit one without a guarantee.

With the benefit of nearly eighty years' hindsight, it's now possible to say that the attitude of the Germans running Starachowice provided us with a lifeline. They were far more pragmatic than the Nazis in Berlin, who were ideologically committed to the complete annihilation of the Jews. The main concerns of the Starachowice directors were meeting production targets and ensuring that ammunition supplies to the *Wehrmacht* – the German military – were maintained.

After the Red Army's victory at Stalingrad a few months earlier, German forces were engaged in a debilitating rearguard action. Soviet confidence surged, as did production rates in the Communist arms industry. The rate of attrition along the 800-mile-long Eastern Front, where the two mighty armies clashed, was crippling. German ammunition stocks needed constant replenishment.

So the simple logic at Starachowice was that the munitions factories required a steady supply of workers to keep production lines operating. If large numbers of labourers were sent to the gas chambers, production would falter and so would the German army.

Therefore, it made sense to keep the Jews alive. In this small corner of the Third Reich, we were fortunate that there were some influential Germans who were bold enough to defy Hitler's zealots.

But that didn't mean we were safe. Far from it. We were now isolated from our friends from Tomaszów Mazowiecki. Back there, we knew who we could trust. We had been among them all our lives. We had a network we could rely on. Here, we were strangers, and so was everyone else. We had to be more wary and tread carefully. The guards ringing Starachowice and posted in the towers were Ukrainian volunteers. They had joined the Nazi forces of their own free will because they shared their pathological hatred of the Jews. If anything, the Ukrainians were more fanatical than some Germans. They wouldn't hesitate to kill us, given half a chance.

As we unpacked and settled in, Mama laid out the rules to ensure that I stayed alive.

'Your father and I will be gone most of the day. We will be working at the ammunition factory. You will be on your own and responsible for your own safety. During the day, someone will give you something to eat, and we will give you something more when we return at night.'

This was going to be a radically new experience. I had never been on my own before. I knew no one here apart from Rutka, one of my friends from Tomaszów Mazowiecki, who was among those who'd been brought to Starachowice. But we had no idea where she and her family had been billeted. As it transpired, during our entire incarceration in the *Arbeitslager* – the labour camp – I never once saw Rutka. That's how big it was.

On the night of 5 September 1943, I could have slept on

my own for the very first time. But I didn't dare, and instead, I climbed into bed with my parents.

The next morning, before she went to work, Mama drilled into me the rules of Starachowice etiquette.

'You must behave like this. If you don't, the Germans might kill you. Do you understand?'

'Yes, Mama.'

'Always step to the side when a German is passing you. Do not run, just step to the side.'

'Yes, Mama.'

'Whatever you do, do not look them in the eye. You mustn't do it. Look at something else. Like their belt. No higher than that. And make sure that if you have a head covering, like a scarf or a hat, you take it off.

'And last of all, put your hands behind your back and clasp them together. Have you got that? Are you sure?'

'Yes, Mama.'

To make sure this submissive behaviour became ingrained as second nature, she practised with me every day before heading to the factory. She woke me up at five o'clock in the morning and pretended to be a German, strutting loudly around the room, as if she was wearing jackboots. I did exactly what she taught me: I stepped out of the way, bowed my head and put my hands behind my back.

Then my parents would kiss me and climb onto one of the waiting trucks. The factory where they worked was about half an hour away. It would barely be dawn, and I would not see them until late at night.

I could have stayed alone at the barrack, but the silence scared me. All the adults had gone to work and at first, I didn't see or hear any other children. The place seemed to be totally empty. So I went outside, because that felt safer, even though the Ukrainians were watching me from the towers. Other children must have made the same decision. I did not see many girls, but I spotted a group of boys running around and playing rough games beneath the gaze of the guards.

When I tried to join in the boys' games, they would only accept me if I played the Jew. They were all Jewish and always wanted to be the Nazis. (Children often identify with an aggressor, and having been exposed to such behaviour, it's not surprising the boys wanted to replicate the power and supremacy of the Germans.) Being a girl and younger, I never got a chance to play the Nazi. And as I couldn't fight, I was always the victim. They pretended sticks were rifles, and I had to run as fast as I could, while they chased me, making gun noises and yelling, 'Stop, you dirty Jew. Or we'll kill you.'

If they caught me, they would hit me gently with sticks. Sometimes, one of the boys would get carried away, forget it was just a game and hurt me. Then I'd run and hide among the barracks and wait until my parents came home. Or I would run to our building and shelter underneath. But I soon forgot the pain. I chose to be outside with the other children and risk a beating. It was more important for me to have any kind of relationship than none. What's interesting to me now is that I preferred to be more frightened than alone. Psychologists would recognize that I was presenting the characteristics of someone in an abusive relationship. That's an understatement when it comes to describing my life at the time.

Re-enacting our daily tribulations in play made us even hungrier than usual. Sometimes, in the middle of the day, someone would give us some food. It was usually a piece of bread or some soup. But it was never enough, and we were constantly hungry. We used to head to a building containing a kitchen and scour the garbage bins. We rarely found anything edible. If we did, we devoured it. But at the end of the working day, I was always certain to eat. My parents were fed during their shift at the factory. The German management wanted their slaves to keep their energy levels up. And Mama would always save something for me.

All the while, we were acting out childhood fantasies under the watchful gaze of the Ukrainian guards in their towers. Although they looked menacing, I never saw them open fire. But there were frequent reminders that the boundary between life and death in Starachowice was razor thin.

One day, everyone in the camp was summoned to the central parade ground, the *Appellplatz*. There were loudspeakers throughout the complex and the tone of the harsh voice making the announcement left no room for doubt. Attendance was compulsory.

'I'm going to take you now, and I'm going to show you what's going to happen to you if you don't follow the rules,' my Mama said. 'And the reason I'm doing this is because I'm not here to take care of you. You have to take care of yourself.'

Hundreds of people shuffled into the square looking nervous. I gripped Mama's hand as tightly as possible. Everyone's eyes were drawn to a woman who was attached to a pole with a rope. Her hands were tied behind her back.

Putting a bullhorn to his mouth, a uniformed officer outlined the nature of her 'crime'. The woman had, in the Germans' eyes, broken one of the cardinal rules of the Starachowice camp. She had displayed disrespect.

The woman had had the audacity to come face to face with a German soldier inside the camp. She had maintained eye contact and refused to yield the right of way. As a child, I was shocked that an adult didn't know the rules as well as my mama and had behaved wrongly. There was only one sentence for such a wilful act of defiance.

Mama squeezed my hand, and whispered, 'Remember what I taught you? Watch.'

Most mothers would have urged their children to look away, or clasped a hand over their eyes to shield them from witnessing further atrocities. Not my mama. These were extraordinary times and Mama was doing her utmost to keep me alive. She was trying to teach me that actions had consequences and I needed to see them for myself to understand the reality of the world we inhabited.

I watched as the officer walked up to the woman. He pulled the pistol from his holster, and shot her in the head at point-blank range. She slumped to the ground. Her husband and their three children screamed and ran sobbing to her body as it lay contorted around the pole. All four of them collapsed on the ground next to her, rocking back and forth, weeping hysterically. The crowd dispersed, abandoning them to their grief.

I turned to my mother and whispered, 'Mama, you promise me you will obey all the rules?'

She nodded and replied, 'And so will you'.

That night, silence descended on the camp as people contemplated the execution and its implication. Even here, although the Jews were useful as slave labourers, they were, ultimately, dispensable.

Over the ensuing months, fewer and fewer people came home from the factories. There were industrial accidents in the steelworks. Some died in the weapons plants following exposure to toxic chemicals.

'Some workers are careless,' Mama said. 'They inhale a yellow powder which destroys their lungs. You always have to be on guard, even at work.'

I remember they called it the yellow death. I now understand that the victims were poisoned by TNT, the explosive compound in bombs and shells. There was probably little the slave labourers could do to protect themselves from chemicals, short of covering their faces with a damp cloth.

Almost every night, my parents had a similar conversation: as long as they were careful and useful, they would be kept alive. But how long would it last?

Time passed slowly in Starachowice. A long, frigid winter came and went. My routine never seemed to vary. The most important thing for us as a family was that we were still alive and together, although my parents spent most of their waking hours on the factory floor.

The major discomfort was our growing hunger. The amount of food we were given started to tail off. I had no concept of measuring time, apart from an innate sense of when I expected to be fed. My stomach was a very reliable clock. I would look forward to lunchtimes, when Rivka, a pregnant Jewish woman who lived in the family barracks, provided us with a small serving of soup and bread. Normally, after eating, we would return to our rough game of Catch the Jew.

But one afternoon, in the spring of 1944, when I was about five and a half years old, Rivka kept us with her longer. I remember the day well. It was sunny and warm. On the floor, next to our table, Rivka had constructed a makeshift stove by laying a square of bricks, covered with a piece of tin. She had left enough space to ignite a small fire from paper and twigs. We all had a mess tin each, into which she poured some flour. She mixed some flour and water in her own mess tin to create a simple dough. Then she poured just the right amount of water into our tins and said, 'Now copy what I have done. Try to make sure all the flour is moist and make the dough as smooth as possible.'

All the children embraced the lesson. I remember the sense of joy of being taught something new and of my fingers getting sticky.

'Now flatten the dough with your fists, until it is as even as you can make it. Use your hands to get rid of any lumps. It has to be as flat as possible.'

Then she showed us how to take a fork and put holes in the dough.

'Children, you have to do this as quickly as possible. Hurry up.'

We all responded to the urgency in her voice. I assumed she was exhorting us to speed up because what we were doing was illicit. Out of the corner of my eye, I could see the guard towers. Their machine guns were pointing in our direction. I was afraid the soldiers would cut us down if we didn't finish quickly enough.

Rivka put each of the mess tins in turn over the flames. The dough baked very quickly. And the finished product smelled delicious. I wanted to feast on mine straight away.

'Now children, I know you are starving,' she said, 'but you are not allowed to take even one bite. Under any circumstances. What you must do is to take it home to your parents and then you will share it tonight. Do you understand?'

It was difficult for me to comply because Rivka was right – I was starving. But by now, being obedient was second nature to me.

As usual, my parents returned to the family barracks late. It might have been ten or eleven o'clock in the evening. I was fast asleep, clutching my creation. Gently, they woke me up.

'Look what I've made for you,' I said, bursting with pride.

My father carefully broke the cracker into three equal pieces and said a prayer. My mother burst into tears. 'Oh, it's the first night of Passover,' she sobbed.

Mama had toiled so hard in the weapons factory that she had lost track of time.

'Do you remember Passover last year?' she asked my father.

'Yes,' he replied. 'It was the day the Warsaw Ghetto uprising began.'

'So much has happened since then,' said Mama. 'I simply can't believe it.'

'And we didn't have matzah to break,' said my father. 'But we still had family and friends. Thank you, Tola, for this wonderful, thoughtful gift.'

Tears flowed down Mama's cheeks as she thought about the loss of her family and their Passover celebrations in the past.

Passover is one of the most important festivals in the Jewish calendar. Each springtime we celebrate Moses leading the escape from Egypt of the children of Israel after 200 years of servitude. The essence of that story is liberation, and matzah symbolizes the hardship of slavery and the Jewish people's escape to freedom. We call it the bread of affliction.

Passover during the Holocaust years was especially poignant. It's hard to imagine another time in the entire history of the Jewish people when its symbolism would have evoked more pain.

When I look back, I realize that as I let the cracker melt in my mouth, savouring the taste and the time capsule it was creating, that was the moment I understood that certain foods have spiritual significance that transcend the notion of fuel for the body.

For the first time in my life, I was eating something that was fuel for the soul. When Rivka told us to hurry up, it wasn't because the guards were going to shoot us, although if they had known what we were doing they might have been tempted. It was because Jewish tradition dictates that the process of making matzah is concluded within eighteen minutes, from the first moment the dough is prepared to the second it is fully baked. We were replicating the experience of our ancestors all those centuries earlier: back then, the matzah ingredients were the only provisions the Jews had and they didn't have enough time to let their dough rise as they made their escape. The message is that they trusted God to provide. And He didn't fail them.

Baking matzah in wartime conditions, under the noses of the guards, was a lesson with several layers of significance that has stayed with me all my life. Not only was it an act of self-determination and sedition, but Rivka was also imbuing us with dignity and self-respect. The Germans were wiping us out, but as long as there were children who understood the traditions that formed our identity, our people had a chance of renaissance one day in the future.

On 7 April 1944, in the family barracks in Starachowice, encircled by barbed wire and watchtowers and trigger-happy Ukrainian fascists, my parents wondered how much longer they would have to endure their own slavery. As my little family finished off the last crumbs of our matzah in deepest, darkest occupied Central Poland, the question hanging in the air was: when will God deliver us from the evil of the Nazis? No answer was forthcoming.

In fact, life was about to become more precarious. And I was the canary in the coalmine who detected that the air was becoming toxic. I didn't realize it back then, but the long hours I spent apart from my parents were helping to make me street smart. I was developing a strong inner core of self-reliance and independence. I was observant, and my radar for detecting potential trouble improved with every passing day. Little did I know that those skills would soon be invaluable.

Roaming relatively freely within the confines of the barbed wire, I began to notice that people were disappearing. I wandered around the family quarters looking for friends to play with and discovered that more and more rooms were empty. Most doors were ajar and when I went inside, I understood what had happened. The ghetto had schooled me well. I saw the abandoned furniture, clothes and toys. I knew these people would never return.

Occasionally, I found some leftover food. I ate it but touched nothing else. I was troubled when I went in search of one of my closest friends on the other side of the main square and there was no trace of her or her family. The other rooms near by were also silent. I broke the news to my parents when they returned home that night.

'I knew it,' my mother gasped. 'That whole street has probably been taken. The rumours about *Selektion* must be true.'

'We've got to find a hiding place,' said my father.

A few days later, early in the morning, just as my parents were due to start their shift at the munitions plant, we heard that the SS were rounding up children from the family barracks.

'Quick, they're coming. You've got to hide,' Papa shouted.

I watched as he opened a trap door that he had created in the ceiling. I hadn't realized it was there. He had camouflaged it with a small rack of hanging clothes. Papa stood on a bed, lifted me up and pushed me into the gap between the ceiling and the sloping roof. I looked down and saw Mama squeezing herself through the trap door, being pushed from behind by my father.

As soon as she was in, he closed the flap and rearranged the clothes below. I crouched in my mother's lap, and she clasped her hand over my mouth. I couldn't believe the strength in her hand. She had my face in a vice-like grip.

'Tola, you've got to stay completely silent,' she said. 'It's absolutely essential. Don't make a sound. If you do, we both could die.'

I grunted an indecipherable response. Then I heard the door of our barrack block burst open, along with the terrifying fusion of running jackboots, guttural commands and weapons being cocked. My father had closed the trapdoor just in time.

Through the thin ceiling boards, I heard soldiers shouting at him.

'We told you to get out. Why are you still here? Get out!'

'Ok, I'm leaving.'

I heard Papa walk out of the room. Suddenly there was a burst of gunfire through the ceiling. I felt a gale of bullets whistling past my body. Some of them slammed into the beams of the attic above my head. I felt like screaming. But my mother had her hand so tightly over my mouth, I couldn't make a sound, even if I'd wanted to.

Her breathing was slow and quiet. I exhaled in sync with her. Eventually, we heard the soldiers leave the room and Mama slightly relaxed her grip. There was a chink of light through a rotten wooden plank in the roof and I was able to look down into the square. I had a clear view of soldiers manhandling children into trucks. I think they were SS, as they looked similar to the troops at the massacre at St Wenceslas Church in Tomaszów Mazowiecki.

I saw the kids that I'd played with. They were all around my age – five, six or seven. It was *Kinderselektion.* Children's selection. It was their time to die because the Nazis were liquidating the camp and they didn't have room for children. They were making it *Kinderrein.* Child pure. Cleansed of children.

Mothers were pleading in vain as they were separated from their children. I can still hear their screams if I close my eyes and replay that scene in my mind. Some parents tried to get into the trucks with their children. With their guns raised, the soldiers forced them back. The parents were fighting for their children's lives against impossible odds.

There was one sight I will never ever forget. A mother was engaged in a tug of war with a soldier. Caught in the middle was a baby. The mother was clutching her child's upper body under the arms, while the brute in uniform was pulling the baby's legs with all his might. Neither would yield. They were using such strength that the baby was dismembered.

The parts of the child's body were hurled onto the truck. It was the worst thing I ever saw and gives me nightmares to this day. Although I have done my utmost to block out the image, it's lodged deep inside my brain. I never talked about that incident with my mother to try to keep it at bay, but it keeps coming back to haunt me.

Infanticide is the most despicable act of war. The Germans were aping evil empires from the beginning of time that eviscerated their enemies' spirits and hopes for the future by slaughtering their children.

The mother's cry was the most harrowing I ever heard. I knew that I was supposed to remain silent, but in the face of such barbarity, my self-restraint faltered. As ever, Mama was one step ahead and clamped her hand tighter than before, stifling the scream that was rising in my throat.

I watched through the gap in the roof until the round-up was finished. I should have averted my eyes, but something inside compelled me to bear witness. The arguing and wailing in a jumble of German, Polish and Yiddish seemed interminable. But there was only ever going to be one outcome. The trucks pulled away and not long afterwards the early summer air was punctured by bursts of distant machine-gun fire. My playmates tumbled into a mass grave dug by their parents earlier that week. My father had been among them. Not only had he been forced to prepare a tomb for his parents, but at gunpoint, he had also had to dig a grave for his child. Me. But somehow, I had cheated death. Again. The Nazis used us to bury our own people. To me Poland is nothing but a mass grave for the Jews.

Eventually, when the commotion had subsided, my father returned to our room. He opened the hatch to the roof space and helped Mama and me climb down. My face was black and blue from my mother's grip. The bruising lasted for weeks.

The mass murder of the children of Starachowice changed the pattern of my life immediately, as the light went out of my world.

'Tola, you can't play outside again,' said my mama. 'It's far too dangerous for you. You saw what happened to those other children.'

I was more of a prisoner than ever before. For endless hour upon hour, I would be in solitary confinement in what I knew as the Dark Room. The sensory deprivation of such treatment is hard enough for an adult to bear. Imagine what it's like for a child of five and a half who has been exposed to more than four years of carnage close at hand. A child whose experiences of life were far worse than any flights of nightmarish fantasy the mind can conjure.

The next day, I briefly caught sight of the dawn of a summer's day through the open door as my parents left for their shift at the ammunition factory. I knew that I wouldn't see them until long after the sun had set. My mother secured a blanket over the window. Not a chink of light penetrated the gloom. I was under strict instructions to stay away from the window.

'The guards might be able to see your shadow on the blanket if you go too close to the window,' Mama explained. 'Under no circumstances, are you to touch the blanket or peek outside. It has to appear as though our room is empty, that no one is home. You must be invisible. Do you promise to obey me?'

'Yes, Mama.'

'Okay. Be brave. We'll bring you some food when we return.'

After hugging me with tears in their eyes, they closed the door and the slash of dawn disappeared. I took the piece of bread they had left me and ate it. It was still early, and I plunged into a deep slumber.

When I woke, I began to worry what would happen if my parents didn't come back. No one would find me. Maybe I'd starve to death. I contemplated the alternative. What would happen if the Germans conducted a search and discovered me? I knew what the consequence would be. That thought alone was enough to keep me away from the window.

I sat on my bunk debating with myself. I convinced myself that my parents would never abandon me. I was certain of their unconditional love. But then I remembered the yellow powder that the workers sometimes inhaled and the stories my parents recounted about their colleagues succumbing to the yellow death. What would happen to me if they were careless and they too were poisoned at the factory? There were graves near the factory where the victims of the powder were buried. Would I ever see Mama and Papa again? The questions kept going in circles in my mind and they spun so quickly that I became almost dizzy.

I have no idea how many days I spent alone with my fears in the darkness while the summer sun shone on Starachowice. My isolation might have lasted for weeks. I yearned for the sound of other children, just to be reassured that I wasn't completely alone.

Although I was silent, and I strained to listen to the world beyond the blanket at the window. I didn't hear the voice or laughter or tears of another child, or a mother's words. I began to wonder whether all the other Jewish children in the world were dead. Was I the last remaining one on earth? If so, I had to survive.

In my braver moments, I convinced myself that it was better to be alone. I no longer had to play Catch the Jew with those rough boys. I didn't have to run away frightened. I didn't have to endure the beatings with their stick guns. I persuaded myself that I was fortunate I wasn't one of those children on the trucks who had been driven away and had never come back. My internal argument was supported by the regular sound of gunfire far away in the distance. But the solitude always overwhelmed me. My mind would begin to float. Things became unreal and I became detached from my circumstances. I was no longer frightened or worried. I zoned out.

I know now that the clinical term for what was happening to me is dissociation. It is a condition where the mind activates a protective mechanism when a person is unable to cope with a situation. A person feels disconnected from themselves and the world around them. It's a way of dealing with stress or trauma. In the most extreme cases, it becomes a personality disorder that can last for years. But I believe my condition back then was short-lived. My survival instincts were so strong, even at such a young age, that I had the mental resources to be able to handle reality when it really mattered.

One day in particular stands out. For once, I was not in solitary confinement. My mother had stayed home for some reason. Before the *kinderselektion* I used to chat away brightly to my parents when we were together in our room. Since the murders, I had learned to keep my voice down, because officially, I didn't exist. Mama and I were having a whispered conversation when we heard boots approaching. We stopped talking immediately. To our horror, there was a rap on the door. For a moment Mama was paralysed with indecision. The soldier knocked again, less patiently this time. Mama had no choice and knew she had to open the door.

Without being told, I understood what I had to do. I jumped behind her and tried to minimize my profile behind her skirt, keeping my arms by my side and breathing as gently as I could. I can't remember the nature of the conversation over the threshold, but it continued for an agonizingly long time. I could sense my mother's relief when the soldier turned on his heel and she was able to close the door. I have no idea to this day whether I truly was hidden from view, or whether the soldier had seen me and had chosen not to notice. Either way, it was yet another close call.

The next day, Mama didn't return to work again. When I asked her why, she replied, 'They are closing the camp'.

My heart soared. At last, I could leave the darkness. I savoured the thought of stepping over the threshold in the morning, enjoying the warmth of the sun on my face and the breeze in my hair.

Then my radar kicked in. I noticed my mother was unusually quiet. She had begun packing a small suitcase. I studied her face. Her eyes weren't focusing on clothes but on an image somewhere inside her head. She looked stunned and shocked. Clearly, the imminent change in our circumstances was not benign.

'Where are we going?' I asked.

'Auschwitz.'

CHAPTER NINE

INTO THE ABYSS

Starachowice labour camp, German-occupied Central Poland,
Saturday 29 July 1944
Age five

After nearly five years of Nazi Germany's occupation of Poland, they came for us with the trains of Europe's death railway. The Soviet Red Army was moving in from the east and it wouldn't be long before they were within striking distance of the munitions factory at Starachowice. The Germans were shutting it down and moving production closer to the Fatherland. They were being squeezed. And now, so were we.

'We're going to have to let them see her,' said my father, with anxiety etched across his face. 'We can't keep her hidden any longer.'

'There's nothing more we can do,' my mother replied. 'I don't think they'll do anything to us or her. Why would they bother now, as we're going to Auschwitz?'

I knew my parents were talking about me. And I sensed the terror coursing between them as they tried to come to terms with the realization that this time, they really were trapped. We'd had an extraordinary run of good fortune – better than millions of others – but now, as slave labourers, my parents had reached their expiry date. For them, and therefore for me, there could only be one outcome, the one-way journey that millions of others had taken.

I'd heard the name Auschwitz before. And I knew it brimmed with evil connotations. People enunciated the word with a combination of fear and awe. They used the same tone when they spoke the names Treblinka or Majdanek, another extermination camp east of Starachowice where an estimated eighty thousand perished. I was smart enough to know that when people went to those places they vanished. But nobody seemed to know how. I had overheard whispered conversations where the word gassing was mentioned. But I didn't know what it meant. And Mama had taught me that if you obeyed the rules and didn't do anything stupid like staring at an SS officer in the eyes, you would survive. And so going to Auschwitz didn't hold any horrors for me. Imbued with the innocence and optimism of childhood, I believed that we would be fine.

Anything, even Auschwitz, had to be better than staying in the darkness in a single room for weeks on end, not being able to look out of the window past the blanket. Besides, it was a beautiful day. Mama had brushed my light brown hair, which now reached down beyond my shoulders. She had created a centre parting and twisted the back into two braids. I could feel their weight as they bounced around behind my head while I skipped outside our building in the labour camp. It was the first time in months that I had been outside.

Mama carried on doing chores inside. She had packed the one small suitcase we were allowed to bring. She'd selected clothes, some other essentials, and a few small black and white photographs of her family that she cherished. No matter where we ever went, Mama always carried her family with her.

Mama performed one last chore before we left. She took a broom and swept the floor. We were about to travel to the deadliest place on the planet and she was cleaning a room to which we would never return. Why did she do that? Did she find sweeping therapeutic? Did she need to do something to divert her mind from the journey we were about to make? No, I think she was doing it for me. She was trying to portray an air of normality. She was displaying remarkable composure at a time of unimaginable stress.

Mama was putting on a bold front for the benefit of her husband and me. Women are the glue that binds families together. When they crack, families fall apart. That image of Mama with a broom will stay with me for ever. She had my best interests at heart, every minute of every dark day.

Too soon, the soldiers came. My playtime in the sunshine ended.

The three of us began walking to the railhead. From every corner of the camp, clutching small suitcases, other inmates emerged from their barracks and headed in the same direction, as if lured by some magnetic force. Some were on their own. Others were with their spouses. I looked for other children. But there were none. Perhaps I was indeed the last Jewish child on earth. I suddenly found myself wanting to be invisible. After all, I wasn't supposed to exist.

Yet none of the guards covering our progress with their machine guns seemed to register surprise or concern that a lone child was at large. My parents had been worried about attracting attention, but if anything, the soldiers manifested an air of studied boredom.

The round-up was going to plan. There was no drama. The Jews were obediently heading towards the black engine snorting steam and cinders into a cloudless Polish sky.

Over the years, I've often wondered why they didn't shoot me on the spot. They probably just assumed that within a few hours, we would all be turned to ashes and asked themselves, why waste a bullet?

After walking for maybe fifteen minutes, we approached the train, and my courage faltered. It wasn't the sight of the cattle cars stretching endlessly behind the locomotive that shook me. And I knew the power of guns – they had my respect, but they didn't intimidate me.

I was unnerved by the dogs. Those German Shepherds. Beneath the fur there was nothing but muscle. They were lean because they were permanently hungry. The dogs were straining on their leashes, baring teeth, panting in the heat and salivating. They wanted nothing more than to be let loose. They smelled our fear and wanted to feast on it. When one barked, they all barked, and they never stopped. My ears rang from the endless loop of their snarling.

I didn't dare catch the eye of any of the soldiers surrounding the cattle cars, but I observed expressions from oblique angles. They were facilitating genocide, yet their faces revealed no hint of sorrow or empathy for the doleful creatures before them; not a trace of shame that their battle honours included herding defenceless slaves onto cars that were barely fit for cattle. But of course, their consciences – if by chance they had any – had an escape clause. They were only following orders.

Mama picked me up and I wrapped my legs around her. My mother's chest was heaving as she gripped me. I looked up at my father for reassurance, and saw something I had never seen before, except when he had helped his parents to their own deaths. He was crying. He was kissing my hair and whispering to me to be good. With tears cascading down his cheeks, he kissed Mama goodbye. They were convinced they were being sent to oblivion. And to make it worse, they were going to be forced apart, separated for the first time since their marriage in 1936.

The Germans put an end to their goodbyes. All the men were

ordered to move towards cattle cars at the back of the train. A soldier strutted up to my father, stuck a gun in his ribs and forced him to join them. All the women – their wives, mothers, sisters and nieces – were commanded to board the cattle cars closer to the engine. This was my first experience of men and women being segregated.

We moved towards a car with its wooden door wide open. It was too high for me. Mama lifted me up and I climbed inside. She followed behind. It was empty, apart from one woman sitting on the floor with her back against the side of the cattle car. We sat down next to her.

A quizzical expression transformed her face. It was as if she saw an apparition before her. 'You have a child?' she asked in a tone that suggested such a thing was impossible. 'May I touch her?'

My mother nodded. The woman gently cupped my face in her hands. There was reverence, kindness and deep sorrow in her eyes. 'How did you save a child?' she enquired. Tears tumbled down her face. 'I lost three children. They were just ten, seven and four. They were taken by force in the last selection. I will never see them again. I know I won't.'

My mother leaned forwards and hugged her in silence. Their embrace was cut short by other women climbing into the cattle car. They kept coming. All three of us – the bereaved mother, Mama and I – were forced to stand to make room, as scores of women were shoehorned inside. As the numbers increased, so the car darkened. My mother pointed to a large vessel in a corner that was supposed to be a latrine. It was the only concession to our bodily needs. Neither water nor food was provided. It was high summer. And Central Europe at that time resembled a furnace.

Still more women were squeezed inside. There were, perhaps, some hundred and fifty souls inside the car by the time the Germans deigned that it was sufficiently full. A guard slid the door along its runners. It slammed shut with an ominous clang, and the rattle of a bolt and chain confirmed we were sealed in. Escape was impossible. All we could do was shuffle our feet a couple of inches either side of our position. Cattle would never have been treated so inhumanely. They would have been given more space.

We were consumed by darkness. The only illumination came from a small barred window to one side near the roof. Scores of hands reached towards the thin shafts of light. I couldn't see the colour of flesh. The women's hands were silhouettes. They fluttered like a murder of crows. A chorus of screams and cries rose as we lurched forwards.

As the train picked up pace, so did the wailing. Some women prayed aloud. Others, weary of beseeching God in vain, cater-wauled. Stoical as ever, Mama kept her thoughts buried deep inside. Occasionally, she offered words of encouragement. But I couldn't make out what she was saying. Her voice was drowned out by the rhythm of the wheels, the creaking of the car's coffin sides, the women's sorrowful ululation and the jarring chirpiness of the engine's whistle.

For mile after mile, we swayed in unison, as the train trembled over points and navigated bends. Everyone in that car was fighting to remain upright. When someone buckled, anonymous hands reached out in support. We were predominantly strangers, but our collective hunger and thirst bound us together, as did our sorrow and whatever time we had left. Our solidarity was unspoken. There was no need for words. Our humanity remained intact and, where possible, we each shared a little of ourselves with our neighbour to ease their burden. A gesture here, a side-step there.

All the while, the temperature rose. My nostrils filled with the smell of perspiration and fear. My clothes were drenched with the sweat of the bodies propping me up. Thank heavens my mother hadn't made me wear the coat she had packed. I would have died of heat stroke.

I was gasping for water, but there was none. I had never been so hot before. Nor had I been so thirsty in my entire life, and I had no idea if I would be able to drink when we reached our destination. On top of dehydration, the hunger pangs were crippling. Images of food floated in front of my eyes, taunting me. My mother stood helplessly by my side. There was nothing she could do to make it better. I tried to marshal all my willpower and convince myself that I could do without. That I was strong enough.

I rested my head on the small of the back of the woman in front of me. I must have fallen asleep standing up. It was physically impossible to sit down. There simply wasn't enough room. It was a blessing that the woman accepted me using her as a pillow. I felt as if we were suspended in space. I had a sense of weightlessness. The mass of people crushed together meant that our bodies were incapable of moving of their own volition.

I tried to tell Mama that I needed the bathroom. But she couldn't hear me. The rank smell enveloping the entire car told me what to do instead. We did what cattle did. We went where we stood.

Although I was only five, I accepted the situation as if it were destiny. I had heard of so many other people making a similar journey, that I concluded it was now our time.

The strain of standing upright and being crushed, together with the never-ending motion was exhausting. The journey seemed interminable and the few rays of sunshine that penetrated the barred window far above never seemed to reach me. I was desperate for the train to stop and for our journey to be over.

As it was the height of summer, the day was long, but eventually, the last rays of evening light were replaced by the pitch of night. Not being able to see provided me with some respite from the trauma I was undoubtedly enduring. Still, the moans and cries intensified with the darkness. As if I needed reminding that we were heading to a terrible place.

I returned to a state of mind I had visited while alone in our room in Starachowice. I began floating again and my emotions disconnected me from the situation. I don't know how long we travelled, or how long I slept. I entered that halfway station between sleep and consciousness, where your mind loses perspective, the sharp lines of reality become blurred and your brain is peppered with fluctuating nothingness and silent moving images that are at odds with the sounds around you.

We were still moving forwards when the dawn came. Our journey seemed to have lasted an eternity already. In reality, it was about thirty-six hours before the train slowed to a crawl and juddered to a halt, accompanied by a great exhalation of steam. I heard the sound of a steel bolt being manhandled, then we were swamped by the rasp of harsh German commands.

Suddenly, we were blinded by the light.

CHAPTER TEN

FAREWELL, PAPA

Auschwitz II, aka Birkenau extermination camp,
German-occupied Southern Poland, Sunday 30 July 1944
Age five

It took a second or two for my eyes to acclimatize to the brightness. It came from a slash of blue sky above the silhouetted heads of the women through the open cattle car door. The travellers' screams of terror became jumbled with those oh-so familiar guttural commands that needed no translation.

'*Raus, raus, raus. Alle Juden, raus. Schnell.*'

So here we were. At last. Birkenau. The deadliest part of the enormous Auschwitz complex. We had reached the buffers. A small railway marshalling yard, that for 1,100,000 Jews constituted the end of the line and the end of their world.

All the tracks from occupied Europe snaked towards this platform. Everything my parents and I had endured during the previous five years had been leading to this moment. From here, as I was to find out, it was a walk of just a few hundred yards to Crematoria II and III, each with a gas chamber attached. German efficiency at its most despicable.

The chaos was bewildering and impossible for a child to comprehend. Blinking in the harsh sunlight and gasping from thirst, the women clambered down from the train from Starachowice. I saw them wince as the Germans carried on shouting at them. Then it was my turn. My mother helped me down to the platform, and at the age of five and ten months, I stepped into the heart of the Nazis' belief system. A hundred and fifty starved, dehydrated, terrorized, disorientated, bereaved women and me. To the Germans, the passengers of my cattle car were the symbol of all evil. And now the gas chambers of the Birkenau extermination camp beckoned. The multitudes of human beings on the platform towered over me, but if I turned to my left, I could see a cluster of stout brick chimneys, about 30 feet tall, belching foul-smelling smoke. To my right was the Gate of Death, a red-brick gatehouse built over an arch through which trains arrived at the most detestable terminus the world has ever known.

Straight ahead, as far as the eye could see, barracks stretched for miles, almost to the horizon. The camp was as big as a medium-sized town. It was designed to hold more than 120,000 prisoners at any one time. That's three times the size of Tomaszów Mazowiecki.

Mama clutched her small suitcase in one hand and my hand

in the other as we stood in a maelstrom of fear and confusion. All around us were soldiers with guns, shouting orders. But I focused on the barking, salivating dogs that were as tall as I was.

'Mama, the dogs are going to eat me now. They're going to kill me.'

'No, they're not, Tola. They won't touch you. They're trained to kill. But only if you run. You're not going to run, are you?'

'No, Mama.'

'Then you've got nothing to worry about.'

The butterflies in my stomach fluttered away. I was reassured. Mama always told me the truth. And I believed her. She would tell me what would happen, and sure enough, it would come to pass. So I trusted her. As ever, her calmness always steadied me when I wobbled.

I sized up the dogs again to try to get their measure. The soldiers were keeping them on a tight leash. They were muzzled, and I told myself that I would stand so still they wouldn't even think that I was going to run.

Then my mother said something that floored me: 'Tola, I'm going to have to leave you for a few minutes.'

I was stunned into silence.

'I have to find your father. I have to know what's happening to him. You stand right there, and don't move. Don't budge. Hold the suitcase. Don't let anyone take the suitcase. Do you understand? Can you do that for me?'

'Ok, Mama. Of course.'

THE DAUGHTER OF AUSCHWITZ

'Don't worry, I'll be as fast as I can.'

With that she plunged into the crowd and headed down the platform towards the back of the train. I temporarily lost sight of her and felt a stab of anguish. Then, through the seething mass, I glimpsed her again with my father. I wanted to run over and join them. But I stayed put, as Mama had insisted. My parents were hugging and kissing and talking intently.

When I look back now, I'm still amazed at the gamble Mama took and the trust she placed in me. There I was, not yet six, all alone in the most dangerous place on earth, in a throng of confused, and terrified people, surrounded by killers, at the mercy of the SS and just a few hundred yards from the nearest gas chamber.

I focused on the suitcase and gripped its handle as if my life depended on it. I had a job to do. Protecting my family's clothes and our last few possessions was my mission. I concentrated with all my might. I was scared. But having a responsibility gave me courage. Nobody was going to take that suitcase. Remember, this was the girl who, at the age of three, was prepared to fight a German to save her favourite white fur coat.

I tried to turn myself into a statue. I steeled myself because the dogs were staring at me. In my peripheral vision, I saw squads of people in rough striped uniforms climbing into cattle cars. Their eyes took in the tragedy unfolding in front of them and they displayed indifference. Not a trace of emotion. These people had all seen too much. Nothing now could shock them.

They hauled out the corpses of people who had died en route, removed latrine buckets and, trance-like, swabbed clean the wooden floors.

The workers were supposed to make the cars look presentable for re-use, as the train would depart soon for another ghetto or camp to pick up more human cargo. They had to remove all evidence of the cruelty suffered by the women who had propped me up, so the soldiers at the next round-up would have an easier time herding yet another set of victims bound for Birkenau. These Jewish sanitation crews were just another mundane, yet essential component required to ensure the Nazis' genocide ran smoothly.

Although terrified, I was fascinated by the madness swirling around me. It was as if I was in the eye of a hurricane. Clutching the suitcase somehow insulated me from the turbulence on the platform. All the while, I kept an eye on my parents. They embraced for the final time and then my father disappeared. My heart sank.

Mama reappeared by my side, sobbing. 'Tola, you and I are staying in Auschwitz. But your father isn't.'

Somehow, Papa had found out he was being sent to Dachau. But first he had to be tattooed in Auschwitz. He wouldn't be sent to Dachau without it. Wherever and whatever Dachau was. I found it impossible to grasp the enormity of what Mama was saying.

The shocks kept coming.

'Your father's best friend was strangled by a man who went berserk during the journey. But don't worry, Papa is safe. He loves you and he's sending you kisses.'

The victim was Aaron Greenspan, who had lived one block away from us in Tomaszów Mazowiecki. He wasn't the only person killed in my father's car. Several other men died in a mass brawl that took place during the journey. There were no Germans inside the car to intervene, and so there was nothing to stop some men lashing out at others who had wronged them at Starachowice. The settling of scores among rival cliques is highlighted in historian Christopher Browning's book *Remembering Survival.*

Papa didn't have a violent bone in his body. He fell sick after leaving Starachowice, and Mama said his head and body were covered with boils and that he looked dreadful. In all probability, he caught an infection through a combination of stress and the insanitary, overcrowded conditions in the cattle car.

With Papa's disappearance, my security and hopefulness disintegrated. He had been ever present in my life. He always came back at the end of the day, no matter how bad the day was. And now that certainty evaporated. But I consoled myself with the thought that at least he was alive, and I was with Mama.

Then Mama surprised me again.

'Get undressed,' she said.

'Undressed?'

'Yes, come on. Take your clothes off.'

'Why do we have to take our clothes off?' I asked.

'They are checking us for deformities or diseases. If our bodies aren't perfect, this is what is going to happen to us,' she said, pointing to smoke belching from a crematorium chimney.

I wasn't too sure what it meant, but the tone in my mother's voice implied it was sufficiently ominous that I should obey. We stripped off our soiled garments right next to the train. I was surrounded by scores of thin, pale, naked women, trying unsuccessfully to protect their modesty from smirking, leering Nazis.

'How do I look?' I asked, pirouetting naked on the platform, next to the cattle car.

'You look beautiful. Perfect,' Mama replied.

'What about you?' I asked.

After slaving in the munitions factory from dawn to dusk for more than nine months, Mama was ghostly white. She had barely seen the sun in all that time. Her complexion was distinctly unhealthy.

'I'm fine as well,' she said, unconvincingly.

Mama started slapping her cheeks, to give her pallor a crimson tinge to try to pass muster at the inevitable health *Selektion*. It was essential to appear fit enough to work. A sickly demeanour was fatal. Other women had similar thoughts and were busy primping their own skin.

Suddenly, I was mesmerized by two women who had also seen the smoke and had started running. They were stark naked. A German shouted at the top of his voice.

'*Halt. Oder wir schießen.*' ('Stop or we'll shoot.')

The women kept going. There was a burst of gunfire and they fell like rag dolls. I was horrified. Those poor women knew exactly what the chimneys were. They followed their primal instincts to flee, even though it was futile. Now, all these years later, I take comfort in the knowledge that the women were killed instantly. If they'd gone to the gas chamber, it would have taken them approximately ten minutes to suffocate. Ten minutes of terror and the agony of gasping for breaths that never came.

It was a brutal introduction to Birkenau. Yet the male Nazis in uniform passing among the naked women didn't react at all to the shooting. For them, it was just another frisson at the coalface of mass murder.

Mama slapped her cheeks one last time. The Germans were checking everyone's body and hair closely. The inspections were intimate, invasive and all the women were distressed.

'They're looking for weapons,' Mama whispered. 'Even a hair pin could be a weapon here.'

The men reached us. After an unpleasant inspection, we were approved. But the suitcase was taken from us. All that we had left in the world was inside that case. Those photographs. Those last remaining mementos. They were gone. Now we literally had nothing but our memories.

We were sent to a building close to the railway line where we were given clothes. I was handed a long grey cotton shift dress that almost reached my ankles. The shoes I was given to replace the ones that had been confiscated were uncomfortable. But at least we weren't naked any more.

I was quickly learning to appreciate small mercies. But more indignity loomed when we were ordered to enter another wooden cabin. The floor was littered with human hair. Hair of all colours: dark brown, light brown, jet black, red, grey. But very little white hair. The elderly never made it this far.

'My poor child,' said a woman standing by a bench. 'I'm going to have to cut off your braids.'

She lifted me onto the bench, and with two snips, my plaits fell to the floor and lay like stumps of light brown rope on the multicoloured rug of shorn locks. I was mortified. I had been so proud of my long hair, which Mama had spent time braiding every morning. The woman then ran her clippers over what remained, leaving tramlines of stubble. I was scared at how, at every stage of our induction to Birkenau, we were physically abused, humiliated, and belittled.

Ostensibly, we were shaved for hygiene reasons, to reduce the chance of lice, but in truth, it was another element of the Germans' psychological strategy. My hair had been part of my identity. They were dehumanizing us and attempting to demoralize us still further. Of course, there was also a practical reason for shearing us like sheep. They wanted our hair to fill mattresses. Nothing was wasted in Birkenau.

I didn't know how my appearance had changed. I didn't

have a mirror. But it was impossible to hide how aggrieved I felt. The female barber registered my discomfort and gave me a rag to cover my head. I looked around for Mama, but couldn't identify her. Her countenance had changed. She too had lost her shoulder-length dark brown hair to the clippers. I was relieved when Mama placed her hand on my shorn head and, with a brave smile, took my hand.

We joined a column of newly shaved women and were led to a barrack block with row upon row of bare wooden bunks. Each bunk had three tiers. The best place to be was on top because you could sit up there without banging your head. The space between the wooden layers was less than two feet, and the only option was to lie down in them. Our family room in the Starachowice labour camp had at least offered some privacy. The sleeping arrangements here couldn't have been more cramped.

Although there was still daylight outside, the cabin was dark and foreboding. It was what I imagined a big stable to look like. More suited to animals than humans, it was a barn, not a bedroom.

Mama and I were allocated a centre bunk in the middle of the room. Of all the possible alternatives, this was the worst of all. I couldn't climb in because our ledge was too high for me, so Mama helped me up and we sat facing each other, one of Mama's legs dangling over the edge.

A woman appeared from nowhere and slapped Mama hard in the face. 'You are in Auschwitz now,' she hissed. 'You cannot sit any way you want.'

Although the woman wasn't armed, the way she asserted her authority frightened me She wasn't German, but Jewish. She was a *Blokälteste* or block elder – a veteran prisoner responsible for inducting newcomers. Other authority figures were called *Kapos* (from the Italian '*capo*', meaning 'boss'; the mafia uses that same word because of the fear it arouses), whom the Germans appointed as supervisors.

Mama turned to me and gave me another lesson in survival.

'More and more women will be joining us in this bunk. Unfortunately, we won't have it all to ourselves like we did in Starachowice. When we go to sleep, try not to move too much because you will disturb the others.

'Sit and lie down next to me and I will try to make you as comfortable as I can. When you get off the bunk, go down like this, feet first.'

Mama slipped off the bunk as unobtrusively as she could. She seemed unnerved by the slapping and was anxious not to upset the block elder a second time.

'Apparently, we'll be fed twice a day. Some warm soup and a piece of bread.'

She gave me a tin cup, a bowl and a spoon.

'Whatever you do, don't lose them. These things can't be replaced. If you misplace them, you won't get any food and you'll starve.'

Mama was worried about the possibility of someone stealing them. They were, after all, our only worldly possessions. She showed me a place in the corner of the bunk where we could hide them beneath some blankets. How sad we now had to worry about theft. Mama saved the worst news to last.

'Tola, you can't go to the toilet whenever you want. The rules here are really tough. You can only go twice a day. Once in the morning, and once at night before lights out.

It's the same for me as well. We will go together at the same time.'

'But Mama, what if I have to go in between?'

'You will just have to hold it in. You will learn. If you don't, you'll be punished.'

Of all the rules, this one upset me the most. I wasn't sure if I could control myself. But I learned.

By now, it was dinner time. All the new inmates of the barrack stood in line with their cups. We were given a little soup and a piece of bread. I was truly exhausted – too tired to eat. But Mama insisted. And she gave me her bread ration as well. Only now, several hours after arriving in Birkenau, was I able to have a drink of water to slake my thirst.

With the passage of time, I now realize I was one of the fortunate ones from the train. An unknown number of people went straight to the gas chambers. But archives that survived the war show that 1,298 men and 409 women from our train were admitted to Birkenau after the selection process. Not all of them came from Starachowice. Some were picked up from other labour camps in the Radom district of Central Poland.

These details are contained in an extraordinary 800-page book called the *Auschwitz Chronicles*, compiled by a team of historians, supervised by Danuta Czech, a former resistance fighter who was head of research at the Official Auschwitz Museum.

Thanks to this painstaking research, I discovered that also on that day in 1944, five prisoners escaped from Birkenau, four of whom were shot during a pursuit.

All my life I have wondered why I wasn't killed upon arrival. It's estimated that more than two hundred and thirty thousand children entered the Auschwitz complex. Almost all of them were murdered in Birkenau within hours of dismounting from the cattle cars. The Nazis had no use for children. They were a hindrance. They lacked the physical strength to become slave labourers. They required sustenance. They cost money. But more than anything, they represented the future of the Jewish people. And when they grew up, they could be witnesses. As far as the Nazis were concerned, they had to be exterminated. So why wasn't I?

One theory is that we had the good fortune to arrive on a Sunday. As I pointed out, one of the crematoria at the end of the railway line was going flat out. But because Sunday was a day of rest, the murder factory was short of staff to escort us to the gas chamber, and they were either unable or unwilling to fire up another incinerator to dispose of the bodies.

Another theory is that around that time the Nazis were suffering a shortage of Zyklon B, the cyanide compound used in the gas chambers. And one further proposition comes from historian Christopher Browning, in his book about Starachowice, *Remembering Survival*, as mentioned earlier. Citing several survivors' testimonies, Browning suggests that Kurt Otto Baumgarten, one of the more humane managers of Starachowice, 'had intervened on behalf of his former prisoners and sent a letter with the transport, assuring the authorities in Birkenau that the Starachowice Jews were all good workers'.

But if that was the case, why did we have to go through a selection process at the platform?

There is no way of knowing definitively what it was that saved me. Perhaps it was a combination of all the above, but whatever it was, I'm grateful that I survived that first day. The challenge now was to survive every subsequent day in Birkenau.

Mama helped me to climb back onto the middle ledge of our bunk. I moved gingerly, trying not to tread on the women on the bottom layer. Mama climbed in beside me. On this night, we had the bunk to ourselves, although it wouldn't always be that way. I snuggled up to Mama. Her scent was a palliative. In her arms, I was secure. At long last, after the worst journey of my life, I fell fast asleep.

CHAPTER ELEVEN

REFUSING TO CRY

Birkenau extermination camp,
German-occupied Southern Poland, summer 1944
Age five

Those first few days in Birkenau were simply terrifying. Although my solitary time in the darkness in Starachowice had been frightening, it was certainly not as intimidating. At least there I had been on my own, and was spared close contact with the SS and other enforcers; here, I was exposed to them all the time. Mama was close at hand and doing her best to protect me, but I was convinced that they were constantly watching me. All of them. There was no hiding place. And the industrial scale of the extermination camp, the noise it generated, the frequent arrival of trains hauling cattle cars on the conveyor belt of death was overwhelming. I felt that I could be shot at any moment.

The haunted looks of my fellow prisoners, their cowering

demeanour and the overriding sense of terror corroded my spirit. Fear is a virus that is contagious, infecting virtually everyone it touches. Immunity is difficult, if not impossible to acquire.

Although I was only five years old, I could detect that the women all around me had abandoned any semblance of optimism. While I couldn't possibly have known it then, I know now that Mama and I arrived in Birkenau at a time of maximum tension. Having completed the annihilation of more than 400,000 Hungarian Jews, the SS were about to liquidate the *Zigeunerfamilienlager* – the Gypsy family camp in Birkenau.

The mass murder of the Gypsies, as the Roma and Sinti people were called back then, had been two months in the planning. It was supposed to happen in the middle of May 1944, but the Roma were alerted to the plan to kill them and broke into an equipment store, grabbing any potential weapons they could: knives, spades, hammers, pickaxes, crowbars and stones. Among the Roma men were former military veterans who had no intention of going quietly to the gas chambers, and 600 of them barricaded themselves into a barrack building.

Armed with machine guns, the SS surrounded the *Zigeunerfamilienlager* and ordered the men to surrender and come out. When they refused, the SS retreated rather than risk casualties. This moral victory, on 16 May 1944, is now celebrated as Romani Resistance Day.

The Roma's defiance troubled the Nazis. They feared it would trigger a mutiny throughout the camp. So they took their time to dispose of the Roma and did so by stealth. In order to reduce potential resistance they split the 6,000 people in the *Zigeunerfamilienlager* into smaller groups. On 23 May 1944, they shipped out more than 1,500 to other camps within the Third Reich. Then, on 2 August, two days after we arrived from Starachowice, an empty train pulled into the platform not far from our barracks. The SS ordered another 1,400 Roma men and boys on board. At seven o'clock that evening, the train set off north-westwards on a 400-mile journey. The Roma were bound for Buchenwald, another big, notorious concentration camp inside Germany's borders.

About that time, Mama and I were outside our barrack, along with the other inmates taking part in the evening *Appell*. This was a twice daily event. Every morning and evening, we were ordered to parade outside and be counted. Everyone had to be present and correct, or we would be forced to stand outside to attention, until the Germans were satisfied. Rain or shine. They were obsessive about counting. They could do it for hours on end.

Appell was always a tedious and frequently nerve-wracking experience. But looking back now, I realize that day's particular roll call was crackling with tension. The SS knew the Roma were about to die and were on edge. And when the guards were twitchy, prisoners suffered.

After roll call was dismissed, and we went back inside, the SS made their move. With all the Roma men of fighting age locked in cattle cars and heading north, the *Zigeunerfamlienlager* now only contained elderly and sick men, as well as women and children. In total, 2,890 of the most vulnerable. The guards distributed bread and salami and told them they were being taken to another camp. As part of the ruse, the SS loaded them onto trucks and drove them less than a mile to the gas chamber next to Crematorium V, surrounded by pine trees. Their bodies were burned in open pits.

Between 300,000 and 500,000 Roma perished in the Holocaust. Like the Jews, there was no place for them in the ethnically pure world of Adolf Hitler. Dismissed as *Untermenschen*, Jews were at the bottom of the pile of the Führer's distorted racial pyramid. The Roma were just above them. Hitler wanted the Third Reich to be populated by a 'Master Race' of Aryans – blue-eyed, blond-haired people of Nordic stock – wiping out those he regarded as inferior.

While the human race has many variations, there is more that unites us than divides us. From bitter experience, I can tell you we all smell the same when we are cremated. Jews, Roma, homosexuals, people of colour – all those whom Hitler tried to eradicate.

That smell. It is unforgettable. I just have to close my eyes and, nearly eighty years on, the memory assaults my nostrils. It will remain with me to my last breath, as will the overriding sense of fear and hunger at Birkenau.

*

Not long after the Roma camp was liquidated, there was one unforgettable *Appell*. My legs were tired, we'd been standing outside in the heat for hours and I didn't know what time it was. The sun was high in the sky and there was no shade outside our block. It must have been the afternoon, and we'd been there since we'd eaten what passed for breakfast: a warm, indescribable drink and a chunk of bread. How much longer would I have to stand still?

All the women prisoners from the barrack where I bunked with Mama were lined up in rows of five. It was one of the longest *Appell*s we'd ever had. I lost track of the number of times our block elder had counted us. Every time she counted, she reached the same number. That meant there was nobody missing from our barrack. But perhaps there was a shortfall of prisoners in one of the other barracks in this massive complex. Maybe one or more inmates had managed to burrow beneath the electric fence and were making a dash for freedom.

There was a strip of no man's land in front of the perimeter fences, clearly marked with signs stencilled with skull and crossbones and the word *Halt*. The Germans would shoot you if you entered that death zone. They wanted us to die on their terms, not on those of our own choosing. Several times at night, I'd been woken up by shooting. Bad news inevitably followed.

Escapes infuriated the Germans, not least because they didn't want evidence of their crimes to reach the Americans, British or Russians who were slowly but surely tightening their vice around the Third Reich. On the day after we arrived in Birkenau, the bodies of five people shot while trying to break out were strung up at the entrance to the men's camp to discourage others from even thinking about it.

Among the women in our barrack, escapes provoked mixed emotions. Of course, they all hoped the fugitives would evade their pursuers and make it to safety. It was courageous, but such a predictable waste of life, as so many never got much further than the fences before being cut down. But when news of an escape trickled down to our hut, it was always accompanied by a sense of irritation that we would pay the price. Our food rations might be cut, or, as on that day, we'd be compelled to stand to attention at a never-ending *Appell*, shifting from foot to foot to prevent cramp setting in, and anxious that we'd be subjected to a random act of punishment.

Normally, at *Appell*, I would try to stand at the back, so as not to attract attention. But on this occasion, I found myself in the front row. I started to fidget after having been stuck there for so long, but I didn't shift from my position. My mistake was to turn my head around and look behind me.

Suddenly, a female guard towered over me. She was a member of the *SS-Gefolge* – which literally means the SS entourage. The woman was every bit as intimidating as her male counterparts. If anything, she was even more sinister, given that she wore a skirt and Nazi insignia on the left breast of her uniform.

The woman hauled me out of the line and started slapping my face. She was hitting my cheeks with an open hand. First

Tova's father Machel Grossman, 1932.   Tova's mother Reizel Grossman, 1948.

Machel (seated third from right, bottom row) with his theatre group, circa 1931.

A group of German soldiers and civilians look on as a Jewish man is forced to cut the beard of another in Tomaszów Mazowiecki, 1939.

Saint Wenceslas Church, the site of the massacre on 31 October 1942, as the ghetto was liquidated. This building no longer exists.

German soldiers clearing the streets of Tomaszów Mazowiecki after deporting six thousand Jews from the ghetto to Treblinka, 1942.

Above: Tova (in colour on the left) and other child survivors display their tattoos to the Russian photographers following liberation from Birkenau, 1945.

Above: Identification card given to Reizel by the International Red Cross to provide safe passage home from Birkenau, 1945.

Left: Tova, age six and a half, returns to Tomaszów Mazowiecki, 1945.

Left: Tova's Aunt Helen.

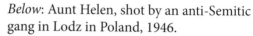
Below: Aunt Helen, shot by an anti-Semitic gang in Lodz in Poland, 1946.

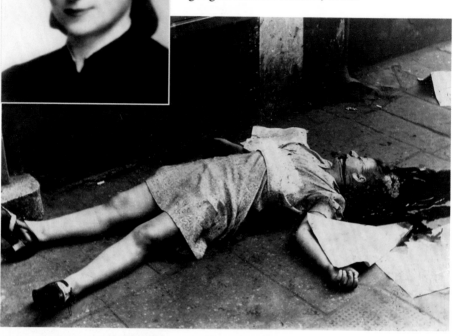

Left: Tova, Reizel and Machel in Landsberg Displaced Persons camp in Germany, 1948.

Above: Tova (seated second from right, bottom row) with her classmates at Landsberg Displaced Persons camp in Germany, 1950.

Above: Machel and Sonia's
wedding in Israel, 1958.

Above right: Tova and Maier's
wedding in Brooklyn, USA,
1960.

Right: Tova with Risa (Ruth),
Gadi and Itaya in Israel, circa
1970.

Above: Tova standing among the remains of a gas chamber on her first return to Birkenau, 1999.

Above: Tova, Maier and their eight grandchildren, 2014.

Left: Tova and her family at her grandchildren Ari and Eitan's Bar Mitzvah, 2014.

Left: Tova's daughter Ruth and her children.

Below: Tova shares her story at Calvin University's January Series in Michigan, USA, 2015.

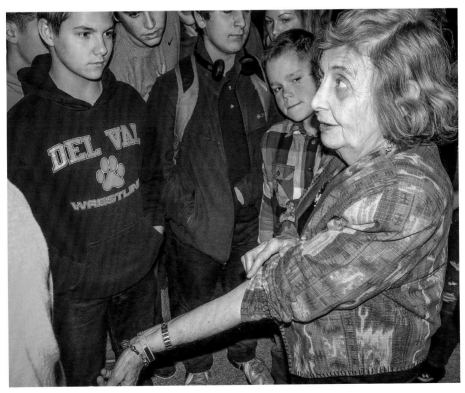

Tova with students at Delaware Valley Regional High School in New Jersey, USA, 2016.

Tova returns to Birkenau with her daughter Itaya and four grandchildren, 2016.

Above: Tova and Maier Friedman, 2019.

Right: Tova attends the 75th anniversary of the liberation of Auschwitz with other survivors, 2020. She is holding hands with Ronald Lauder, the President of the World Jewish Congress.

one side, then the other. I had to lift my face up towards the guard. I knew that was what she wanted. I glanced over at my mother, and Mama looked back at me, but she didn't say anything because she didn't know what the consequences would be. So she had to keep quiet, even though she felt like coming to my aid. I knew she couldn't interfere. But we communicated with our eyes.

Hold on.

The blows kept coming. The SS guard used all her strength. I looked her square in the face as she laid into me and I thought to myself, You can hit me until you kill me, but you will never know how much it hurts.

My cheeks were burning from the attack, but I refused to cry. Even at that age, I had no intention of being a victim. I didn't know what the word resistance meant. But intrinsically, I felt it. I refused to be broken and nobody was going to destroy my inner core. Not one tear for my abuser.

My mind used that same coping mechanism I had first encountered in Starachowice: dissociation. As the slaps rained down, my consciousness took a ride and I had another out-of-body experience. It was as if I was floating above the barrack and watching the scene from on high. Down there, a woman in black was beating a helpless, starving Jewish child. The helicopter view helped to numb the pain.

I don't recall how long the assault lasted. She was trying to knock me to the floor, or at least make me cry. But I remained standing and silent. I wanted the punishment to finish, but I wasn't going to let her know. Eventually, she became too tired to continue. I looked at her hand. It was bright red. My cheeks stung and began to swell.

'Next time, stand still,' she hissed as she pushed me back in line and walked away.

I was numb. I just stood very still next to Mama. We didn't say anything. We didn't need to. My body was heaving with the shock of the violence and relief that it was over. Only after the woman had walked away did I allow the tears to fall in silence. And they continued silently in my bunk for the rest of the day. I had learned an important lesson. As a prisoner, I would never ever cry in public, even if it meant the punishment lasted longer. It only encouraged our tormentors. They fed on our weaknesses.

I wasn't very far from Mama every moment of that beating, but I felt very much alone. We were trapped in a living nightmare. In a nightmare, nothing makes sense; everything is scrambled and unpredictable. So was our war. Neither Mama nor I knew what would happen if she had intervened. Mama could have been shot. I could have been shot. Or we both could have been killed. There were no rules. Even if there were rules, they kept changing in a way you could never anticipate. All we could do was cling on and trust in luck.

*

I remember the time I spent with Mama in the first month in Birkenau vividly, although it was quite routine and mundane. Our days never started well because nights were invariably rough and there was no such thing as restorative sleep. Mama and I rarely had the bunk to ourselves, as a constant rotation of bed mates was imposed upon us. The whole bunk structure would creak and shift as scores of women twitched and rolled over at random. People tried to be considerate, but their pasts conspired against them and there would often be screams as a flashback roared to life and traumatized them once more.

Women whose contours became familiar during the night, would suddenly disappear. We never knew where they had gone. Maybe to another barrack, or another work camp in the Auschwitz complex. Or they had been put to sleep in one of the gas chambers at the end of the railway line. Or perhaps they just couldn't take any more and had made a dash for the nearest electrified barbed-wire fence.

We spent endless hours waiting in lines. Reaching the latrine in the morning tested bladder control to the limit. Hundreds of women needed to relieve themselves at the same time. The latrine had a barrack all to itself. A slit trench ran down the middle, covered by a series of raised wooden planks, punctuated every few feet with holes designed to accommodate women, not children. The size of the holes troubled me. I used to cling onto the planks for fear of tumbling into the reeking cesspit below.

Sometimes, I was able to pay an unscheduled visit to the

latrine. Usually, it would happen in the evening, when our block elder was in her room and had 'company'. It was strictly *verboten* (forbidden) for Germans to fraternize with Jews. But proximity to death is a heady aphrodisiac. No doubt, the elder received something in return for her favours. Perhaps a few extra days on earth. Or another bread ration. People did whatever they needed to do to survive. Mama would wait for the elder's latch to click shut and she would tell me to hurry to the latrine and back.

If we weren't waiting in line for the cesspit, we were lining up to be fed. There was no good place to be in the food line. Near the front, the gruel was warmer than when you were at the rear. But if you were among the last to be fed, there might be more chunks of lukewarm or cold turnip at the bottom of the tureen.

I was always hungry. But despite the malnutrition, my body was growing, as was my appetite. Mama tried to alleviate the pangs by giving me her bread ration. I rarely saw her eat. She seemed to survive on air. Life improved slightly when she was put to work in a potato warehouse. Occasionally, she stole a potato and I would eat it raw. Supplementing our diets in this way was perilous: if she'd been caught with a potato in the fold of her dress, she could have faced summary execution. But Mama was wily and got away with it. Sometimes she would trade a potato for a hunk of bread, which she would always give to me.

Our routine rarely varied. Life was a blur of basic functions. Sleep, wake, latrine, eat, *Appell*. Repeat. It's extraordinary what you can become accustomed to and how much hardship you can endure. Luxuries were little things: an extra mouthful of bread could improve your day; an unexpected smile would lift the misery for an hour or more. This was my world and I accepted it, along with its all-pervasive stench of roasting flesh from the crematoria. I even got used to that.

But the stink of the latrine was hard to take. Once, I was bursting to breaking point. I ran to the latrine and jumped up onto the wooden platform. I was in such a hurry that I misjudged my leap, and because I was so small, I slipped backwards through a hole and into the slurry. The indignity and stench were bad enough, but worst of all, I couldn't climb out. I was stuck up to my knees and surrounded by squealing rats swimming through the waste. My screams alerted Mama who was never far away. She was horrified. Other women came to help. I was wedged beneath the wooden plank for what seemed an eternity. After several attempts, the women gripped me under the shoulders and pulled me to safety. Mama hosed me down, but without soap, the smell lingered for days. It was horrible.

Not long after my dip in the latrine, I fell sick. There must have been all manner of bacteria and germs down there. I woke up one morning and was shocked to realize I couldn't see. A solidified crust of pus had superglued my eyelashes together. I worked away at one eye and managed to free it a touch.

Then, a couple of days later, I woke up and my throat felt like it was on fire, it was so dry and swollen. And my teeth seemed to be bolted together and my jaw had locked up, making it impossible to eat. I started to fret. I might have only been five, but I was smart enough to know that sick people were killed. I was so scared that I didn't even tell Mama. I was afraid someone would overhear our conversation and I'd disappear. My eyes were stuck together with pus again, and I was holding onto the bunks to move around.

Mama soon noticed that I wasn't well. But for the first time in her life, she was unable to control what happened to me next. Matters were taken out of her hands when other women in the block also realized that I was sick. In their weakened state, they were afraid of contagion, and I was taken away.

CHAPTER TWELVE

ON MY OWN

Birkenau extermination camp,
German-occupied Southern Poland, August 1944
Age five and three quarters

I had no idea where I was when I woke up. I could feel my body. I could see and I could hear. But I felt strange. It was warm and I was comfortable. And I was alone in a single bed. The last time I had been conscious I couldn't open my eyelids, but now they moved freely. That was a relief. And that terrible feeling of having my mouth locked had also subsided.

'So you are awake at last,' said a kindly female voice.

'Where am I?'

'You are in the infirmary. You've been very sick. But now you are on the mend.'

'Mama?'

'She's not far away. You've got to stay in bed for a while, until you get your strength back.'

I don't know how long I was delirious. It could have been days, it could have been a week or more. But now it appeared that I was through the crisis. I had been struck down by a combination of scarlet fever and diphtheria. Both were common childhood ailments in the first half of the last century. Scarlet fever is contagious, caused by bacteria and generates a high temperature and sore throat. Diphtheria is also triggered by bacteria. It attacks the respiratory system and it's nicknamed 'the strangling angel' because, in the worst cases, it does just that – it chokes you to death.

I was fortunate to be alive on two counts: I had survived two potentially fatal illnesses. More significantly, I had also survived being sick; given the Nazis' practice of culling the weak and infirm, and their ruthless slaughter of children, I was amazed that I was still breathing.

But history has taught us that infirmaries in camps like Birkenau were often staffed by Jewish prisoners who had been medics in their pre-war lives. And despite being under constant threat of being murdered, nurses and doctors in the camps upheld the sacred Hippocratic oath to treat patients to the best of their ability. Where possible, they masked the symptoms of the sick and shielded them from their Nazi overseers so that, against the odds, their patients could leave the infirmaries, and had a chance of survival. It was an act of compassion and resistance.

I stayed at the infirmary a week longer to recuperate, and then it was time for me to leave. I donned the cotton shift dress that I was issued with when I arrived at the camp. But I had lost the uncomfortable shoes. The nurse went in search of a replacement pair and returned with some white lace-up high-top shoes. I slipped my feet into them, and stood by the bed, perplexed.

The nurse looked at me quizzically.

'You don't know how to put them on, do you?'

I nodded. I had put the right shoe on the left foot and vice versa.

'How old are you? Five and a half? A girl of your age should be able to put shoes on.'

She showed me how to do it. Then she took my hand. 'Come with me. We're going to your new barrack.'

'Are you taking me back to Mama?' I asked.

'No, you are going to the *Kinderlager*.' (The children's camp.)

My heart started pounding. I was distressed by the news that Mama and I would be apart. I had become accustomed to being by myself in the hospital. But that was easy. The atmosphere was benign. I couldn't comprehend the enormity of what being totally alone would mean.

My war was about to take on an entirely different complexion. Little did I know that everything I had been through over the past four years had been preparation for this moment. The only weapons I possessed were the things I had seen and the lessons I had learned. I had my wits. My powers of observation and self-preservation. I had no alternative but to be self-sufficient and resilient. I remember being sad that I wouldn't be returned to Mama, but I didn't cry. I wasn't about to share my emotions with anyone else.

We left the infirmary and walked towards the chimneys spewing fumes. I felt as if everyone was staring at me as I walked with the nurse in my white lace-ups. I didn't like the direction we were taking. The smell was getting stronger.

But then we turned right, crossed a road and cut across the railway tracks in front of a steam engine, puffing away. We reached a barbed-wire fence with a big wooden gate. The nurse spoke to the guard, showed him a paper and we were nodded through. I didn't know where we were. But I do now. We were in what had been the *Zigeunerfamilienlager* – the Roma family camp. We walked in a straight line for about five minutes or so. There were anonymous barn-like barracks on either side of me. I wondered how far we would go because the camp seemed to stretch for ever. But after we walked past a laundry on our right, and a latrine reeking in the midsummer heat on our left, we reached our destination. Barrack Number Eleven in the *Kinderlager*. The nurse led me in, turned abruptly and walked out.

I was surprised at how many other children were there. There might have been fifty or seventy or so. One or two were smaller than me, but most were bigger and older. Where had they all come from? Had they been hiding in the camp? Maybe I wasn't the only Jewish child in the world, after all? But where were their parents? There weren't any adults in this section. I might not have been on my own, in that I was now part of a group, but without Mama by my side, nothing was the same.

To my surprise, I recognized two familiar faces from Tomaszów Mazowiecki and my heart skipped a beat: Frieda and Rena were standing at the entrance. They were cousins who were five and six years older than me. At that moment, I felt slightly less alone. Unfortunately for me, they weren't in the barrack for long. Somehow, shortly after my arrival, their mothers managed to smuggle them out of the *Kinderlager* to a different part of the camp. I didn't see them again until after the war.

But at least there was another friend from Tomaszów Mazowiecki. Rutka Greenspan was much closer to my age and had apparently been on the same train that brought me to Auschwitz. It was her father who had been strangled in the cattle car on the journey from the labour camp at Starachowice to Birkenau. Rutka did a double-take when I walked into the barrack. I was overjoyed to see her. She was delighted to see me as well and we hugged each other tightly. I didn't know whether she knew that her father was dead. The manner of his death was so awful, I decided to keep it to myself. I was trying to be kind.

But I must confess that occasionally I was a little cruel. Sometimes, in the middle of the night, hunger pangs woke me up. I would slip out of my bunk and squat on the line of warm bricks that ran down the centre of the barrack. The bricks radiated heat from a small stove, and I loved the warmth on my bare feet. I was comforted. When I was warm enough, I'd stand up and prance along the bricks as quietly as possible. I felt tall and powerful. I'd tiptoe between the bunks and raise my arms and extend my fingers, as if I was a witch or a monster, casting a spell on the children that I thought were sleeping. It was just a game. But I learned later that Rutka was often awake as well, and on occasions I had towered over her with my arms outstretched like a Nazi eagle. My silhouette terrified her in Birkenau and was the source of nightmares for decades to follow.

There were other nights when I woke up and was petrified. Once, two SS soldiers came into our barracks in the middle of the night when all the other children were asleep, and I was wide awake. I watched with horror as they went from bunk to bunk, peering at the children. I couldn't work out what they were doing. I thought perhaps they were looking for twins on behalf of the Angel of Death, Josef Mengele, the Nazi doctor, infamous for conducting excruciating live medical experiments on prisoners. Mengele's laboratory was not far away, separated from our barrack by just a barbed-wire fence.

The older children in our building were aware of the atrocities that were being perpetrated just a few yards away, and the stories they told us added a new layer of fear to life in Birkenau. We heard that Mengele was fascinated by twins. He would dip one twin in boiling water, another in ice and compare how they reacted. Mengele was a psychopath who abused his medical skills in the sick pursuit of racial purity. He conducted amputations without anaesthetics. He injected the eyes of twins with chemicals to see if he could change their colour. Mengele was trying to create the perfect Aryan blue for the 'master race' of the future. One twin would be used as the guinea pig, the other as the control. And when the tests inevitably failed, both children would be murdered.

I remember trembling in my bunk, trying to convince myself that I would be safe from the soldiers' attentions because I wasn't a twin. Nevertheless, I lay there fretting that they would hear the pounding of my heart and would come and take me away, murder me, chop me up and use my liver to feed troops on the front lines.

I'm not suggesting the Germans were cannibals, but as a child of Auschwitz, I had seen evidence of the aftermath of dissections with my own eyes: during one particularly strange period, our block elder took us on walks around Birkenau. Supposedly, she did it to give us some exercise and fresh air, in a place where the atmosphere could not have been more putrid. During one ramble, I became separated from the main group and being inquisitive, I opened the door of a small wooden building and saw that it was packed to the rafters with body parts, and long-dead eyes staring back at me. I was shocked by the experience, and slammed the door shut immediately, thinking, This has nothing to do with me.

I tried to forget what I had seen. But the image was planted in my brain and has frequently returned to upset me. Most recently, this happened in December 2021 as we were deep into drafting the manuscript for this book. I found myself thinking about Mengele's evil works and for a few nights I was completely unable to sleep.

Like most Auschwitz survivors, I wish that Mengele had been faced with post-war justice. But he managed to evade Allied investigators and eventually made his way to South America. He apparently died of a heart attack near Sao Paolo in Brazil in 1979.

Living as close to Mengele for as long as we did, demanded a safety valve: humour. Some of the older children in my barrack would pick on the younger ones with a particularly sick joke.

'I've just seen your mother.'

'No, you haven't. I haven't seen her since we arrived here. So how could you have seen her?'

'Would you like to see her?'

'Yes, of course.'

'See that smoke, that's where she is. She's coming out of the chimney.'

Of course, the dark humour was a defence mechanism to try to ward off the fear that we all experienced. We all felt vulnerable and alone without our parents. Still, a sense of cama-raderie permeated the *Kinderlager*. We were bound together by our situation. But ultimately, I knew I could only depend upon myself.

Today, nearly eighty years later, I occasionally experience a similar sense of solitariness. Although I might be at the centre of a large gathering of people, I still feel my family's absence. It's a phantom pain, as though part of me has been amputated. The sensation even surfaces when I am surrounded by my four children and eight grandchildren, during holidays like Hanukkah and Passover, when extended family enriches the experience. I'm reminded that my mother was the sole survivor of the Pinkusewicz family who lost 150 members. Then there were my father's parents, five of his siblings and all their families. They all perished. I still miss my Uncle James after all these years.

I too was slated to die once my number came up. All I have to do today is look down at my left forearm and there it is: the constant reminder of who the Nazis wanted me to be. A-27633. Just a number waiting to be gassed. Over time, the tattoo has come to represent the exact opposite of what the Nazis intended. It was meant to dehumanize me. To reduce me to a number. To brand me. Like cattle or sheep. Instead, it has empowered me. It is also affirmation of my personal humanity, and of my obligation to those who weren't as fortunate. In a way, it is symbolic of my ultimate moral victory over Hitler and his kind.

Only once was I embarrassed by the tattoo, when I was about twelve, not long after I arrived in America. I was strap hanging on the subway in New York. Everyone in the carriage seemed to be staring at me and zeroing in on my left forearm. Nobody said a word. They just looked at the tattoo. I suddenly felt incredibly hot. I wanted to cover it up.

Not long afterwards, I had a doctor's appointment as part

of a refugee resettlement programme. In common with other refugees, I was checked out to make sure I was healthy.

'I'm going to give you a gift,' said the doctor. 'I'm going to take away the number with a little plastic surgery. You'll never know it was there. It'll be just a little cut.'

I was only twelve. I might have been a refugee, but I was full of chutzpah. I pointed to my forehead and said, 'If the number had been right here, I wouldn't take it off. I did nothing wrong.'

I was angry that the doctor had even suggested it. The tattoo is my witness statement. I was there. I saw what happened.

I do know a few people who had their tattoos removed when they were young. They all regretted it. I can still remember the young Jewish woman who gave me my tattoo a few weeks after I was installed in the *Kinderlager*. Most prisoners were tattooed as soon as they entered Auschwitz. I don't know why I wasn't. Perhaps German bureaucracy had its shortcomings.

When our turn came, we all had to line up. Starving hungry and hoping for an extra ration, some girls pushed and shoved to reach the head of the line. Rutka from Tomaszów Mazowiecki ended up right in front of me. She was given the tattoo number A-27632.

The tattooist was about seventeen or eighteen years old. Back then, at my young age, I thought she was quite old. She was very nice and very careful, but her hand was shaking, and I thought to myself, This lady doesn't like to do what she's doing.

I watched every single move. I was fascinated by the mechanics.

The needle hurt a little, but concentrating on what she was doing helped minimize the pain.

She didn't have a machine like they do nowadays. She had a sharp needle which she dipped in a bottle of ink. She went backwards and forwards making pin pricks. Every dot was made separately. The woman talked to me gently as she was working.

'I'll give you a very neat number. If you ever survive, you can buy a blouse with a long sleeve and nobody will know what happened to you. You won't be embarrassed. Find yourself a cold wet rag to press against your number. It will hurt less. And from now on, you don't have a name. You only have a number. Memorize it. It's important.'

Not long after she inked me, the tattooist was killed. Like so many others, she spent ten minutes choking to death. Why did they kill her? After all, she was working. She was just a small cog in the war machine, yet she was, in Nazi terms, gainfully employed. Perhaps she was too slow. Perhaps she was too gentle and too kind as she carried out a function she clearly despised. In Nazi terms, showing compassion was a crime, punishable by death.

The tattooist was right. I had to memorize the number. Even though I couldn't read or write and didn't yet know my numbers. At morning and evening roll call, when all the children gathered, I never once heard the block elder yell the name Tola Grossman. There were so many numbers that sounded like mine. I taught myself to hear the numbers grouped together. If the elder ever shouted out A-27633, and I failed to reply 'present', she would stop and repeat it. And she would get angry, and life would become more unpleasant. There would always be some form of retribution for upsetting her. I was reminded that it was best to be anonymous, not to draw attention to myself. I had learned that lesson with my parents in the ghetto and the labour camp. But now I could see for myself the wisdom of that strategy.

The block elder at the *Kinderlager* had a range of punishments that she would administer. I already knew I could withstand her slaps without any difficulty. She was nowhere near as powerful as the SS woman I had aggravated in August. Most commonly, we were made to remain at attention at roll call for extended periods. Nobody wanted to stand for ever. Reducing the food ration, however, was the most painful sanction. I was missing my mama's physical presence, her love and nurturing soul. But now I understood how much I had relied on the morsels of bread she had given me from her own ration. Without that extra bread, I was hungrier than ever. The watery soup we were given in the *Kinderlager* was as insubstantial as it was in the barrack I shared with Mama. But there seemed to be even less of it. The hunger pangs lasted longer than before and I was permanently famished. The Nazis may not have slated us for the gas chamber yet. But they were certainly starving us to death.

Mama was obviously worried about the impact of the Birkenau diet on me. One day, a woman came up to me and gave me a little pouch on a piece of string. It was 7 September 1944.

'It's from your mama,' she said. 'It's your birthday present. You're turning six.'

My mama was still alive! I looked inside the pouch. It was a chunk of bread. Never has a present meant as much to me as that morsel. It was full of my mother's love and reminded me that she was thinking of me, and despite our terrible conditions, fighting for my life. I later discovered that my mother had stolen a potato to trade for that piece of bread. She was spotted and brutally beaten about the head. The punishment was so severe that Mama suffered acute headaches for the rest of her life. But she had managed to cling onto the bread.

The present lifted my spirits. I was so hungry I could have eaten it there and then. But I resolved to save it for the moment when I was about to die from starvation. Death. Isn't that what happened to every Jewish child? In my innocence, I thought that the bread could save my life and bring me back from the brink. So I put the pouch underneath the front of my dress and fell asleep on the bunk that I shared with another girl, who was about twice my age.

Squeaks and a stampede of tiny feet all over my body woke me up in the middle of the night. Rats had found my gift. I felt their claws on my skin. Several of them dived into the front of my dress and stole the bread, running off into the darkness to devour their prize. Other rats jumped off the bunk in pursuit. I felt for the pouch, but the rats had taken it all. There wasn't a crumb left. Needless to say, my sixth birthday was not a happy one.

*

Each long day in Birkenau seemed to melt into the next one. But because I know what happened on my birthday, I'm able to give a precise date to my encounter with the rats. While researching the timeline in Auschwitz, I learned that two days earlier, on 5 September 1944, a girl called Anne Frank arrived at Birkenau from a transit camp called Westerbork in the Netherlands. The cattle cars contained 1,019 Dutch Jews, including seven who had been living in hiding for over two years in a narrow canal-side house in Prinsengracht 263, Amsterdam. Among them were Anne Frank, then aged fifteen, her sister, Margot, her mother, Edith, and father, Otto. Anne Frank's final diary entry, written in the Secret Annexe, hidden behind a bookcase, was on 1 August 1944, three days before her arrest by the Gestapo, after the family was betrayed.

In her diary, perhaps the most famous literary work of the Holocaust, Anne Frank wrote, 'Our many Jewish friends and acquaintances are being taken away in droves. The Gestapo are treating them very roughly and transporting them in cattle cars to Westerbork, the big camp in Drenthe where they're sending all the Jews.'

She added: 'If it's this bad in Holland, what must it be like in those faraway and uncivilized places where the Germans are sending them? We assume that most of them are being murdered. The English radio says they're being gassed. Perhaps that's the quickest way to die.'

But the Holocaust was unpredictable. Anne Frank didn't

die quickly. She toiled as a slave labourer in Birkenau until November 1944 when she was transported to the Bergen-Belsen concentration camp north of Hanover, where she died of sickness and exhaustion in February 1945. We never met, but we endured the same regime of malnutrition that ultimately contributed to her death.

The physical pain of starvation has never left me. It is the worst feeling in the world. You may not see the scars, but I feel them still, eighty years later, gnawing at my stomach. Hunger has a lasting effect, emotionally and physically.

Starvation triggered a very telling dream in Birkenau. It was so extraordinary that to this day, I can still recall its entire hallucinogenic weirdness. Naturally, it revolved around the thing that I was missing the most: food.

I was out walking and suddenly I came upon a lake that consisted entirely of egg yolks. They stretched as far as the eye could see. After surviving on gruel and stale bread, it's obvious why I was fantasizing about eggs, my all-time favourite comfort food. I took off my white shoes, carefully broke the membrane on top of the egg lake and immersed myself up to my neck. I had the sensation of floating in a warm bath, and I began swimming, breaststroke. My eyes were level with the yolks, and I swallowed one whole with every stroke driving me forwards. I swam and ate. Swam and ate.

I'm sure that my fellow prisoners fantasized about something similar. Starvation is difficult to describe. Imagine a monster inside you, devouring every single cell. Food becomes an obsession. You become crippled by a sinister inner chill. Every nook of your body craves sustenance because every internal organ, every joint, every cartilage is atrophying from a lack of nourishment. Your body is dying from the inside, in slow motion. Imagine feeling like that as a child, and not being able to explain what was wrong.

Although I was only six, I could identify people on the verge of death. They seemed to collapse in on themselves until they were doubled up. In the slang of the camps, there was a word for them. They were known as *Muselmann*. Literally, it translates as Muslims – because they looked as though they were bent over in prayer. The term was used to describe those who were overcome by exhaustion and starvation, and who were so worn down that they accepted death was imminent and even a relief. Once a prisoner had reached this stage, there was virtually no way back.

The twelve-year-old girl who shared my bunk presented all the symptoms of a *Muselmann*. I knew she was dying from starvation. Her body was shutting down and, sure enough, the girl passed away in the middle of the night sometime in the autumn. I woke up in a panic and found her immobile and cold next to me. I was sad that she had died, but also worried that we'd be kept standing for hours on end at *Appell* when the girl failed to respond to her number being called. I was also concerned on behalf of the block elder who had to count us. If the numbers didn't add up, and there was a suspicion someone had escaped, the elder would be in trouble with the Germans. I was scared of the elder, but I knew, even at that young age, that she was a victim of the Nazis as well.

The corpse was my responsibility because we shared a bed. I still could not read her number, but as I had heard it called many times over the past few months, I knew I would recognize the sound pattern. At dawn, I dragged the body to the barrack entrance and pulled her next to a pile of other children who had died in the night. Although the girl was little more than skin and bones, she was extremely heavy for a six-year-old to haul. At *Appell*, her number was called. I remember feeling an unusual sense of pride in dealing with the problem, despite not understanding numbers.

I raised my arm and responded triumphantly, 'She's dead'.

CHAPTER THIRTEEN

THE LONGEST WALK

Birkenau extermination camp,
German-occupied Southern Poland, autumn 1944

Age six

I remember the best breakfast I ever had in the extermination camp. If I close my eyes and think about it, I can still taste it and feel the texture on my tongue. For once, it wasn't a coarse hunk of stale bread and watery soup. I don't know what it was precisely; at the time I thought it was porridge, whereas now I believe it was more likely to have been a standard German comfort dish, farina pudding: semolina cooked with sugar, and maybe condensed milk, which every German soldier carried in his knapsack as part of his hard rations. Whatever it was, for children like me who were starving and craving proper food, it was delicious.

'We have a special treat for you this morning,' said an adult voice. 'Eat up, it's cold outside, we are leaving.'

This meal was everything I wanted. I had been yearning for something sweet. It had substance and filled me up. I wolfed down the semolina and scraped every sticky grain off the tin cup with my spoon.

Ours was the last remaining children's block. We all instinctively knew where the walk was going to take us. It didn't matter. Our bellies were full for the first time in a long while. We were living from minute to minute. And in that moment, we were just thankful for the gift of food. When I think about that breakfast now, I find it distressing that even with children, the Nazis played mind games. They manipulated us to ensure we did exactly as we were told.

After we'd eaten, we came out of the barrack. Outside it was freezing. The ground was rock hard and covered in frost. I can't be certain when it was, but it was probably the end of October or the start of November 1944. We turned left, and walked towards the railway track. Our breath was steaming from our mouths. There must have been over fifty children aged from four to twelve, escorted by two female members of the SS. I was one of the smallest, extracting every ounce of warmth from the rough coat I wore over my shift dress. I was still wearing my white lace-up shoes and no socks. I was at the back of the line with another little girl, and we were talking as we walked.

Dead bodies, all thin, sharp angles, covered with frost, lay scattered on the ground, not far from the path we were taking. Their eyes seemed to follow us. Death could strike at any time and in many forms. People didn't always die in their bunks like my bed companion had. I knew that they just dropped dead on the spot from starvation, exhaustion and disease. Maybe these people had just died in the past few minutes. Or maybe they had passed away the night before and hadn't been yet been collected by the *Leichenkommando*, the work teams responsible for corpses. Either way, the sight didn't disturb us. The cadavers were merely part of the landscape.

We walked past another of the children's barrack buildings. It was empty. We hadn't seen those children for a few days. Some of the older ones in our line surmised that the SS had come for them, and they'd been taken to the crematorium.

'Maybe it's our turn,' I said to my companion.

As ever, I had already accepted the idea that death was my fate. I wasn't exactly sure what death was, or what happened afterwards, but I remained convinced that all Jewish children had to die. As we were walking, whispers trickled down from the front of the line to the back. Someone had asked where we were going. The answer seemed to be that we were indeed heading to the gas chamber.

We kept on walking. The German breakfast was doing what it was intended to do. I was nervous but not excessively distressed. For once, I had a full stomach, and that inner cold that comes from starvation had, for the time being, disappeared.

Suddenly, a woman's loud voice pierced my consciousness.

'Tola.'

I was confused. That was my name. For months I hadn't heard it spoken outside the children's barrack. To adults, I wasn't Tola any more. I was A-27633.

'That must be my mother,' I said to my companion. 'She's the only grown-up who knows my name. Yes, I'm sure it's her.'

I looked to my right and there were all these thin women, who seemed to be half naked, pressed up against a barbed-wire fence. They all looked terrible, displaying the hallmarks of starvation.

'Tola, where are you going? What's going on?' my mother shouted.

I couldn't see Mama in among the crowd. All I heard was her voice.

'We're going to the crematorium,' I replied, almost jauntily.

Suddenly, all the women behind the wire began screaming and ululating. We carried on walking and the screaming became louder and more desperate. I turned to my young companion and said, 'I don't understand why they are crying. Every Jewish child has to go to the crematorium. What are they crying about?'

We must have been walking for about fifteen minutes. Then, just before we reached the railway track, we turned right, close to a long, single-storey T-shaped building with sloping roofs. It resembled a large community hall, apart from the incongruous annexe on the side with a squat brick-built chimney emitting that foul-smelling smoke. The warmth of the breakfast was wearing off. We were freezing, especially those who didn't have shoes.

'Go down the steps,' ordered a soldier in an SS uniform.

We did as we were told, and entered a stark, bare concrete room with grey walls. Coat hooks lined the walls. What a sinister and scary place it was. This was the anteroom for the gas chamber in Crematorium III.

'Hang up your clothes in such a way that you will know exactly where they are when you come out. You are going to have a shower now.'

The concrete walls amplified the bitter temperatures. I undressed and immediately began shivering. Rarely in my life have I felt so cold. I stood on tiptoe, hung up my clothes and placed my shoes neatly beneath them. I looked down to see if there were any landmarks on the floor that I would recognize later. Then I looked to the left and right to determine which children were on either side of me for when we emerged from the shower. Except, I had this sixth sense that we wouldn't be coming out.

Still the guards maintained the delusion that we would. Some of the older children were sobbing. Some quietly. Others less so. The noise upset the German desire for order and more than once, they told us to shut up.

The guards distributed ragged threadbare towels, reinforcing the fiction that we were only in this dungeon for a shower. The towels didn't pacify the older ones. I was given a small orange one which I wrapped around myself by tucking it under my arms. It gave me momentary warmth, although I soon started shivering again. Echoes of whimpering children, suffering from the cold and sheer terror, filled the room. Some were swept along by the sense of doom that descended on us. Not me. I remained silent. I didn't cry. I had resigned myself to my fate. Whatever that may be. As long as I could escape the cold.

We all huddled together in that concrete waiting room, a few feet from the shower doors. I didn't feel afraid. And I didn't miss my parents. This event, whatever it was, was something I had anticipated. Wrapped in our thin towels, freezing, shivering and shaking, we clung to each other for warmth. We watched and listened as, on the far side of the room, uniformed SS guards with clipboards barked at each other. They seemed to be confused. Ordinarily, German operations ran like clockwork, but on this frigid morning, the mechanics of the Nazi war machine appeared to have malfunctioned.

We waited and waited. The tension was excruciating. The whimpering was getting under the skins of the Germans who repeatedly yelled at us to be quiet. We remained standing, wrapped in our towels for hours. Suddenly, a harsh command snapped us to attention.

'*Raus, raus.*' ('Get out, get out.')

We were ordered to get dressed as quickly as possible and to go back to our barrack.

'It's the wrong block,' I heard someone say. 'We'll take them another time.'

We filed out of the waiting room, back up the stairs and

retraced our steps towards the *Kinderlager*, escorted again by two SS guards. This time the women's camp was on our left. The same gaunt women who had seen us pass before pressed themselves against the barbed-wire fence once again. This time, however, their voices were full of relief and amazement.

'Tola, what happened? Tell me what happened?' Mama yelled.

Once again, I couldn't see her in the crowd.

'They got the wrong block,' I yelled back. 'They're going to take us another time.'

Matter of fact, as always, even at that young age.

In the history of the Holocaust, of all the millions who entered gas chambers in Poland, such as Auschwitz, Majdanek, Chełmno, Treblinka, Belzec and Sobibor, there were very few who somehow survived the experience. Our group of fifty children was probably the largest number to live to tell the tale.

I always thought my escape was a miracle of the Holocaust. To this day, I don't know if we were saved because, as I thought at the time, there was confusion over which children were scheduled for extermination. But if we were indeed the last children in Birkenau, how could the SS have been expecting another group to be gassed?

During the research for this book, another possibility has surfaced. If our entry to the gas chamber took place on or after 2 November 1944, it's entirely feasible that we were saved by Heinrich Himmler, the second most powerful man in the Third Reich, and one of the architects of the 'Final Solution'. Because on this date, Himmler decreed that there were to be no more gassings using the cyanide-based Zyklon B. His order defied Hitler, who was insistent that the extermination of the Jews continued until the task was completed.

One of the catalysts for Himmler's decision was recognition that the Allies were by then aware of the scale of the genocide being perpetrated by the Nazis. The turning point happened in late July 1944 when, in a lightning-fast attack, the Soviet Red Army captured the Majdanek extermination camp, 220 miles north-east of Auschwitz. The Russians took the place intact, before the Germans had a chance to destroy the gas chambers and other infrastructure. Evidence of Nazi war crimes was then indisputable.

The prime witnesses were workers called *Sonderkommandos*. Predominantly Jews, their function was to do the most revolting tasks to save the Nazis from further soiling their bloodstained hands. The Germans tried to make the *Sonderkommandos* complicit, forcing them to lead their fellow Jews to the gas chambers, sometimes shepherding their own friends and families to their deaths. Then, after the cyanide had done its work, they were required to remove the corpses and load them into crematoria. And when the crematoria were overwhelmed, they burned cadavers in open pits.

The *Sonderkommandos* were the walking dead. They knew too much. They saw everything the Nazis did. As potential witnesses, they posed a threat to the Germans, if justice ever presented itself. Performing tasks the Germans weren't willing to undertake prolonged the lives of *Sonderkommandos* by a few months, maybe a year. They enjoyed slightly better rations than the average Birkenau prisoner. But they were doomed the moment they were coerced into joining.

On 7 October 1944, after hearing that they were about to be killed, 250 *Sonderkommandos* staged the biggest revolt in the short bloody history of Auschwitz-Birkenau. They made improvised bombs and hand grenades using mess tins and explosives smuggled to them by female slave labourers who'd been working in a munitions factory. After attacking SS guards with knives, rocks, hammers, and crowbars, they managed to damage Crematorium IV, which like Crematorium V, was set in pine trees that were almost in a direct line with the front door of our barrack. Three members of the SS were killed, including one who was thrown into the open furnace of the crematorium. We cowered inside as the fierce battle took place just a few hundred yards away. Using blasts from exploding oxygen canisters and resulting fire as cover, some of the prisoners tried to escape. The *Sonderkommandos* had seen what had happened to their predecessors and preferred to go down fighting. None of them made it. The SS killed all 250. A further 200 co-conspirators were killed.

The Nazis then investigated how the explosives had fallen into the hands of the *Sonderkommandos*. Four women prisoners were sentenced to death, tortured for weeks and subsequently hanged in Auschwitz. The *Sonderkommandos'* last stand did, however, achieve one notable success: Crematorium IV was damaged beyond repair and had to be demolished.

After Himmler's decree that gassing operations cease, work on dismantling the other gas chambers and crematoria began. Women prisoners like my mother were ordered to start demolishing Crematorium III and its gas chamber, the one that almost claimed my life. They had to remove the metal tracks that led to the line of ovens. The tracks' purpose had been to speed up the process of cremation. *Sonderkommandos* would load up small carts with bodies and pushed them along the tracks to the individual ovens.

The women were ordered to lay grass turf over all the pits that had been used for burning corpses when the crematoria couldn't handle the load. They were also required to sift through human ash remains before they were dumped in the nearby Vistula River. Some women tried to hide bones, so they could be used as evidence later. The women knew that the Russians, and with them maybe justice, were on the way. It's extraordinary to think that at a time when the German Third Reich was facing its greatest threat, from the might of the Soviet Army, the SS were ordering women to plant trees on the sites of the former burning pits, to make it look as though nothing had happened.

The last time I was in a gas chamber was on 26 January 2020. I returned for the seventy-fifth anniversary of the camp's liberation.

I walked into the preserved chamber, in Crematorium I, near the famous entrance gate to Auschwitz, with its sardonic welcome, *Arbeit Macht Frei.* The relatively small chamber, with three or four ovens and metal trays for pushing corpses into the flames became redundant because it couldn't handle the industrial-scale extermination at the heart of the Final Solution.

I thought I was tough enough to cope with entering a place replete with nightmarish personal memories and which symbolizes the crimes against my people. But after a couple of minutes, I could hardly breathe and had to leave quickly. The experience was too much for me.

CHAPTER FOURTEEN

DELIVERANCE

Birkenau extermination camp,
German-occupied southern Poland, mid-afternoon,
25 January 1945
Age six

After my close encounter with the gas chamber, the next moment of maximum peril came at the end of January 1945 as history closed in on Auschwitz-Birkenau.

Just because the Nazis had been ordered to stop gassing us, that didn't mean murder had ended. Although the gas chambers were now out of action, life wasn't any safer. They were still executing people. Prisoners were still dying from sickness, malnutrition and exhaustion. But for the first time since the Nazis had swept to power, their priority was now self-preservation. Although our guards, the fanatical SS, took pride in their reputation for being the cream of the German military, but like many bullies, they became cowards when confronted by opposition.

There were bombing raids by American planes on factories attached to the Auschwitz complex. Despite the danger to the slave labourers inside, the attacks were welcomed by them as a sign that liberation might soon be at hand. The rumble of artillery grew louder as the Soviet Red Army moved in from the East. When they approached the city of Kraków, 40 miles from Birkenau, on 17 January 1945, prisoners witnessed a state of panic and chaos among drunken SS personnel.

The Germans were now in a race against time. Prisoners didn't need newspapers or radio broadcasts to know what was happening. They overheard soldiers' anxious conversations. The SS were experiencing pangs of real fear, perhaps for the first time. Birkenau had been a soft posting. All it entailed was murdering harmless civilians. Nobody in their right mind volunteered for the Russian front, where no quarter was proffered by enemy nor winter. Now the Russian front was on their doorstep. The sacrifice of Stalingrad was fresh in the Soviet memory. More than a million Russian troops and civilians were killed there, the bloodiest battle of the Second World War. The Soviet victory on the banks of the River Volga in the winter of 1942 finally turned the tide of the war in the east against Germany. Retribution was on the tip of every Red Army bayonet. Storming westwards, the Russians swept aside all opposition. They were just a few days from arriving at our gates.

The Germans began the evacuation of Birkenau on 18 January 1945. The worst genocide in the history of humankind had taken place within the confines of these electrified fences. The Nazis attempted to sanitize the crime scene, or at least leave as little evidence as possible. They blew up Crematoria Two and Three. Only Crematorium Five remained intact. They incinerated the records and files so diligently gathered over the previous few years, but their biggest problem was that there were so many witnesses left. Sixty thousand prisoners remained in Auschwitz, Birkenau and Monowitz, the main components of the Auschwitz complex.

The Nazis started gathering prisoners to either transport them or force them to march westwards towards Germany. On the first day of this operation, some five thousand women and children left Birkenau, wearing clogs or barefoot and in columns of 500 escorted by SS guards. Anyone who was too sick or weak was summarily shot. Like wounded animals, the Germans were at their most dangerous now that they felt threatened. Over the course of the next week, the mayhem intensified as the Russians drew ever closer.

On the morning of 25 January 1945, the block elder in Mama's building said the evacuation of the camp was nearly finished. She told the women that those who could walk would have to leave, and all those who couldn't, would be 'taken care of'. Mama knew what that meant. She waited for her opportunity and when the elder's back was turned, she slipped out of the barracks to fetch me.

Mama understood the enormity of this day: it offered the prospect of freedom. After six years of slavery, starvation and degradation, liberation was perhaps just hours away. In her own small way, Mama had resisted for the duration of the war. Every day that she and I survived was an act of defiance. On this day of all days, she couldn't afford to be passive. It was unthinkable that we might succumb to the Holocaust in these last turbulent hours. For the first time in the war, Mama had a slight chance to dictate how her day might end. Her sixth sense, her intuition, had served her well in the past. She had to follow her instincts while keeping her eyes wide open.

The confusion in the camp, the smoke from the fires and the murk of winter all worked in our favour. Mama achieved her objective. She managed to take me to the infirmary and hide me in a bed with a covered corpse.

What Mama didn't know, and what I've learned since, is that at two o'clock that afternoon, large numbers of SD troops were sent into our camp to force all the remaining Jews out into the open. SD stood for *Sicherheitsdienst*, the security service – possibly the most dangerous outfit within the German armed forces. Their function was to act as mobile killing units.

As soon as I heard their boots, I snapped out of my day-dream about the doll with the green face. I was instantly alert. I had time to mould myself as close as possible to the shape of the corpse and then I remained as still as possible. My presence of mind in staying calm and clutching the cadaver a little tighter was testimony to the education in survival Mama had given me.

'*Raus, raus,*' the Germans bellowed. '*Alle Juden heraus. Heraus, schnell, schnell.*'

My heart began pounding. I couldn't see anything. All my nerve endings were on fire. But I remembered Mama's parting words: 'No matter what you hear, do not move until I return.'

My body went rigid. I heard shooting and screaming as patients were hauled from beds, jarring their emaciated frames as they fell to the floor. I heard the fear in their voices, as guttural German commands zapped like machine pistols around the infirmary. Leather gloves smacked skin and bone. A woman cried in pain. There was a shot, quickly followed by another.

Now it was my turn. A soldier approached my bed. He moved slowly and deliberately. Gravel trapped in the soles of his jackboots ground on the floorboards as he drew closer. He was breathing heavily. I kept my breaths as shallow as possible so the blanket wouldn't move. I breathed towards the ground. And then I held my breath for as long as I could. The soldier seemed to take an age assuring himself my bedmate was dead. Eventually, he moved on. I fought hard not to gasp as I exhaled. I listened as soldiers went from room to room, dragging patients from beds onto the floor. They were shooting people in the building and outside. The screaming and the shooting camouflaged the sounds of my breathing. I did not budge an inch.

Then it went quiet. I tried to work out whether the Germans

had left the infirmary. I wanted to rip off the blanket and look. But I didn't dare move. Mama had told me to stay put. I trusted Mama. I lay there waiting and listening. Time had no meaning. I had no way of telling how long I lay there.

Then I smelled smoke. At first it was bearable. But within minutes the smoke filled my lungs and started to crush them. I struggled to breathe. Yet still I hugged the cold corpse and stayed beneath the blanket. I refused to cough. I could have choked or burned to death. I was following Mama's instructions to the letter. The smoke intensified. I was finding it harder to breathe. I was desperate for fresh air but still resisted the urge to cough. Suddenly, the blanket was tugged from the bed.

'Quick, we've got to get out of here. They've set the building on fire.'

She sat me up.

'They've gone, Tola. They've gone.'

It was Mama. She'd kept her promise. Mama had come back. She too had been clutching a corpse and pretending to be dead.

There was astonishment in Mama's voice and a sense of joy that I had never heard before.

'Where are your shoes?' she asked.

The white lace-up shoes I had worn since the previous summer had vanished.

'We'll have to leave without them. We have to go. We don't have much time.'

I scanned the barrack. All around me, women were climbing out of beds. The half dead were pushing cadavers out of the way. They fell to the ground with a soft thud. It seemed as though corpses were flying off the beds. Floorboards cantilevered into the air as coughing, skeletal figures in rags prised themselves out of hiding places and shook off dust and dirt. It looked like the dead were coming back to life.

I grasped Mama's hand and walked barefoot out of the burning infirmary and into the snow. Scores of buildings were on fire. Birkenau truly was an inferno. Fresh corpses littered the frozen ground. These were the people I'd heard being executed outside. They had been cut down because they were physically incapable of joining what would be later termed the Death March. That could so easily have been Mama and me.

There were no SS, no SD, no Nazis of any description to be seen. They had all vanished. Our astonishment was shared by other surviving inmates of Birkenau, as the realization dawned that the guards had abandoned their posts and fled. As the crowd ventured towards the railway tracks that had brought us all to Birkenau, I could see silhouettes in the gathering dusk, across the flat terrain more than a mile away, beyond the Gate of Death. The last group of prisoners to leave under guard numbered around three hundred and fifty children, women and men. I have no idea what happened to them. Perhaps they suffered a similar fate to those on the Death March, who were murdered on the way or died from starvation and exposure.

I was finally free to cry. But I didn't. I was too hungry. More than anything, I was craving food.

Now free to roam, the prisoners broke into storerooms and found enough rations to feed an army. Word rapidly spread that there was food aplenty. Collective madness descended as people sought to alleviate their hunger pains. Using whatever implements they could find, they forced open cans of processed meats and other delicacies.

That night, Birkenau glowed every shade of red. Flames flickered in barrack blocks torched by the Germans. Some had been reduced to cinders. Abandoned prisoners in thin rags, clustered around bonfires, warmed their bones and tried to grasp the concept of freedom. For the first time in six years, flames meant life, not extinction. Searchlights no longer beamed from watchtowers. And although there was no power in the electric fences – electricity and water supplies had been knocked out during a recent Allied bombing raid – most prisoners stayed inside.

Mama and I wandered back to her barrack block and clambered into a bunk together. For the first time in almost five months, I snuggled up to her as tightly as I could possibly get. Her body had changed. There was much less of her than there used to be. But she still had the scent of my mama.

Thankfully, that night no other women shared our bunk. I descended into the most secure, tranquil sleep I had enjoyed in ages. I even slept through a huge explosion in the middle of the night when an SS demolition squad blew up Crematorium

Number Five. It was the last military action by the Germans in Birkenau.

For me and Mama, the war was over. Now, new battles began. We had to fight the complications of peace. And our demons.

CHAPTER FIFTEEN

LIBERATION

Birkenau extermination camp,
Soviet-occupied Southern Poland, mid-afternoon,
27 January 1945

Age six

For two days, the sounds of fighting grew louder and closer. Although our Nazi oppressors were nowhere to be seen, there was an underlying fear that they might return. We found ourselves in a peculiar hinterland between incarceration and freedom. Our jailers had fled, but the survivors left inside the barbed wire not only had no place to go, but also were confused, traumatized, sickly and, of course, exhausted. The trepidation and dire conditions, however, were counterbalanced by a wave of optimism, an emotion that had been absent among my people for my entire life.

'The Russians are coming, the Russians are coming,' was the repeated refrain as the day wore on.

And for once, optimism was rewarded. As the light was fading, we caught the first glimpse of our liberators. I stood next to Mama at the barbed-wire fence, looking towards the red brick Gate of Death. We were lost in a crowd of mainly women who had the physical strength to stand for hours in the freezing cold. Although most were little more than skeletons, they managed to shout and scream and cheer and whistle. It was the happiest sound I had ever heard.

Marching behind a giant red flag, with a gold hammer and sickle in the corner, the soldiers pushed open the gate to a roar of welcome. Some prisoners were dancing, fuelled by adrenaline and affirmation that against all odds, they had defied extermination. Women rushed forwards and kissed the soldiers on the cheeks. So did some of the men. Others fell to their knees and kissed the boots of the victorious Russians.

The soldiers hugged the frail stick people in rags and returned the kisses. A giant of a soldier picked me up and, with a big grin on his face, held me over his head. He said something that I didn't understand. I looked at Mama and she was smiling, too. So I told myself that what he was doing was ok.

Until then, I'd thought that all soldiers wore the intimidating steel helmets and black and grey uniforms of the SS. The Russians were clad in dark green greatcoats. Some had helmets, others had squat fur hats decorated with unfamiliar insignia. What distinguished the Russians was their demeanour and empathy. Contempt and hatred had filled German eyes. The Russians' were full of joy. But their expressions quickly changed from jubilation to shock at what they had stumbled upon. Even I could tell that they couldn't quite believe what their eyes were seeing.

As night fell, the Red Army troops pitched tents inside the barbed wire. Some occupied empty buildings. Days after the Germans had set them on fire, some blocks were still burning, and the Russians extinguished the flames. The soldiers gave everyone something from their ration pack. It was one of the most extraordinary nights I've ever known. I've always regarded 27 January, the date of the official liberation of Auschwitz, as my alternative birthday, because it was the first day of the rest of my life.

I had something to eat. I was warm. I felt safe. And I was with Mama.

The Russians, having recovered from the shock, were raucous and the camp was filled with the unfamiliar ripple of laughter. Those young men radiated the happiness of being alive. Their laughter was a lullaby that rocked us to a deep, untroubled sleep.

At first light, I awoke to an aroma I couldn't identify. The Russians had set up a field kitchen near their makeshift hospital and the cooks were baking bread. The smell was incredibly enticing. Everyone lined up and was given a warm loaf. It was beyond delicious. I wolfed it down as fast as I could. Once I had finished, I raced back to the line. I told the cook I was an orphan and hadn't received any bread. He recognized me, grinned and handed me another. Mama saw me with the second loaf and gave me one of her silent, all-knowing looks.

'Somebody gave it to me,' I fibbed.

My eyes were bigger than my stomach, and I only managed to eat a couple of mouthfuls because I was so full. But I hid the loaf beneath a blanket to consume later. Not long afterwards, the mouth-watering smell of simmering meat wafted through the camp, overpowering the lingering stench from the crematoria lodged in my olfactory nerves. The cooks were stirring huge vats of pork stew that was a staple for the Russian soldiers. I was itching to run towards the new food line, but Mama stopped me.

'We can't eat this. Our stomachs aren't ready yet. If we eat it, we'll get sick. For the next few days, it's bread only for us, I'm afraid.'

Although I was disappointed, I was too disciplined to contradict Mama. So while many of the other inmates threw caution to the wind and devoured the stew, we ate only bread for two days. On the third day after liberation, Mama slathered butter on the bread. It was wonderful. By day five, I'd graduated to bread with butter and sugar. Life was definitely improving.

Several days later, she allowed me to sample the stew. Although pork is forbidden in Judaism, if you are starving and only non-kosher food is available, then it's permissible. I devoured the stew – a real meal for possibly the first time in my life. I sensed the nourishment percolating through my core. And Mama's wisdom was validated once again: I managed to keep the food down, but as we wandered around the camp, we saw scores of starving people whose stomachs were in turmoil.

Most were convulsing, vomiting uncontrollably or suffering from dysentery or diarrhoea. In the worst cases, the reaction to the very ordinary Russian rations was fatal. How tragic that people who had survived the starvation of the Holocaust should be killed by food as freedom beckoned.

That winter was one of the coldest of the twentieth century. Temperatures hovered well below freezing point. Mama needed warmer clothes. I had a coat that was barely adequate for the conditions. Along with other survivors, we tramped through the snow to the warehouses in the pine trees known as *Kanada*. Some of the buildings had been destroyed during the Germans' scorched-earth retreat. But six blocks remained standing. They were filled with the contents of all the suitcases that more than a million people had carried on their final journey to Birkenau. Who knows – perhaps the possessions I had guarded in vain six months earlier were in there? If so, it would have been impossible to find them. The cornucopia of belongings was staggering in its scale. The *Sammlungstelle* in Tomaszów Mazowiecki, where Mama and I had sorted clothes, was minuscule in comparison.

Many of the garments lying in heaps in the warehouses had clearly been expensive when purchased. After wearing rags for six months, it was tempting to take the prettiest clothes, but Mama maintained her principles of frugality and propriety.

'I need a warm coat,' she said. 'But I'm not going to take a fur or anything else that looks expensive. We will not benefit from the murder of someone else.'

Mama sifted through a pile of clothes and emerged with a man's dark overcoat that swamped her and reached all the way to the ground. Although it was far from glamorous, I thought Mama looked beautiful. My eyes then caught a rag doll poking out from between some clothes.

'Can I have that, Mama?' I pleaded.

'No, Tola, I'm afraid you can't. It was taken from a little girl who died. We are only taking what we need to protect us against the cold.'

A week or so later, I left Birkenau for the first time. Along with other children, we were transported in a truck by the Russians to the main Auschwitz camp, the one with the famous arched metal sign saying *Arbeit Macht Frei*. The Russians had summoned a film crew to record for posterity the horrors they had discovered.

Shepherded by nurses and a Russian commissar in a fur hat, I held hands with two of the youngest children, and we walked along a narrow path with now harmless electrified barbed-wire fences on either side. Then the Russians told us to roll up our sleeves and reveal our tattoos. That sequence became one of the most iconic of the Second World War. I'm the girl in the left of frame in the tattoo shot, in a dark coat and wearing a tightly tied headscarf.

Unlike the adults in the same Russian film, who were little more than skeletons, none of the children looked gaunt. A few days of eating decent Red Army food had enabled us to get our weight back on track. The footage was testimony to the natural resilience of children. When filming was over, I was taken back to Birkenau.

Seventy five years later, three of us from that famous picture, including Michael and Sarah, standing to the left of me, found each other in New Jersey. By coincidence, Sarah taught my grandchildren. What a small world.

The first few weeks of our liberation were exhilarating, such was the bliss of no longer being scared, cold or hungry. But life under the Red Army's protection soon palled, thanks to a combination of vodka and testosterone. The Russians became rowdier and aggressive, towards each other and especially towards women. They roamed the camp at night in packs, pushing, shoving, shouting and occasionally brawling. I noticed that Mama tried to avoid them whenever possible. Other women weren't so fortunate. I couldn't understand the change in their behaviour.

Nights became nerve-wracking experiences once again. They reminded me of the ghetto when the Germans turned up full of malice.

Russians would enter our block when we were sleeping. As soon as Mama heard their steps, she'd wake me up, dress me quickly and we'd run out and find another barrack to sleep in. Some nights, we'd be pursued and would race from building to building to avoid them. Ever watchful, Mama lay awake for hours, listening, just in case. The need for constant vigilance was exhausting.

One night, while we were outside, an inebriated Russian soldier grabbed Mama by the arm and made his intentions crystal clear.

'Go away, leave me alone,' she screamed.

By now, Mama had regained her strength and she managed to wriggle free from his grasp. We ran away and hid. He bellowed a few drunken curses, staggered a few steps and gave up the pursuit. The next morning, when we went to collect our daily bread, we saw Mama's assailant slumped outside a building, fast asleep, still clutching his bottle.

'We have to leave,' Mama said. 'As soon as possible.'

Our chance came as the war in Europe entered its final stages. The Russians were in Berlin and advancing towards the Reichstag, and the American-led Allies were closing the vice from the west. Rumours that Adolf Hitler was dead buzzed around the camp as the International Red Cross turned up to register survivors and offer us assistance. Mama was relieved. She was handed a stamped document giving us free passage on Polish public transport.

'We're going home,' she said, with a smile.

Spring was about to become summer. I had grown and needed to replace the dress and coat that I had been given almost a year earlier. There was still a vast array of garments to choose from.

Mama took me back to the *Kanada* warehouse, and I picked a dark blue dress decorated with a white apron, a skirt with a white blouse and a warm jacket that fitted me perfectly. Thinking of the children who wore these before me made me feel bad, but I had no choice.

Our next stop was a storeroom containing thousands of suitcases. I wondered whether ours was somewhere in the pile. We took a small case and filled it almost to bursting point with food, mostly bread, cheese and jam taken from army rations. There was just enough space for my extra dress. All we possessed was that small suitcase and our memories. I was full of optimism because Mama promised we would meet her wonderful family.

'You will now know your background,' she said.

We were among the fortunate few to leave behind the Auschwitz motto, *Arbeit Macht Frei*. But work did not set us free.

We walked out of Birkenau, hand in hand, one morning in April 1945. Mama said one word.

'Remember.'

CHAPTER SIXTEEN

THE WELCOME

Tomaszów Mazowiecki,
Soviet-occupied Central Poland, summer 1945

Age 6

After leaving Birkenau, we had about 130 miles to travel by bus and train. We walked to the station in the nearest town, Oświęcim (that's Polish for Auschwitz). People averted their eyes and gave us sideways glances as we passed by. They knew where we had come from. They knew what had been taking place on the other side of the barbed-wire fence. Just like us, they had smelled it.

After taking a series of crowded trains and buses, we arrived in Tomaszów Mazowiecki around dusk. We'd been away for almost two years. We weren't really sure where to go. Mama didn't know what to expect. Like a homing pigeon, she'd been drawn back to Tomaszów Mazowiecki. But where was home? My grandparents' place? The big ghetto? The small ghetto?

Tomaszów was now occupied by Russian soldiers and some of the town had been damaged in fighting between the Germans and the Red Army. Mama had trouble finding her bearings. Then she recognized a woman she'd known before the war. Someone who'd been a friend. Mama picked up the pace to greet her. But when the woman approached, she hissed, 'What are you doing back here? I thought Hitler killed you all.'

That was our welcome back to Tomaszów Mazowiecki.

Mama did not reply. She squeezed my hand. We crossed the street and walked away quickly. I was really shocked. I wanted to ask why the woman was so angry at us, but I knew Mama was upset and so I kept quiet.

We continued wandering aimlessly as the cold and darkness deepened, until Mama found a cellar with a door ajar. It smelled warm and clean and we were too tired to go any further. We had nowhere else to go. The cellar was used as storage for potatoes. We sat down on a pile of clean, folded burlap sacks and ate the remaining provisions we'd brought with us, until we fell asleep, exhausted.

When I awoke the next morning, Mama was already up and busy.

'Tola, we're going to stay here for a while, until we find our family,' she said.

Mama had come to an arrangement with the owner of the house who gave us blankets and boxes to use as tables. The cellar had an earthen floor. It was rudimentary, but it offered shelter from the elements. I quickly learned how to sprinkle water on the floor to keep the dust down. I'm not sure how Mama provided for us, but we didn't go hungry.

Every day she took me for a long walk, pointing out the buildings where her family lived before the war. Most of the apartments were now occupied by strangers and we never went inside. Mama was hurt by the reality that homes which embraced her before the war were now off limits.

One building where Mama had once lived with her siblings was now in ruins. We sat on the rubble as she told me all about her life at home before the war and before she met Papa. She was trying to make me appreciate that I was part of a big, loving family with a proud, distinguished history. Every day she bought me a jam doughnut and reconstructed the Pinkusewicz family tree. She told me about the festivals and holidays they had enjoyed and the many songs that were sung around the Sabbath table of her very observant family. By talking about them, she was trying to keep the flickering candle of hope alive. Yet there was a quiet desperation in her voice. The stories she was compelled to recount mostly served to accentuate her loneliness.

'Hopefully, some of them will return soon and then you'll meet your family.' Mama mouthed the words, although I'm not sure she believed what she was saying.

Together with the Red Cross, the now tiny Jewish community established a centre where they registered all survivors returning to Tomaszów Mazowiecki and provided them with supplies and other assistance. Just 200 returned. Every morning Mama checked the list in the hope that some of her relatives might be alive. Every day she came back home, shaking her head. As hope ebbed away, we stopped our daily walks, although Mama scrutinised the list every morning. As time passed, she became more and more despondent.

Mama wanted me to go to first grade at the local Polish school. But she gave up trying to persuade me. If she dared mention the word, I ran out of the cellar and disappeared.

However, the grim mood changed dramatically for the better when my father's three sisters suddenly appeared in Tomaszów Mazowiecki. They had not been named on the Red Cross list, and everyone was surprised to see them. I was especially happy to be reacquainted with my wonderful Aunt Helen, the widow of my Uncle James. Like Mama and me, Helen and her sisters, Ita and Elka, were all tattooed. They had spent several months in other parts of Auschwitz where they had worked as slave labourers for private German companies. As the Russians closed in, they were forced to join the Death March to Germany. Somehow, despite the cold and the violence, they'd all survived, found each other and decided to return to the town they regarded as home.

Mama's spirits soared. The sisters' arrival provided proof that some of Papa's family had defied death. But where was he?

Aunt Ita was a gifted tailor, and she set about working immediately. The five of us moved into a tiny two-bedroom apartment. Ita created a workshop in the sitting room. She soon had a full order book, especially from Russian soldiers. Mama and my aunts helped as well. Although we were forced to share beds, nobody complained.

However, Mama's elation at my aunts' return was short lived. Her despair returned and intensified as she acknowledged her own family wasn't coming back. She slept more and ate less. By nature a quiet woman, Mama retreated deeper inside herself. My aunts exchanged worried looks as they cared for her, and I was left free to roam. I was adventurous and enjoyed pushing the boundaries. I wandered the streets of Tomaszów Mazowiecki, following the Russian army as they marched, sometimes in time with a band. I was enchanted by the music and the spectacle. I got lost several times following their parades, until my aunts managed to find me.

The Russians in Tomaszów Mazowiecki were as ill-disciplined off-duty as those in Birkenau. They were frequently drunk and convinced of their entitlement to force themselves on women who took their fancy. Aunt Elka was the oldest of the sisters and very pretty. The Russians were always banging on our door.

If that wasn't bad enough, our Polish neighbours were almost as hostile as the Germans had been. There was no sympathy for the ordeal we had endured.

'Why have you come back? Why aren't you dead? You should be,' were some of the insults repeatedly hurled in our direction.

Weary of the Russians, the anti-Semitism, the provincial attitudes of Tomaszów Mazowiecki and our cramped living conditions, Aunt Helen decided to move 40 miles away to Lodz, Poland's third-biggest city. She was now in her mid-twenties. Helen had been a widow most of her adult life, and there were more prospects in Lodz, which had a bigger Jewish community.

We escorted Helen to Tomaszów Mazowiecki station, from where the majority of the town's Jews had been transported to Treblinka. As the train departed for Lodz, she poked her head through a window, smiled, waved and blew me a kiss. Although they understood Helen's desire to leave, her sisters and Mama were worried because Poland was awash with stories of attacks on Jews returning from the camps. The worst took place in July 1946 in a town called Kielce, 100 miles north-east of Auschwitz. Polish troops, police and civilians attacked a gathering of Jewish refugees, killing forty-two and injuring forty. It was the worst pogrom since the end of the Second World War. After everything the Jews had suffered, the attack provoked international outrage and completely undermined our sense of security.

I was around seven years old at the time. As a distraction from the harshness of daily life in Tomaszów Mazowiecki, Mama introduced me to music and dance. She took me to the cinema to see Shirley Temple in the comedy *Bright Eyes*. I was enthralled by her rendition of 'The Good Ship Lollipop'. The film was dubbed in Polish and years later, I was surprised to discover that Shirley Temple wasn't Polish.

We also went to see *The Red Shoes*, one of the finest films of the age. It is an adaptation of a Hans Christian Anderson fable about a girl who could not stop dancing. The dancing and music mesmerized me and I can still picture it vividly in my mind. But the cinema only offered Mama a brief respite from her melancholy thoughts.

Then, one day, at last there was some uplifting news. Mama's obsessive survey of the survivors' noticeboard paid off. She found Papa's name. He was coming home from Dachau. Papa had discovered where we were living from a list that was compiled and shared by a group of teenagers travelling from town to town, trying to find lost relatives.

The day of his return was bittersweet. There was a gentle knock. Mama opened the door and screamed with joy. She threw her arms around Papa, and they held each other. Then he lifted me up and hugged me. All three of us stood in the doorway clutching each other and weeping with happiness. Ita and Elka joined in the embrace.

But then Papa broke away and limped into the sitting room. He opened a newspaper to a page dominated by the photograph of a murder victim, lying on the floor of the shop where she worked.

'Look what I found on the train,' Papa sobbed.

I could barely make out what he was saying.

Mama and the sisters took a closer look at the newspaper. The victim was my beloved Aunt Helen. She had been shot by a marauding gang of anti-Semitic Poles.

Besides being traumatized, Papa wasn't in great shape. He

had been shot in the leg by an SS officer in Dachau and needed to recuperate.

My parents and aunts began discussing whether it was time to leave the country. We were intimidated by the Russians and the all-pervasive anti-Semitism. But Mama refused. She was afraid that if her family came back and she wasn't there, she would never find them again.

As for me, Papa's return meant I could no longer avoid going to school. My days as a vagabond on the street were now over. I was seven and a half and Papa insisted I begin my formal education.

The first day was an utter disappointment. The teacher put me at the back of the class and I had no idea what was going on.

'I don't understand why those children sit at those little desks doing something with a pencil on a piece of paper,' I told Mama. 'It's a complete waste of time.'

But my parents were resolute and took me back the next day. Once again, I was marooned at the back of the class trying to comprehend what was happening. In the middle of a lesson, all the children were told to go to the chapel. I didn't have a clue what that meant and was left alone. I decided to head home. As I walked away, I felt something hit my back. I turned around and saw some of my fellow pupils throwing stones at me.

'You dirty Jew,' they screamed. 'Why are you alive? You are just a dirty Jew.'

I pleaded with Mama and Papa not to send me back, but

they insisted. So I stole some money from my mother's bag and bought a crucifix on a chain. The next day, I proudly wore the cross around my neck for all to see. The children started laughing at me.

'You aren't Christian.'

'You don't belong here.'

'You are a dirty Jew. You killed Christ.'

I cried all the way home and kept asking myself how I could have killed Christ? I didn't even know him.

I told Mama what had happened.

'I want to be a Christian. I don't want to be a Jew any more.'

Mama was furious and smacked me hard.

'How dare you say that? After everything we've been through. We've made it and survived. You should be proud of being Jewish. Never forget that.'

Although Mama had survived physically, she was struggling psychologically. A hundred and fifty relatives had disappeared. They weren't coming back. Her depression was so severe, we couldn't even get her out of bed. She stopped eating altogether and wouldn't wake up. Papa decided we had no alternative but to leave – to try to save Mama's mind and possibly even her life.

One day, I was told to dress with everything I owned. As Poland's borders were officially closed, Papa had to pay a smuggler to get us out. Aunt Ita stayed behind with her new boyfriend Adam, who had just been discharged from the Russian army. But Aunt Elka and her fiancé, Monyak, joined us.

Of all the ironies, we headed into what I thought was enemy territory. Under cover of darkness, we crossed the border into Germany. Our destination? Berlin.

Once we had crossed the border, Mama turned to me and said, 'We will no longer be speaking Polish. It's a very unwelcoming country.'

And so I began to learn Yiddish.

We vowed never to return to Tomaszów Mazowiecki. Today, nearly eighty years after the war, the town doesn't have a Jewish community.

CHAPTER SEVENTEEN

SLEEPWALKING IN BERLIN

Germany, 1947

Age eight

The night terrors began with a vengeance in our new home over-looking Checkpoint Charlie in the American sector of post-war Berlin. I dreamed that I was being chased. I had to run away and save myself. My nightmares were so intense that they took me over and I started sleepwalking. I got out of bed in our two-bed, second-floor apartment, went downstairs and continued to flee along Friedrichstrasse, one of the main streets in the area. It was the front line of the embryonic Cold War where US and Russian troops faced off against each other in the tense, divided German capital.

My sleepwalking dismayed my parents. Sometimes they heard me get up and could catch me in the street and take me back to bed. When I awoke later, I had no recollection of what I'd done.

I was eight and a half years old at the time. Sleepwalking was not uncommon among child survivors of the Holocaust. After everything I had experienced, it was not surprising that my sleep was disturbed. Mama and Papa did everything they could to alleviate my suffering, as they were worried that my nightly excursions could do me considerable harm. A doctor assured them that sleepwalking could be easily disrupted by putting wet sheets and towels on the floor by my bed. His theory was that when I got up, I'd feel the cold, wake up and go straight back to sleep. But his suggestion didn't work. Then he recommended placing big bowls of water by the bed to wake me up. That failed as well. I just knocked the bowls over as I fled from the people pursuing me in my dreams, flooding the floor in the process. Thankfully, the area where we lived was safe, and during my nocturnal escapades, I never strayed too far before being rescued.

My parents didn't always catch me in the act, however. Sometimes they slept through. Once, I was found near the checkpoint in a trance-like state by a friendly American soldier called Jim, whom I had met before when he was on patrol. Jim carried me back upstairs to my parents. They had no idea that I'd vanished.

A few days after we'd settled into the Berlin apartment, together with Aunt Elka and Monyak, Mama allowed me to explore. Although bomb- and shell-damaged buildings bestowed the neighbourhood with a somewhat ghostly air, she judged it to be safe. The presence of patrolling American soldiers generated confidence that I would come to no harm in daylight hours. For the first time in my life, I encountered troops who behaved in a civilized manner, and Jim's kindness made him stand out. The first time he saw me, he offered me an orange, and followed it up with a piece of chocolate. Then he gave me chewing gum, which I swallowed immediately. We smiled at each other, and I rushed home with the rest of my treats. Neither of us understood what the other was saying, but whenever we saw one another thereafter we always waved.

The night terrors, however, curtailed my daytime activities. I was exhausted from sleepwalking and often compensated by snoozing through daylight hours. Although the American GIs weren't intimidating, my parents felt strongly that we should move to a place with a minimal military presence. Berlin was teeming with soldiers. Besides the Russians, there were also French and British troops guarding their sectors of the city. Mama and Papa thought that the presence of uniforms and guns was contributing to my trauma. My parents didn't need to take me to a string of consultants to be assessed. My mother's intuition was unerring. She knew exactly what I required. A tranquil, secure environment.

Ironically, my healing process began in the pretty medieval Bavarian lakeside town where Adolf Hitler wrote *Mein Kampf*, his blueprint for controlling the European continent and exterminating Jews.

Mama, Papa and I moved to the Displaced Persons' (DP) camp

in Landsberg am Lech, west of Munich in the American zone. Aunt Ita and Adam had joined us in Berlin, but now both aunts moved to the Leipzig DP camp with their partners. During the war, Landsberg was an annex of the Dachau concentration-camp complex, forty-five minutes away, where Papa was incarcerated. Landsberg had a dark history of slave labour, starvation, disease and executions. Jewish prisoners were put to work digging massive underground bunkers intended for aircraft production. An estimated fifteen thousand Jews died, amid terrible conditions. American troops who liberated Landsberg in April 1945 found 5,000 survivors. Physically and emotionally, they were too sick to leave. They had nowhere else to go and so they stayed.

Liberation did not bring instant relief. Conditions inside Landsberg remained deplorable for some time. The survivors' psychological and physical welfare were neglected, until the administration of the camp was transferred to the relief agency of the fledgling United Nations. By the time we arrived in early 1948, Landsberg DP camp had been transformed into a model community, full of hope, energy and optimism.

Similar camps were established across Germany, Austria and Italy to provide temporary safe havens for 250,000 dispossessed European Jews. Being stateless and homeless were the only entry requirements.

Everything about Landsberg was conducive to healing and recovery, especially for children. We had very pleasant family accommodation in the stout former military barracks. The communal kitchen had a gigantic oven where we prepared meals for the Sabbath, which is such an important element of Jewish life.

For the first time, I went to school and didn't object. There were only about ten children in my class. We learned the Hebrew alphabet, not Latin script. Our teachers were volunteers from Israel who were psychologically trained to be aware of the traumas we had experienced and knew how to relate to us. I have especially fond memories of one called Rena who was extremely sensitive to our emotional state. She framed her questions in a way that encouraged us to concentrate on the present and future instead of mourning the past. Rena didn't want us to forget what had happened. Far from it. But she wanted us to have a new perspective on life.

I considered myself fortunate to have both parents. Every child in my class had a tragic story to tell. Some of my fellow pupils were orphans and were cared for by relatives. Others had lost entire families and were being nurtured before starting new lives in Israel.

I met my best friend, Clara, in Rena's class. Clara was a year older than me and lived in the DP camp with her father. Clara, her little sister, and their parents had spent much of the war hiding with a Polish farmer whom they paid well. But then a neighbour had discovered them and informed the Gestapo. Clara and her father had run into a forest and escaped, but her mother and little sister were caught. Clara clung to the hope that her mama and sister had also been liberated from a camp somewhere and that eventually they would all be reunited. Their plight reminded me of my mama's never-ending quest to trace her lost relatives. We were all still searching and hoping, all too frequently in vain.

Landsberg's secure, peaceful atmosphere was designed to facilitate the renaissance of a people who had been crushed physically, emotionally and spiritually. Our Jewish pride was restored. We began the process of metamorphosis from victims to survivors to thrivers, helped by an education system that offered classes from pre-school to college level. The camp also contained a ritual bath, a kosher kitchen, cinema, theatre, radio station and had its own newspaper. A premium was placed on physical wellbeing and people who a few years earlier were little more than skeletons found themselves participating in sports competitions. The aim of the camp hierarchy was to prepare displaced people for life in what was called *Eretz Israel*, or the Land of Israel. Because despite everything we had faced, Jewish refugees remained unwelcome in many countries around the world, and if it had not been for Israel many had no place to go. The need for the Jewish people to have their own homeland, where they could live free from persecution and rejection, was now beyond question.

My family's passion for Zionism was reinvigorated. I remember walking in a parade on 16 May 1948, a few days after the new State of Israel was formally inaugurated. I was nine years old and all the other children were lined up with Israeli flags. At last, the Star of David was no longer a symbol that marked us out for destruction. How times had changed. It was on display in Germany, and of all places in a town that was strongly associated with Hitler's tyranny.

In Landsberg we were able to breathe again. We were among our own people. No longer persecuted, we could revive our traditions and reassert our values free from fear. Everyone benefited from an experience akin to summer camp for families. My parents weren't required to work. Papa regained his strength after Dachau. He resumed acting, his great love. Mama recuperated physically, although she still suffered headaches as a result of the beating she received in Birkenau for stealing a potato. The agony of losing her family had not diminished. But through her pain, Mama devoted herself to raising me. My night terrors abated and I stopped sleepwalking.

Mama began reading and listening to music again. Her favourite instrument was the piano and she decided I should learn as well.

'You've seen such terrible things,' Mama said. 'I want you to see that life can also be beautiful.'

She found a piano teacher for me about five blocks away from the DP camp. A nice, young married German with long hair and three small children, he was classically trained and had no interest in popular music. He spoke to me softly in German. It was significant because at last the language wasn't accompanied by the threat of violence. The teacher insisted on practice,

practice, practice. It was hard work, but I persevered and made good progress. And the tables had turned: the music teacher and his family were hungry, as Germany was in ruins and food was in short supply. He was grateful that we paid for the lessons with cans of peas and carrots that we received from the Americans.

Papa was also determined that our family should embrace culture once more and he introduced me to the theatre. He adored Shakespeare. Mama and I basked in pride and reflected glory as we watched him on stage in the roles of Othello and King Lear in Yiddish productions. The journey to the theatre in Munich to watch him perform was also memorable as the train from Landsberg was very posh.

Although the DP camp was preparing us for life in Israel, Mama and Papa decided to emigrate to the United States, as the economic conditions in Israel were difficult. But their plans were interrupted by the discovery that I was suffering from tuberculosis (TB), a bacterial disease that scars the lungs and can be fatal if untreated. TB is contagious and the American authorities wouldn't permit our family to enter the country until I was cured. At the turn of the twentieth century, it was the main cause of premature death in the United States and was still a problem in the post-war United States.

Mama took me to a sanatorium in Bad Wörishofen, a small town renowned for the healing properties of its waters. I went there to breathe the pure mountain air. Today, TB can be cured by a sustained course of antibiotics. In Central Europe in the late 1940s, however, treatment followed the methodology advocated by Hermann Brehmer, a nineteenth-century German physician. Brehmer theorized that the cardiovascular capacity of tuberculosis sufferers could be improved by breathing air at high altitude where there was less oxygen. The lungs could be repaired by a combination of cleaner, thinner air and the extra effort required to breathe. Bad Wörishofen lay 2,000 feet above sea level. At that altitude, there is 10 per cent less oxygen in the air. The oxygen depletion wasn't so extreme that I felt woozy, but it was sufficient to get my heart pumping.

My treatment is brilliantly described in the novel *Magic Mountain* by the German Nobel laureate, Thomas Mann. Vigorous hikes were prescribed, complemented by extended periods lying down in the fresh air while swaddled, like a newborn, in blankets. The Dominican nuns who ran the sanatorium bound our blankets so tightly that it was virtually impossible to move, and we had to lie on beds outside for three or four hours at a time, no matter the weather. If the temperature dipped, more blankets were applied. Lying there in my cocoon, I pictured the other places where I'd had to lie still and was unable to communicate with anyone.

Once again, I was separated from my parents. I tried to push the thoughts away, but I desperately wanted my mother. However, the trip from Landsberg was quite expensive and I was only able to see her twice in my nine months of treatment.

After being released from bed rest one day, I took a walk that led to my second flirtation with Christianity. I have always loved to wander and explore. Birkenau taught me self-reliance, and consequently, I felt comfortable investigating on my own. As I strolled through the narrow streets of Bad Wörishofen, I was captivated by a Catholic church attached to the nuns' monastery. The sisters were charming. They served me breakfast and afterwards, one of them fashioned my hair into braids, like Mama used to do. When the nun left me, saying she had to go to chapel, I was intrigued. Although Poland was, and still is, a very Catholic country, I had never entered a church before.

I followed the nun and was enchanted by the interior. Beautiful frescos decorated the ceiling. The story of the Nativity was conveyed by a display of mechanical dolls, and at the push of a button, along came Jesus, Mary, Joseph and the Three Wise Men. I didn't know who any of these people were, but the nun who wove my braids promised to teach me the story.

She spoke to me in German and taught me the catechism, which is a summary of Christianity in the form of questions and answers. The nun practised with me every day, until my responses were perfect. She also started to teach me the Latin alphabet. Until then, I had only learned the Hebrew alphabet. I found the High German script hard to grasp, not least because the Gothic handwriting was so flowery and complicated.

I was in the sanatorium for so long that the Jewish education from Landsberg started to wane in my mind. I missed my classmate Clara and I made no friends at the sanatorium. I was also very lonely without my parents, so it wasn't surprising that I gravitated towards the nun because of her warmth and kindness.

One day Mama paid a visit. She brought a large bottle of carrot juice, which she was told would help to cure my TB. We sat down together, and as I was drinking the carrot juice, I regaled Mama with what was happening in my life.

'The food is delicious,' I said. 'And I go to this place where they've got somebody called Jesus, and someone called Joseph.'

'What place is this?' Mama asked.

'I don't know what it's called, but I'll take you there, and it's beautiful.'

We walked to the church and went inside. We came out almost straight away and Mama confronted me.

'What on earth do you think you are doing?' she demanded.

I didn't understand what I'd done wrong. I had forgotten the conversation we'd had in Tomaszów Mazowiecki after I bought the crucifix to try to blend in with my Christian classmates.

Mama complained to the sanatorium administration about the apparent attempt to convert me to Christianity. It transpired that I hadn't been correctly registered as a Jewish child, but from that moment on, I was schooled in Judaism by a rabbi.

Rabbi Asher, who was also a Holocaust survivor, somehow instinctively knew how to reach me. And I was drawn to him. He introduced me to our Torah, the Old Testament and laid the groundwork for my love of Judaism. I enjoyed listening to the classic tales of biblical heroes Abraham and Sarah, and stories like Noah and the Flood. I especially loved the tale of baby Moses who grew up to deliver the Jews from slavery. Although I never mentioned it, I always wondered where was our Moses when we needed him? I went to the synagogue and did everything the rabbi told me to reinforce my Jewish identity. I felt guilty about having upset Mama. And the more I learned about Judaism, the more I loved it.

After about nine months in Bad Wörishofen, the doctors determined that I was no longer contagious. I returned to Landsberg where my parents were finalizing the paperwork that would enable us to join my aunt Elka who had emigrated to the United States just a few months after arriving at the DP camp in Leipzig.

My best friend, Clara, and her father didn't have a relative like my Aunt Elka to sponsor them for emigration to America, but were instead heading to Israel.

Clara hugged and kissed me on the day we left for Bremerhaven in Northern Germany for the voyage to New York. As a farewell gift, she gave me a box of matzah.

'Don't forget,' she said. 'You will be celebrating Passover on the ship.'

We hugged once more and never saw each other again.

CHAPTER EIGHTEEN

NEW YORK, NEW YORK

USA, 1950

Age eleven

Lashed by thick hawsers to the moorings in Bremerhaven, the ship towered above me. I felt a flutter of excitement in my stomach at the dockside. What an adventure, I thought. We were leaving everything behind to start afresh. A new school, new language and new friends all awaited. This boat was the beginning of the next chapter of my life. I was eleven and a half years old.

The vessel was called the *General R.M. Blatchford*, but to us and everyone else mounting the steep covered gangplank on 26 March 1950, it was the Ship to Freedom. I was number 263 on the passenger manifest. Mama and Papa were assigned the two numbers before me. There must have been about a thousand exhausted and emotionally drained refugees on board, each with their own dream and plan for life in America.

Although the *General Blatchford* was only five years old, she had clearly seen better days. This was no luxury transatlantic cruise liner. Rust patches scarred her paintwork. The interior was austere, commensurate with a vessel designed to carry 3,500 American troops across the ocean to the front lines of Europe. The soldiers who sailed before us must have been hellishly cramped, because even though the ship was only a third full, the cabins were overcrowded. The conditions evoked memories of confinement in the ghetto, but I quickly banished those thoughts because I recognized the difference in the two situations.

At first, we made good progress and the sea was relatively calm. After a day or so, we entered the English Channel and were able to see the White Cliffs of Dover off to starboard. But as we left England behind and entered Atlantic waters, the voyage took a turn for the worse. Buffeted by strong winds and tall waves, the *General Blatchford* lurched unpredictably, pitching up and down and from side to side. An epidemic of seasickness engulfed the vessel. Even veteran crew members were throwing up. It was impossible to keep your footing on the floors of cabins, corridors and restrooms that had been transformed into foul-smelling skid pans. Motion sickness was contagious. The sight or sound of someone hurling triggered a similar reaction from those near by.

Mama was violently ill as the ship was tossed around like a toy. Her head hurt. The claustrophobia of the cabin and stench of vomit were unbearable. We moved our mattresses top side onto the deck where small groups of passengers huddled together, trying to keep upright. When the wind subsided and balance was easier, animated Yiddish reverberated around the deck as people shared stories from the war. Everyone had been touched by tragedy. Muffled sobs were lost in the wind as Holocaust survivors found themselves overcome by memories. Although we were dampened by the spume and lacerated by the wind, the air was fresh and so much better than inside the cabin. Mama didn't seem to notice the difference, though. She gripped her mattress beneath the blankets. Her headaches intensified and she barely ate. I was convinced she would die if I left her. Throughout the entire crossing, I remained by her side.

'You take such good care of your mother,' observed a woman sitting nearby on a mattress with her husband and their beautiful young daughter.

'She saved my life,' I replied, rather defensively.

'I couldn't save my two boys or their father,' she replied. 'But I met my husband in a DP camp, and as we both lost our families, we are determined to start again,' she said, pointing to the girl, who must have been born after the war and about three years old.

Will it never end? I wondered. This constant reminder of the past.

I was still tending to Mama as we approached New York.

'We're almost there,' said Papa. 'Go to the bow and take a look at the Statue of Liberty. It's a sight you'll never forget. I'll look after Mama.'

I was stunned by the size of the monument and how Lady Liberty's eyes seemed to follow us as we steamed slowly by. Our teachers in Landsberg had prepared us all with photos, but I was completely enchanted by her sheer magnitude and the serenity of her face. Years later, when I read her inscription, I appreciated our welcome even more.

> Give me your tired, your poor,
> Your huddled masses yearning to breathe free,
> The wretched refuse of your teeming shore.

There and then, I resolved to do good on this earth. I had no idea how, but I promised to leave the world better than I found it. The pledge I made when I was eleven years old has influenced my relationships, my profession and my entire life.

After the turbulence of the Atlantic, the flat calm of New York Bay came as a relief to Mama, and she had rallied a little by the time we disembarked. We were greeted at the pier by a representative of the Hebrew Immigrant Aid Society, proffering coffee and doughnuts.

The woman from Immigrant Aid was under the impression we were heading to Massachusetts.

'More travel?' Mama exclaimed. 'Never again, and I don't care about Boston, wherever that is.'

The woman checked her clipboard and vanished. She returned with an official-looking man who spoke Yiddish, telling us we had to leave New York. Rain began falling but Mama refused to budge from her perch on her suitcase. Her determination paid off. Along with other refugees, we were taken to temporary accommodation in a hotel in Manhattan.

It was 4 April 1950, the fourth day of Passover. I was still clutching Clara's unopened box of matzah and found myself thinking back to that Passover in Starachowice when freedom was nothing but a fantasy. Here and now, though, the promise of freedom was real and at the hotel we joined several other families to celebrate Passover and liberty.

The next morning, and every following day, we stepped out of the hotel on the Upper East Side and explored Manhattan. We were overawed by the scale of New York and its vitality. The skyscrapers made me feel physically small, but I was infected by the energy of the people. After so many years of being constrained by barbed wire, watchtowers, gun muzzles and German Shepherds, it was unbelievably liberating to be able to walk down any main avenue or side street of our choosing. I remember us suddenly finding ourselves in front of the Empire State Building, then the tallest structure in the world, and being completely mesmerized. It seemed to touch the clouds.

Papa relished playing the tour guide, pointing out parks, cinemas, restaurants and other landmarks. He couldn't pass a street musician without stopping to enjoy the performance. It was as if he was rediscovering the joy of live music. The excitement of finding something new around every corner distracted me from tired legs and aching feet. Sometimes we visited Aunt Elka and Uncle Monyak who were living in Upper Manhattan.

More often than not, Mama felt unwell and stayed behind in the hotel. But the walks I took with Papa weren't just sight-seeing excursions. Wherever we went, Papa was always seeking job opportunities.

'I know I'll find a job here,' he said. 'It may take some time, but in this country there is plenty of work for everyone.'

Despite Papa's efforts, Manhattan failed to yield employment, so he extended his search to the outer boroughs, and after three weeks he was successful.

'We won't be living on charity any longer,' he announced with a smile. 'I've found a job and a small apartment in Astoria, Queens.'

My first apartment. I bounded up the three flights of stairs to our new rooms in Astoria, across the East River from Manhattan. I loved the place. Even if I had to sleep on the couch. What luxury – our own kitchen, bathroom, radio and even curtains!

At last, my formal education could begin. The first days in school were upsetting because I only spoke a few words of English. The principal and Mama decided that I should start in the fourth grade, and I was placed in a class with children two years younger than me. I felt humiliated, but I was determined to progress through the grades as quickly as possible to catch up with my English-speaking peers.

At the same time, although I only spoke Yiddish, Mama

insisted that I begin my Jewish education, too. She handed me a slip of paper and told me that I was expected at a Sunday school in Manhattan. She wasn't going to take me. I had to make my own way there. Initially, I was daunted, but then my old independent spirit kicked in and I told myself that if Mama had enough faith in me, I could do it. So I took the piece of paper and entered the New York subway system alone for the first time.

I showed the address to women I encountered along the way and they all pointed me in the right direction, helping me to navigate the various lines and the complicated subway map. I switched trains several times but arrived safely.

Mr Gupkin, the Yiddish-speaking principal, welcomed me warmly and introduced me to seven or eight classmates. The class was learning Yiddish, but the instructions were in English. After a while, the bell rang. Everybody disappeared and I was left alone in class, bewildered. Then one of the boys returned. He had very dark eyes and a full head of black hair.

'They all went to lunch. Did you bring any?' he asked, in perfect Yiddish.

I didn't understand the question, even though it was in Yiddish, because I didn't know what the word lunch meant. The boy took me by the hand and led me to the nearest drugstore with a food counter. I didn't say a word and nor did he. He ordered a cheese and lettuce sandwich and gave it to me. I was touched by his warmth and kindness. His Yiddish was immaculate as he talked to his grandparents every day. At the age of eleven, I made my first friend in America. Maier Friedman, the man I would marry.

That summer, while my parents worked long hours on a factory production line, I never left the apartment in Astoria, so that I could memorize the picture dictionary from A to Z, although I still couldn't properly string together sentences in English.

At the beginning of the new school year, the teacher made me feel like an outsider. She told me to never discuss the war as it upset people. Once, when I showed my tattoo to a curious classmate, she called me into her office and admonished me.

'Tola, you will never fit in unless you forget all that. It makes people uncomfortable, and we really don't want to hear it. The best thing would be to cut your braids, wear long sleeves and change your name to Susan.'

So, I did all three. I cut my hair short to look and feel less European and more American, as the teacher suggested. But I only remained Susan for a few weeks because remembering my new name was a challenge. People addressed this person called Susan and I didn't realize they were talking to me. And then I thought more deeply about what the teacher was trying to make me do. Asking me to be Susan meant forgetting my past and my identity. I thought about the young tattooist from Auschwitz who gave me small numbers and had also told me to cover my arm to spare myself any embarrassment.

Why should I feel shame? I wondered.

I came to the conclusion that only an unkind world would pressure me to cover up the war crime against me. My number was now inextricably part of me; it showed what had been done to me, and that I was lucky to be alive. I compromised by giving up Susan, going back to my real name, but never talking to my classmates about the war again. That did not stop the other children from shunning me, however.

And it wasn't just at school that people were unfriendly. In our neighbourhood, our predominantly Italian neighbours were standoffish to the point of hostility, which puzzled me, as they seemed so kind and loving towards their own children.

I was envious of the Italians' large families. I wished I had a little brother or sister to make me feel less lonely, but Mama felt that this world wasn't meant for children. For her, it was too cruel and destructive for small, innocent beings. Papa and I were the centre of her life, but beyond us, Mama rarely experienced joy. Society had failed her and stolen 150 members of her family.

Mama struggled with her faith, and although she never rejected God entirely, she questioned a deity that would tolerate its most faithful being cut down. She found it impossible to look forwards with any optimism and mainly dwelled in the past.

I acknowledged that I was destined to be an only child and made my peace with that reality. Education was my refuge. Constant study offered an escape and a way of coping with loneliness. Lively voices on American radio kept me company while I buried my head in books. Gradually, my English improved and I caught up with my class. To my parents' surprise and delight, I graduated the eighth grade with honours.

After a year in Astoria, Mama and Papa could no longer bear the district's latent anti-Semitism. Very soon we were on the move again.

CHAPTER NINETEEN

TRANSITION

Brooklyn, USA, 1951

Age thirteen

Brooklyn was a significant upgrade on Astoria. The borough had a substantial Jewish population as well as over 1.5 million people from other immigrant backgrounds. To me, as a teenager, impatient to formulate a new, meaningful life, 1950s' cosmopolitan Brooklyn was hugely exciting, vibrating with the energy of 2 million strangers committed to achieving their version of the American Dream. It was impossible not to be infected by their enthusiasm. New York's most populous borough was, for me, a potential springboard to create a new existence and leave the traumas of war behind.

Our new apartment in east New York was basic, but for the first time in my life, I had my own room, and it became my sanctuary. I could close the door behind me whenever I got tired, shut out the city, lie on my narrow bed and, without interruption, read to my heart's content. My small window opened onto a dark alley populated by battalions of feral cats. During steamy, airless New York summers, my consumption of literature and poetry was accompanied by a soundtrack of feline fighting and flirting and tomcats doing what tomcats like to do.

After years of deprivation, books provided me with a passport to explore the world in my imagination. I was especially grateful to the English teachers who instilled in me a love of poetry and drama. I gravitated towards poets whose wordscapes painted images of journeys full of discovery and adventure. Walt Whitman, America's great writer, was my favourite.

In *Leaves of Grass*, Whitman offered an escape from my urban existence with his reflections on the vastness of my new homeland's landscape.

> See, pastures and forests in my poems – see, animals wild
> and tame – see, beyond the Kaw, countless herds of
> buffalo, feeding on short curly grass,
> See, in my poems, cities, solid, vast, inland, with paved
> streets, with iron and stone edifices, ceaseless vehicles,
> and commerce

I embraced English poets as well, visualizing William Wordsworth gazing at a field of daffodils. In my mind, I sailed with Samuel Taylor Coleridge in his *Rime of the Ancient Mariner.*

I was a pupil at Brooklyn's Thomas Jefferson High, which had a reputation as one of the most illustrious in the New York schools' system, producing a string of distinguished alumni, especially in the arts. Imparting knowledge was just one of the goals of Jefferson's teachers. Collectively, they were committed to turning their multiracial immigrant pupils into high-achieving American citizens. I joined the Justice Club, which provided my first experience of democratic process. Guilt was determined by proof, not prejudice.

Despite its credentials for educational excellence, Jefferson had a dark side, in that many students were intimidated by gangs roaming its corridors. Brooklyn was a melting pot and each gang was made up of clusters of boys from the same ethnic group. Once in a while, the police were called in to confiscate a weapon.

I, however, was impervious to the undercurrent of violence. Is this what they call dangerous? I wondered. They have no idea what real danger is.

Once, on the way to school, a tough kid blocked my way just outside the gates. I stood rock steady, staring him down. The bell rang with its injunction to head to class. Glaring intensely into each other's eyes, we both held our ground, each challenging the other to flinch first. Summoning all the menace in his possession, the bully inched ever closer. When he realized I would not be intimidated, he turned away and never bothered me again.

During those school years, I made some lifelong friendships, but mainly outside of Jefferson High. Most of my new friends were European Holocaust survivors. To our American peers, we were all greenhorns, but our diverse experiences during the war bound us together and more than compensated for us being outsiders. We were mature and responsible beyond our years. Our survival instincts were finely honed, as was our commitment to protecting our traumatized parents.

Among our number were those who had hidden from the Nazis in the forests of Central Europe, foraging in the wild and supplementing nature's bounty by 'liberating' foodstuffs from local farmers. Others had been concealed by their Gentile neighbours after shelling out small fortunes for the privilege and then worrying about their fates when the money ran out. Not everyone had been pushed to the limits of endurance by the Germans, however. Some had suffered at Russian hands, spending most of the war years as forced labourers in Siberia's frozen tundras.

Our personal histories were recounted casually, as if hardship was routine. Occasionally, stories were punctuated by heroic vignettes of stealing food, evading the enemy and helping the partisans. We were united by a sense of pride in overcoming adversity and shared a determination to integrate into a wonderful society that opened its arms to us when so many nations had pulled up the drawbridge. We also felt as though we had to protect each other from America's dominant culture until we were each ready to enter. The American kids didn't accept us. We spoke with accents, our clothes weren't stylish, and few of us participated in school sports because many had to work to help their parents financially.

Nevertheless, we also had a lot of fun. For many of us, this was the first time in our lives we could actually exhibit our youthful exuberance freely. We spent some afternoons on the beaches of Coney Island and Rye, a coastal town in upstate New York, and evenings at gatherings. In spite of our emotional baggage, many romances and marriages resulted.

But acceptance into the greater American culture took time. To that end, I began calling myself Toby. It was American, short, unassuming and easy to remember. I shed my name Tola with pleasure this time, and with it, I hoped, my painful wartime memories.

We spoke what the dictionary defines as Yinglish – English with Yiddish phrases intertwined. Most of us didn't expect to go to college because we needed to support our parents. I was an exception, as Papa managed to scrape together a living. I hoped I could advance to higher education because Brooklyn College was free. I just had to find a way to pay for course books. Money at home was so tight; we never ate out in even the cheapest restaurants and buying snacks from street vendors was the height of luxury.

But almost everything in my life paled in significance compared to Maier Friedman, the first boy I met in Hebrew school. He lived about twenty blocks away from us and I frequently dragged one of my best friends there, just so I could look at the light in his closed window.

'But you see him every Sunday,' she protested.

'That's nothing,' I told her. 'I need to see him every day.'

'But you don't,' she countered. 'His window isn't open.'

'Yes,' I replied. 'But I can imagine him behind it.'

Maier constantly occupied my thoughts. Family history repeated itself: I joined a Zionist group just to be close to him, twenty years after my mother had done the same thing, so she could get to know my father.

The group was called Habonim, a cultural youth movement committed to social justice and Zionism, the creation and protection of an Israeli state. Its meetings were platforms for powerful debates about egalitarianism, politics and human rights. Whenever he spoke, Maier was mesmerizing and charismatic – a brilliant analyst of core issues. His self-assurance and knowledge were magnetic and attracted me to him on all levels – physically, emotionally and intellectually.

While I was still a sophomore, Maier graduated from Stuyvesant High School, one of the top-ranking institutions in the country with its emphasis on maths and science. From there, it was a natural progression for Maier to enrol at the Cooper Union for the Advancement of Arts and Science – a free private university that attracted the best candidates in the country. At the same time, he was accepted to MENSA, the high IQ society. Our feelings for each other deepened, yet somehow neither of us expressed them. I hoped to marry him and live on a kibbutz in Israel, although I kept my dreams to myself.

My optimism was not reflected at home, where life was a constant financial struggle. Papa had started a small tailoring workshop. Sewing bespoke garments for both men and women was far from lucrative, and he worked very long hours. Papa's absence and my outside interests exacerbated Mama's loneliness and depression. She was no longer able to work because of her deteriorating health. Her continuing debilitating headaches, caused by the beating in Auschwitz, confined her to home. She no longer immersed herself in the English-speaking world in which she was living, and her language skills faltered.

Occasionally, glimpses of Mama's former self flickered to life. On a rare trip to the cinema, she mentioned to Papa how much she admired a coat worn by one of the actresses. Papa recreated it entirely from memory and presented it to her a few weeks later. She loved the coat and reserved it for special occasions. However, the vitality of Brooklyn failed to penetrate Mama's consciousness. Four thousand miles from Birkenau, the Holocaust remained omnipresent. It hadn't retreated with liberation.

Little by little, my intelligent, courageous, beautiful Mama deteriorated before my eyes. My love for her was boundless, but my need to belong to my new world was equally strong. I was constantly conflicted. When I was home, I wanted to be out and when I was with my friends, I knew I was needed at home.

Ultimately, my adoration and concern for Mama triumphed over my own needs. I stopped going out after school and came home directly. Mama was always waiting with a glass of milk and a jam doughnut. We would sit at the table in our small, windowless kitchen, and Mama would hum the Sabbath songs that she used to sing with her family. She wanted me to commit them to memory. Mama talked in great detail about members of the Pinkusewicz family who were no longer with us. Stories that began as happy reminiscences always ended with the horrific conclusion that her family had been massacred and that she was the sole survivor.

Being subjected to a constant barrage of gloom was unbearable. I zoned out, put up a defensive screen and nodded in the right places. I heard her, but I didn't listen. Some of the stories struck a chord and remain with me. But the names didn't stick. Memories of a whole generation were lost because of my insensitivity. Back then, I had no idea just how precious that time was. I would give anything now to turn back the clock, to hear the stories and names again, so I could at least light a memorial candle for them and keep their memory alive.

Similarly, the festive spirit of most Jewish holidays always disintegrated into painful memories. Before the war, these feasts were large family gatherings; now there were only three of us at the table. While Mama appreciated our survival, her belief in God was shaken to the core. She constantly questioned why her entire family of observant Jews had been slaughtered. Her guilt was overwhelming.

'If there is a God,' she would say, 'He is utterly unjust and doesn't deserve to be worshipped.'

Nevertheless, she maintained Jewish traditions, keeping kosher and lighting candles on the Sabbath. Doing so kept her close to her family, if not to her religion. In preparation for holidays and Fridays, I would accompany Mama to an open market. We would come home with a freshly butchered chicken or a live carp that Mama then hit over the head before making gefilte fish, a traditional Sabbath delicacy. But I could see that the light in her eyes had dimmed.

At the age of forty, Mama was diagnosed with breast cancer. The doctors caught it early, and her spirits rose after she apparently recovered and entered remission. She began to read in Polish again, and found the energy to socialize once more, spending time with my Papa's sisters. Aunt Ita and Uncle Adam had moved from Israel to Brooklyn with their two children, Pearl and Ben, and we were frequent visitors to Aunt Elka and Uncle Monyak and their son Marty in Upper Manhattan.

For a time, Mama's mood improved even more, which, to my relief, allowed me to concentrate on my own activities. But after graduating from Jefferson High, my plans to get a college degree ran into opposition from both parents.

'Get married, I want to see you safe before I die,' Mama said.

Papa took her side, but I insisted. So I went ahead and registered to study psychology at Brooklyn College. There, I began by studying the individual psyche through the works of Freud, Jung and Carl Rogers, an innovative American psychologist who was a pioneer of client-centred therapy.

I was more fascinated, however, by the field of group psychology. Trigant Burrow, an influential psychoanalyst who pioneered group therapy, caught my attention. I also pored over the work of German-born Kurt Lewin, recognized today as the founder of modern social psychology. A German soldier wounded in the First World War, and later a professor at the University of Iowa, Lewin proposed that behaviour is shaped by the interaction of individual traits and the environment.

I wanted to understand how an entire nation could be brainwashed and led by an individual who was clearly deranged. The Holocaust was never far from my mind.

One psychiatrist whose work I was introduced to at that time was Viktor Frankl who, like me and my parents, survived the Shoah. Later in life, when I became a therapist, I studied his survival theories in greater depth. In his book *Man's Search for Meaning* Frankl proposes that one has the choice to behave morally even under the direst circumstances and one can find spiritual meaning by helping others:

'Every day, every hour offered the opportunity to make a decision, a decision which determined whether you would or would not submit to those powers which threatened to rob you of your very self, your inner freedom.'

Those words resonate with me whenever I think of how my parents behaved throughout the war.

CHAPTER TWENTY

POSTCARDS FROM MAMA

Brooklyn, USA, 1957

Age nineteen

After my first semester studying psychology, Brooklyn College offered an inexpensive trip to Israel in the late spring of 1957. I was desperate to visit a land that until then had only existed in discussions and dreams.

Israel was still tense after the 1956 Suez Crisis. Egypt's hawkish President Gamal Abdel Nasser had nationalized the Suez Canal, on which Europe's oil imports depended. Israeli armed forces had invaded Egyptian territory, advanced towards the waterway and were reinforced by British and French troops. The invasion was a debacle. Egypt emerged victorious. The British, French and Israeli troops had all been withdrawn by the time my trip was due, but the situation was far from ideal.

'You can't go,' Mama said. 'It isn't safe. There's a shortage of food, especially eggs.'

'Well, in that case, save some for me,' I laughed.

I was not to be dissuaded. I wanted to see if my passion for Israel would be confirmed. Another strong motivation was the prospect of seeing Maier, who had a summer job in Jerusalem.

Nevertheless, I was anxious about leaving Mama. I consulted our family doctor who assured me that she would be fine.

'Your mother is well. Go,' he said. 'It's just a two-week trip and if you don't go now, you will never be able to have your own life.'

So I left for my first visit to Israel. As soon as I arrived in Jerusalem, I was greeted by several postcards written in poor English by Mama, which made me chuckle. I assumed that the doctor's confidence had been justified and that she was healthy.

It was on that trip that I fell in love with Israel. I had heard and studied much about it, but my expectations were far exceeded. The beauty of the Judaean Desert enchanted me and Jerusalem's history fascinated me. When Maier and I met up at a kibbutz, we acknowledged that we both loved Israel and resolved to return in the future.

But throughout the trip, I could neither shake nor identify a feeling of foreboding. And it transpired that my intuition was correct. When I returned to Brooklyn, I discovered that Mama had died two days into my trip. Someone else had mailed her postcards.

Mama passed away on 29 June 1957. She was forty-five years old. My sense of guilt was overwhelming.

'She died of a broken heart,' Papa told me, accusingly. 'She went to sleep with a headache, took some aspirin and never woke up.'

We never discovered the true cause of her death, because no post-mortem was conducted. But we believe she suffered a brain aneurysm and fell into an irretrievable coma. Strong emotions, including grief, can contribute to an aneurysm, as can head trauma. Certainly, in physical terms, Mama had never been the same after the beating in Auschwitz. Although she died twelve years after the war ended, she was unquestionably another victim of the Holocaust.

But at the time, I was convinced that I was the cause of her death and that she would have lived, if only I hadn't gone to Israel. I dropped out of Brooklyn College and stopped socializing with my friends. I was overwhelmed by grief and guilt. I kept thinking about how much my smart, beautiful, sensitive mother had sacrificed for me. Her intelligence and courage were the main reasons why I was still alive. I owed everything to her.

Papa blamed me for Mama's death, which I felt was cruel and unfair. But deep inside, I convinced myself he was speaking the truth. Our individual mourning drove a wedge between us. Papa buried himself in work and I just stayed at home in our small apartment. When Papa came back from the workshop, we circled each other like strangers and barely spoke. I cried myself to sleep every night for weeks.

A few short months after Mama's death, Papa made a dramatic announcement.

'I am going to Israel,' he said.

Days later, he bade me farewell, handing me $1,000 and the keys to the apartment. My sense of abandonment was complete. I was eighteen years old. Any feeling of optimism completely evaporated.

My two aunts would have taken me in, but they had no room. In the depths of feeling not only hopeless but homeless, I remembered Mama's faith in my ability to take care of myself. Her early lessons in survival served me well. She had imbued me with inner courage. I'm in good hands, I thought to myself. My own.

I called a close friend who was studying for a Ph.D. in maths at UC Berkeley, California, and he invited me to join him on the West Coast. As soon as I arrived in Berkeley, two weeks after Papa left for Israel, I realized I'd made a mistake, although my friend went out of his way to make me feel welcome. He shared a small apartment with three adults and two children who all slept on mattresses strewn on the floor. I found the arrangement extremely uncomfortable. I enrolled in a few classes in the hope they'd distract me and make me happier. And I took a job in a bagel shop whose profits helped the Hopi tribe of Native Americans, whom we visited once a month. In solidarity with their status as a marginalized minority, I was paid with meals instead of money.

Although I was surrounded by people, I felt very much alone. The nightmares, which I thought had been banished, haunted me once again. I was homesick for a home that no longer existed, and I couldn't adjust to the California lifestyle. In desperation, I contacted the Berkeley campus rabbi who was very sympathetic.

'What's a nice Jewish girl from Brooklyn doing here?' he asked. 'Go home.'

Before I left, he gave me the telephone number of a psychiatrist in Manhattan named Lillian Kaplan. Our special relationship changed my life.

For the next four years, I had weekly therapy sessions with Dr Kaplan, who specialized in helping young trauma victims, including those from the Holocaust. In the safe atmosphere of her office, for the first time in my life, I was able to express all my pain, sorrow and fears. I wept as I unburdened myself about the guilt I harboured over Mama's death and all my painful war memories that I could never share with my mother because I wanted to spare her feelings.

Dr Kaplan secured for me a place in 'The Club' – a residence for homeless Jewish girls attending school, run by the Jewish Childcare Association. The beautiful brownstone building stood in the residential district of Park Slope near the Brooklyn Botanic Garden and the Brooklyn Museum. I lived alongside girls from wildly different backgrounds and with a wide range of traumas.

They often acted out. Some had been abandoned by their families or expelled from school. Some had spent time in psychiatric institutions. Others were fugitives from abusive homes or, like me, became homeless after one or both parents died. Besides offering shelter, the Club provided emotional support through dancing, music, art and counselling. These activities were tailored in a therapeutic way to help us overcome our individual traumas.

After almost a year away, Papa returned from Israel in the middle of 1958. He was accompanied by his new wife, Sonia – a survivor of a Soviet labour camp in Siberia. Sonia was beautiful, kind and intelligent, and although she didn't have any children of her own, she was extremely sensitive to my feelings. She was smart enough not to try to replace Mama in my affections, but her moral support and kindness mitigated my sense of loss. With Dr Kaplan's help, I accepted Sonia and the guilt over my mother's death subsided. I recognized my good fortune in having such a wonderful therapist and she inspired me to follow in her footsteps. She had planted the seed for my future vocation.

After graduating from college in 1960, I resolved to move to Israel. To my surprise, after years of not keeping in touch, Maier Friedman, who had been studying at the Massachusetts Institute of Technology in Boston, appeared one day at the Club.

'How did you find me?' I asked him.

'I never lost track of you,' he responded.

When I told him about the vaccines I had just received in preparation for my trip, he said simply:

'Let's get married first and we'll move there together.'

We had known each other since I was eleven, but we had never actually discussed marriage before. Now we both just knew we were meant to build a life together in Israel.

We were married in Brooklyn two months later, on 11 June 1960. It was a traditional Jewish wedding, and while representation on my side was small, Maier had a large, sprawling family. I considered myself fortunate to be embraced by the Friedmans. At last, I was part of a big, loving family and felt accepted, protected and no longer alone. But I missed Mama terribly. She had been gone for three years already, and it made me profoundly sad that she never lived to see me marry.

Maier and I didn't have time for a honeymoon. We drove straight to San Diego in California where Maier had a new job lined up. But West Coast living didn't agree with us. We missed our family and friends, not to mention the vibrancy of New York, and after only six months, we returned.

Maier had a brilliant mind, and he inspired me to strive harder. He began a Ph.D. in biochemical engineering at Columbia University, and I enrolled in a master's programme in English literature at the City College of New York. Both schools were located on the Upper West Side, and we decided to move to nearby Harlem. In 1961, Harlem was considered a dangerous part of Manhattan and we would definitely be a minority there. Our decision stunned our family and friends.

'How are we going to visit you?' Papa protested. 'It's so dangerous in that neighbourhood.'

'It's not too dangerous at all,' I replied. 'There are police everywhere.'

We weren't just motivated by a convenient commute. On our West Coast road trips, we had been affronted when we encountered segregated restrooms, restaurants and water fountains. Coming from the north-east, we had not come across the daily effects of segregation and our sense of indignation stayed with us when we returned to New York. Maier and I were actively trying to live by our abiding principles. Our membership of Habonim, the Zionist organization, had not just strengthened our belief in the right of Israel to exist, it had also reinforced our commitment to genuine equality across the racial divide.

By the time we were husband and wife, America's Civil Rights movement was in full swing as African–Americans demanded an end to segregation and discrimination. Jewish activists played a significant part within the movement, not least because Judaism stipulates that we have a moral obligation to uphold the fundamental rights of others. We marched alongside African–Americans in Washington as they called for integration. Talking about equality wasn't sufficient. We decided to live it.

We moved into a nice two-bedroom apartment overlooking the famous Apollo Theatre, on 125th Street. We were the only white kosher Jewish couple among nearly 800 African–American and Latino tenants in our twenty-one-storey building.

At first, our neighbours were hostile and didn't acknowledge us, even in the tiny elevator. I hoped the ice would break somehow but wasn't sure about the best way to approach even the people on our very floor. We avoided eye contact and passed each other silently in the hall. Months passed before neighbours began to even nod when they saw us.

It's a start, I thought to myself.

But Maier and I knew we were getting somewhere when we joined a tenants' meeting and a few familiar faces smiled at us. I began to attend various smaller meetings in individual apartments, where tenants discussed safety, cleanliness and sanitation. I wanted to contribute, and I saw these meetings as a bridge towards acceptance. So it proved. At first, I invited myself, but after a while I was asked to attend. The barriers had come down. Our neighbours saw that we had the same concerns as they did.

Every day, on my way to college, I passed the Apollo and heard the music pulsating through the walls, but had neither the money nor the nerve to enter. The Apollo was the beating heart of culture in Harlem. It started out as a whites-only music hall, but by the mid-1930s it had become a showcase for a broad range of African–American talent. Over time, it evolved, promoting jazz, big bands, comedy, opera, gospel and soul music. Performers who trod the Apollo's boards in the early stages of their careers became household names the world over: Ella Fitzgerald, Louis Armstrong, Duke Ellington, Richard Pryor, Aretha Franklin, the Staple Singers, Ray Charles, Otis Redding, the Jackson Five and

Stevie Wonder, to name but a few. The building, its stars and audiences, gave off such a positive vibe, that just walking past, you could tell something extraordinary was taking place inside.

My best discovery in the area was the public library at 135th and Lenox, now called Malcolm X Boulevard. On my first day there, the librarian tried to be civil, but behind her plastic smile, I sensed I wasn't welcome. To her annoyance, I began to browse. My attention was drawn to glass cases protecting original manuscripts of African–American writers. Through gritted teeth, she explained they were part of the Schomburg Collection, an archive of material focused on black culture.

I spotted an article lying on the desk about an African–American called Richard Wright who had died in Paris from a heart attack a year earlier at the age of fifty-two. The article stated that although Wright had written a number of works, very few people had heard of him. I was intrigued and borrowed *Black Boy*, a non-fiction work published in 1945 – the same year I was liberated from Auschwitz.

Black Boy chronicles Wright's experiences in America's deep south, as he endured poverty, illness and racism. I was shocked that an American child could be subjected to such terrible abuse and violence, not only at the hands of society, but his family as well. Soon after, I announced to my professor that I would write my MA thesis on Richard Wright. But I needed his approval first.

'I am not sure that a white woman not born in America will understand the Afro–American experience,' he said. Nevertheless,

I wouldn't take no for an answer, and I ultimately obtained permission after pressing my professor to consult with other committee members at the college.

While Wright's sexual and violent imagery led to widespread bans on his books, I appreciated his honesty and empathized with his pain. He blamed institutionalized racism in America for the degeneration of his characters. They were intelligent, tortured and violent, which often led to murder. Searching for social justice, Wright joined the Communist Party for a decade, but eventually quit, disillusioned by the lack of justice and its sheer hypocrisy. A party that supposedly stood for total equality among the working classes also espoused segregationism, which meant more racism. In an article called 'The God That Failed', Wright expressed his disappointment and disgust with communism. He died in self-imposed exile in 1960, disenchanted and unaware of his influence on other writers.

I felt a certain kinship with Richard Wright. Even though we had very different backgrounds with different religions and skin colours, we both had endured abusive childhoods and had struggled to find meaning as wounded children in a harsh, racist society. His torment resonated with me.

I became pregnant with my daughter Risa while studying for my master's. We named her after my mother. I was determined that any child of mine would have an upbringing free of hatred, unlike Wright's and my own. Some of our neighbours had now become friends, and although money was tight, they gave what they could. Gifts of baby clothes, sheets and diapers made us feel as though we belonged to a community. Risa's brother Gadi was born thirteen months later. During that Christmas, more gifts piled up outside our door and although everyone knew we did not celebrate the holiday, they always argued, 'Why should the children suffer?'

With two babies, life was hectic and there was little time for schoolwork. So we posted a flyer in the elevator offering free English and maths tutoring in exchange for babysitting. After a slow initial response, we gathered a few teenage girls requiring help with short composition essays who we could trust with our babies. A twelve-year-old boy who was struggling with maths also appealed for help. He couldn't babysit because he was already taking care of his two young brothers, but Maier sat with him for hours going through numerical puzzles that became increasingly complex and challenging. The mysteries of maths were unlocked and the boy made great progress. It still warms my heart that our tutoring deepened our relationship with our neighbours. Economic, educational and social differences melted away once we connected on an emotional level.

By early 1967, both Maier and I had finished our degrees and were ready to move on. Our neighbours threw a fantastic farewell party and we were very sad to leave. Little did we know that we were heading straight into another war.

CHAPTER TWENTY-ONE

ISRAEL

Netanya, Israel, 1967
Age twenty-nine

Warm, dry air enveloped me in a welcoming embrace the moment I stepped through the door of the El Al airliner and down the steps onto Israeli soil. It felt good to be back – this time with my husband, Maier, and two young children. I'll always remember the date – 3 May 1967.

All the windows in the car were wound down as we headed northwards along the coast on a thirty-minute drive from Ben Gurion airport to Netanya. Squeezed together, our children, Risa and Gadi, leaned out of the windows as far as they could, like flowers, turning their faces towards the sun. The heat was a balm, easing away the aches of a long flight and residual tensions of New York life. Already, the sensory contrasts between the Big Apple and Tel Aviv were impossible to ignore. We were blinded by the glare of the sun bouncing off white stone houses. The breeze carried the perfume of blossoms and the salty tang of the Eastern Mediterranean.

I could get used to this, I told myself.

Netanya was much smaller than Tel Aviv, but just as inviting. As part of our introduction to this young, developing country, we stayed in a uniquely Israeli educational institution called an *ulpan*, which immersed immigrants in the Hebrew language, along with the culture and customs of their new homeland. We registered for six months, which we thought would be sufficient to acclimatize and establish a solid grasp of the language.

Our *ulpan*'s compound was geared towards young families, and I was touched that a doll and a ball were waiting on the children's beds. The gesture made us feel very much at home. Mealtimes were communal affairs, and the dining hall was filled with a competing chorus of different languages, including Russian, Polish, Spanish, French and English. Our instructor constantly tried to inject Hebrew into our conversations. I decided to change my name to Tova to sound more Israeli. I also chose it because it was close to Tema, the name of my maternal grandmother.

Initially, life was predictably routine and comfortable. Every morning, we'd take the children to nursery, and then head to class for Hebrew lessons. We settled into the sub-tropical rhythm of resting in the afternoon while the sun was at its hottest, and we'd socialize and do homework in the cool of the evening. We loved

Israel's outdoor lifestyle and spent endless hours on Netanya's pristine sandy beach.

Our soft landing in the Middle East didn't last long, however. In the middle of May 1967, we were visited by an Israeli army officer from a nearby base, who announced that war was imminent and that in all probability, we would find ourselves on the front line. This shouldn't have come as a major surprise, but somehow it caught both Maier and I off guard.

We were conscious of sporadic cross-border Palestinian guerrilla raids and the war-mongering rhetoric of Egypt's President Gamal Abdel Nasser. But despite a mutual defence accord signed by Egypt and Syria in late 1966, the perceived threat seemed rather distant. If anything, Israeli towns near the borders of Egypt and Syria appeared most at risk. However, the army officer's visit forced us to focus on potential conflict in our neighbourhood. We lived in one of the narrowest slivers of Israeli territory. Our compound was just 8 miles from the Jordanian border. The Israeli army was afraid that when war came, Tulkarm, a predominantly Palestinian town just across the frontier on the West Bank of the River Jordan, would be used as a fire base.

The officer gave the *ulpan*'s director specific instructions on how to construct rudimentary defences. There was no time to lose. We had to start digging foxholes and trenches immediately. It wasn't a request; it was an order.

'I'm sorry, I can't spare any soldiers to help you,' he said, before returning to his base.

Most of our motley group were originally city dwellers who had never handled a shovel. Not only that, without a common language, we had trouble communicating. It was a daunting time, but Maier rose to the challenge. He had never experienced war but faced the looming conflict fearlessly.

Big or small, Maier dived into every project as though it was his puzzle to solve alone. With his engineering mind, he supervised the digging, organized a rota, taught safety measures and made sure the bomb shelters were reinforced and fully stocked with supplies, in case we were forced to take cover for an extended period.

Maier's upbeat determination was in stark contrast to my mood. For the first time in over twenty years, since the Nazis' liquidation of Birkenau, I was truly petrified. My nightmares had receded again because life kept me engaged. But now they haunted me once more. I was tormented by visions of naked bodies, homeless children, starvation and torture that robbed me of my sleep. I refused to get undressed at bedtime. I was afraid we'd be invaded during the night, and I'd be caught naked by Arab soldiers.

Back in America, my father's wartime nightmares were also resurfacing. He called daily, begging us to fly the children home to him while the borders were still open. When we refused, he bombarded the US Embassy in Tel Aviv with pleas to convince us to send the children to nearby Cyprus for safety, as so many were doing. Papa's entreaties worked. A consular official came to see us.

'Your father has been calling us several times a day,' said the diplomat. 'He made me promise to try to persuade you to evacuate the children.'

We politely declined his offer.

'What will happen to other Jewish children will happen to ours,' Maier said. Principled to the core, he was always an idealist and an unwavering Zionist.

Peace ebbed further away with every passing day. In the middle of May, President Nasser demanded the United Nations remove peacekeeping troops from the Sinai Peninsula where, for more than a decade, they had been a buffer between Israel and Egypt. The 1,400-strong UN force was only there by invitation, so it was obliged to withdraw as 1,000 Egyptian tanks, and 100,000 soldiers – a third of the entire Egyptian army – advanced through the Sinai Desert towards the Israeli frontier, just 30 miles from Tel Aviv.

Tightening the noose still further, Nasser ordered a blockade of the Straits of Tiran, where the Gulf of Aqaba meets the Red Sea. The blockade severed Israel's access to the sea from the port of Eilat, imperilling the nation's oil supply and other key imports from the south. Of all the provocations, the blockade was the most potent. The Israeli government interpreted Nasser's decree as an act of war and announced a full mobilization, which was a highly efficient process. Most civilians of fighting age were reservists and well drilled. Once the call was made, people immediately stopped what they were doing and reported to their military units.

Meanwhile, to the north-east, Syria deployed troops to the Golan Heights, overlooking the upper River Jordan valley. A week later, Nasser signed a defence pact with Jordan's King Hussein. The Israeli army officer had been spot on. The war was going to take place in our backyard.

Risa and Gadi were oblivious to the coming storm. We made up a game that delighted them. We would scan the sky for aircraft, and when one of us spotted a plane, I'd bang a toy drum and they'd dive beneath the bed, which I had turned into a den, full of other toys and snacks. We practised the drill for days, until it was no longer a game.

Air-raid sirens wailed early in the morning of 5 June 1967. This was no false alarm. It was the real thing. I grabbed the children's hands and we sprinted to our foxhole. I held them as tightly as I could and, like my mother before me, tried to shield them with my body. I couldn't see what was happening. But the sounds of rockets and shells were terrifying. The percussive effect of the explosions seemed incredibly powerful and destructive. The children were crying with fear, and although I was terrified, I tried to soothe them. Maier was nowhere to be seen as salvoes whooshed through the sky. He was leading other families to their foxholes and once they were safe, he jumped in with us.

'It's the ones you don't hear you should worry about,' he said. 'The ones you hear have already passed you by.'

His remark meant I was now frightened for my children by the silence in between the shell bursts.

Ranged against Israel, the Arab coalition had a combined force of 900 aircraft, 5,000 tanks and 500,000 soldiers. We, in comparison, had only 175 aircraft, 1,000 tanks and a standing army of 75,000 soldiers, which could be boosted by reservists. The sheer weight of numbers generated a state of high anxiety among the civilian population. It felt like a war between David and Goliath. We had no inkling that our generals were so confident.

In the opening hours of the conflict, I assumed that Israel had been attacked first and that Jordan, just 8 miles away, had started the aggression. In such circumstances, amid the confusion and fear of an artillery barrage, it's hard not to think you are at the epicentre of the action. It was several hours before news reports on Israeli radio filtered back to us and put our plight in perspective.

What had happened was a classic move out of *The Art of War*, the military playbook written thousands of years ago by Sun Tzu, an ancient Chinese general and philosopher. One of Sun Tzu's principal exhortations is: 'Attack the enemy where he is unprepared, appear where you are not expected'.

That is precisely what the Israelis did. Early on the morning of 5 June 1967, the Defense Forces launched a series of pre-emptive strikes to blunt the Arab coalition's military threat. Israeli aircraft destroyed 90 per cent of the Egyptian Air Force's planes while they sat helpless on the ground. Israeli pilots then crippled the air capacity of the other Arab nations in the alliance.

Control of the skies enabled ground forces to confidently advance on their objectives.

Despite the rapid successes of the Israel Defense Forces, we stayed in our shelters. As I clutched my children, I wrestled with guilt. After all my experiences in Poland, how could I put their lives in danger? Was I being irresponsible? Should our desire to live in Israel take priority over their physical wellbeing? After all, this conflict was only the beginning. They would be living in a country surrounded by enemies, facing a perpetual existential threat and struggling for survival. These doubts were in the forefront of my mind while the artillery exchanges continued. We surfaced from the shelter when the guns ceased firing. In the darkness, we could see flames rising from Arab villages across the border.

As the war quickly progressed, and victory was within grasp, my perspective changed. I became calmer. I realized I was providing Risa and Gadi with a gift. Being citizens of a Jewish nation meant they would never experience anti-Semitism, discrimination or shame. They would not have to endure the agonies that my family suffered. The physical danger they faced was transient, but their spiritual enrichment would be permanent. I convinced myself I had done the right thing by not sending them away. They belonged in Israel. Compared to everything I had been through, the risks were within acceptable limits. We had a country with an outstanding army and air force. We were far from helpless. We were strong and effective.

The war only lasted six days before Israel prevailed. The day after victory was declared, Maier and I celebrated our seventh wedding anniversary with some of the other students from the *ulpan*. It was a bittersweet affair. I regarded our triumph as a miracle, and Israeli casualty figures were relatively light. Nevertheless, our happiness was tempered by the wave of funerals taking place across the country. Seven hundred and seventy-six young soldiers sacrificed their lives to make Israel a much more secure country for the rest of us.

As soon as we could, we headed towards the Kotel (or Western Wall), in Jerusalem's Old City which, for so long, had been inaccessible for Israeli Jews. We had waited a lifetime to make this pilgrimage. The Kotel is the only surviving section of the retaining wall that had supported the First and Second Temples built thousands of years ago. It is the most sacred place of worship for Jews,

Before the war, Jerusalem had been split in two. The Israelis administered the western half, while the Jordanians controlled the eastern section, including the Old City, with its crenelated limestone ramparts and diverse holy sites, sacred to the world's three major monotheistic religions: Judaism, Islam and Christianity. After driving back Jordanian forces in house-to-house fighting in East Jerusalem, the Israelis seized control of the Old City on day three of the war.

We could feel the tension when we entered the Jaffa Gate about a week later, although we felt safe because troops patrolled the maze of narrow alleyways inside the walls.

We were overwhelmed by the sights and sounds of the bustling *souk* or market. Stalls brimmed with exotic goods, dresses with intricately hand-stitched embroidery and beautifully crafted pieces of jewellery. Paprika, cumin, cardamon, za'atar and other brightly coloured spices in large open sacks emitted intoxicating aromas. Traces of familiar and strange languages I'd never encountered before mingled with shouted conversations of stall holders in Arabic. Although the *souk* merchants belonged to the losing side, any resentment towards the Jews now exploring their new world was diluted by pragmatism. Given the circumstances, they were reasonably hospitable.

Finally, after navigating the Old City's labyrinth, we reached the Western Wall, rising 60 feet above us and glistening in the sun. Although partially hidden by the dilapidated shacks propped against it, amid reeking donkey dunghills and piles of garbage, the monument was awe-inspiring. I quietly mouthed an ancient prayer known as '*Sheheheyanu*': 'Blessed are You, Lord, our God, King of the Universe, who has granted us life and sustained us and allowed us to arrive at this time'.

For over 1,500 years, Jews have recited the *Sheheheyanu* to express gratitude for new and unusual experiences. It is hard to describe just how sublime this moment was, standing there with Maier, holding our children's hands, before the Western Wall. At last, we, as a people, were able to pray where, for nearly two millennia, our ancestors had also petitioned God.

I felt immense gratitude and pride to be there with my family, touching those giant, ancient stones. As I stood in reverence and silence, I realized the wall represented part of my identity. It was a testament to Jewish strength, tenacity and chutzpah. Furthermore, it was vindication, and a far cry from being defined by the Nazis as *Untermenschen* – subhumans, parasites and vermin to be annihilated. This felt like another moment of liberation. Not surprisingly, it also felt like home. Confirmation that I belonged.

Not long after peace broke out, we left the *ulpan* and rented a three-bedroom house, 5 miles outside Jerusalem in the Judaean Hills, 2,000 feet above sea level, in a community called Motza. The house nestled in knee-high grass among cedar trees and a small orchard brimming with peaches, apricots, apples and pears. After Manhattan's landscape of concrete, steel and glass, it seemed like paradise.

One morning, a tall figure in a robe and sandals appeared at our door. He didn't say a word. Using his hands, he gestured, 'Can I be of help to you?'

In no time, our garden was pristine. He scythed the grass, pruned the trees and disposed of the rotting fruit on the ground. Ahmad, who lived in a small Arab village without electricity or water, became our gardener, babysitter and friend. He honoured our family by naming his two boys Maier and Gadi.

Maier immersed himself in a niche area of cancer research. At the time, international health bodies and food companies were striving to mitigate the impact of aflatoxins, naturally occurring carcinogenic fungi that grow in hot and humid climates and contaminate a wide range of products, including maize, rice, nuts, spices and cocoa beans. In a project sponsored jointly by the Hadassah Medical Centre and the Hebrew University, Maier and a team of researchers developed a fermentation process to produce aflatoxins in order to help other scientists around the world protect the food supply chain and reduce the risk of cancer.

I took a job at the Hebrew University, teaching English to students who required help to matriculate or qualify for entry to university. One of my pleasures was driving past the Dome of the Rock, with its magnificent golden orb, sparkling in the sun. The Dome meant as much to most of my Arab students as the Western Wall meant to me.

My students came from poor, male-dominated villages. In their traditionally patriarchal world, women were discouraged from studying or teaching. Most were indignant that a woman should be their instructor and expressed their resentment in many ways. Some talked ostentatiously during presentations, others stripped off their shirts, and whenever there was political tension or instability, they tuned into Arabic news on small transistor radios. Although I couldn't understand the language, I was aware that their tone was strident, not least because my students always seemed to get wound up.

Ever since childhood, I had always stood my ground. The habit had served me well, and I saw no reason to change now.

The students settled down once they realized that their test grades would reflect their inattentiveness. I understood them and empathized with their plight. They felt powerless, ineffectual and maybe even scared. Being a minority in a dominant culture is always a challenge. But I'm pleased that some of them became high achievers and went on to obtain advanced degrees.

All the while, family life expanded and improved. My father and Sonia settled in Tel Aviv. Maier's parents, Ruth and Leo, also moved from Brooklyn to Jerusalem. They were now close to both their sons, as Maier's brother, Bunim, lived with his family in Tel Aviv. A few years later, my daughter Itaya was born and we moved into Jerusalem itself, as it was nearer to family and more convenient. There, Maier's parents lived across the street and were able to help us raise the children, while the two of us worked full time. Fridays and holidays were often spent with Papa and Sonia in Tel Aviv, but our favourite activity was going to the beautiful Israeli beaches with Bunim, Davida and their three children Shavit, Boaz and Oded. Jerusalem's safe streets also became the children's playground. At that time, young children even rode buses alone and Risa, Gadi and Itaya would take themselves to activities like their sports teams, karate lessons and horse riding.

Being surrounded by a growing family and a widening circle of friends helped to heal the wounds of the Holocaust. I could never replace those who were lost. But now life had real meaning, especially when a new life came along. The sense of belonging enriched our existence, as did our lifelong friendships.

In retrospect, this time we spent with family and friends in Israel was one of the happiest periods of my life.

Although we enjoyed the sea, Maier and I were more suited to living in Jerusalem than the coast. We adored its complexity and history, the timeless quality of its architecture, the crisp, clear air and brilliant light. Treading its streets, I always had the feeling that the stone houses had been there for eternity and would stand ad infinitum. Our fleeting existence in Jerusalem's continuum was a privilege and we made the most of it. Buildings scarred by bullet holes were a constant reminder that our liberty came at a price. I adored the eclectic blend of Arab women in long, colourful dresses, orthodox Jewish women in modest clothing, religious Jewish men in their unique attire and girls in miniskirts bringing a sense of the swinging Sixties to restaurants, stores and falafel stands amid the aroma of cumin and za'atar.

During downtime from work, we explored the four quarters of the Old City, sharing our curiosity with our children and imbuing them with a sense of history. My favourite site was – and still is – the Burnt House in the Jewish Quarter, which was unearthed not long after the Six Day War. Beneath layers of ash, archaeologists discovered the remains of a priest's house that was set on fire and pillaged by the Romans in the year 70AD The contents of the house were a time capsule from the period when the Western Wall formed part of the Second Temple.

In the Christian Quarter, we wandered along the Via Dolorosa, past the Church of the Holy Sepulchre, supposedly the site of

Christ's crucifixion and burial, inhaling the scent of freshly ground coffee from nearby cafés. In the Armenian Quarter, I always felt a sense of solidarity with the residents who fled the 1915 genocide in which 1.5 million of their ancestors were murdered. In that quarter they produce beautiful hand-painted tiles, mosaics and dishes known around the world.

I admired the entrepreneurial ethic in the bustling bazaars of the Muslim quarter. Our sightseeing tours always ended in the Jewish Quarter, with falafel and a cold drink near the Cardo, an ancient Roman market. Although diverse in character and faith, what united these communities was the thread of spirituality.

Every few weeks or so, we'd drive an hour east from Jerusalem to the Masada National Park in the Judaean Desert. We'd hike to the top of Masada, a rock formation 1,300 feet above sea level. We'd get there at dawn and watch the sun rise over the Dead Sea and Jordan and explore the ruins of King Herod the Great's first-century fortress. After our exertions, we'd cool off by swimming in the pools of Ein Gedi, close to the Dead Sea.

These experiences are a sample of how, by and large, after the Six Day War, life in Israel felt safe and comfortable. The children attended an experimental school, which adopted a new approach to education: they didn't mark the pupils' work because they didn't believe in competition. The children loved the school and flourished. The building was close to the Machane Yehuda *shuk*, a 200-year-old market which Maier and I visited every Friday to buy food for Shabbat (Sabbath).

However, we had to live in a state of permanent vigilance. Part of the new normality was the War of Attrition. For almost three years, Israel and its neighbours engaged in frequent tit-for-tat raids, as our Arab neighbours attempted to destabilize Israel and undermine its security with a series of incursions. Still, we took it all in our stride – walking the children to school one day, we passed a bomb squad disarming a device in the middle of our path. We just changed course without thinking and continued on our way. But the children were taught not to pick up toys, food, pens or interesting rocks, even in the playground, because it might be an explosive booby trap. A bulletin board with potential threats was regularly updated and parents organized patrols to monitor the school, classrooms and the grounds for suspicious objects.

And so life went on.

My love for Israel was tempered by one significant area of disappointment: the subject of the Holocaust was seldom raised, even though the country was home to a large number of survivors who migrated in the 1950s with the intention of rebuilding their lives.

Israel's founders had erected a permanent memorial to the Shoah in 1953 (known as Yad Vashem, the beautifully designed remembrance centre was an attraction for people from every country and walk of life), but the Israeli education system discouraged students from visiting it, arguing that the country was too fragile, insecure and vulnerable to teach children about the atrocities that the Jewish people, and possibly even their extended families, had endured.

Israel was trying to develop a new, self-confident, psychologically strong, proud generation, ready and willing to fight to defend their country. Educators claimed that studying the Holocaust could instil self-doubt and undermine the confidence of youth. I was hurt that I could only share my story with other survivors, but I knew many other survivors who agreed with the prevailing sentiment of not addressing the Holocaust. Some of my friends and even my aunts, Ita and Elka, never even shared their experiences with their own children for fear of damaging their egos. Some removed tattoos and never spoke of their past. Consequently, their children only discovered their parents were survivors after they had passed away.

Thankfully, this way of thinking began to change in the 1980s when Israel started teaching the Shoah to high-school students, and today, Holocaust education is core curriculum for all ages. Today, Yom HaShoah, Holocaust Remembrance Day, is observed as a day of mourning and as a pledge to never let it happen again. But back then, I was reminded of the tattooist in Auschwitz telling me to cover my number with a long-sleeved shirt and the teacher in Astoria who told me to forget the Holocaust. I felt the pressure once again and decided to remain silent.

*

It wasn't long before everyone's attention focused on a new conflict. Sirens pierced the air on Saturday 6 October 1973. It was Yom Kippur, the Day of Atonement, the holiest day in the Jewish calendar. Surely this was a mistake, a technical glitch? Galei Tzahal, the national army radio station, assured us that the alarm was genuine, however. Egypt and Syria had launched a coordinated attack to try to reclaim territory they had lost six years earlier. This time, the Israel Defence Forces weren't prepared. Many front-line units were understrength because soldiers weren't at their posts for this High Holy Day. The Egyptians made rapid progress in the Sinai Desert, while the Syrians struggled in the Golan Heights.

Within a few hours, the country had mobilized. Maier reported for reserve duty, taking with him our vehicle, which was requisitioned by the army to help transport the troops. Civilians, young and old, kept the country ticking. Government departments, schools and the post office were mostly staffed by volunteers, supervised by professionals not serving in the armed forces. Even my seventy-year-old father-in-law, Leo Friedman, stepped up to do his part, becoming the local postman.

The conflict lasted three weeks. Fighting was intense. In the Golan Heights, the biggest tank battle took place since the Second World War. The Israelis counter-attacked and destroyed 500 Syrian tanks and armoured vehicles in the Valley of Tears.

Although Israel was ultimately victorious, there was a sense that the country would not always enjoy military superiority.

In human terms, the price was high. Over 2,000 Israelis were killed and many more wounded. Once again, we found ourselves in bomb shelters. This time, I was with my three children aged ten, eight and four. We painted the streetlights and car headlights blue and covered our windows with blackout curtains so as not be targeted by any bombs. The streets were eerily quiet with everyone in their shelters.

Although the war was over fairly quickly, it was six months before Maier was allowed to return home. He was exhausted but returned straight to work. Many Israelis were very angry because prior to the war, the government had been smug, overconfident and had misread the danger signs. The prime minister, Golda Meir, felt responsible and resigned, and the economy tanked because of high inflation and the international oil embargo, imposed by Arab oil producers to create leverage in the wake of the war.

I gave birth to a son – Shani. I had always thought I would have six children, one for every million Jews murdered in the Holocaust. But after having two girls and two boys, we decided that our family was complete.

Unfortunately around this time, Maier's project lost funding and eventually closed. My department at the university also cut its staff by 50 per cent and I found myself jobless. Maier took a position in the solar-energy industry, and I enrolled at the Hebrew University. We desperately tried to hold on, but when Maier was offered a post back in the United States we weighed our options, and reluctantly decided, for financial reasons, that we should pack up and leave Israel after ten happy, fulfilling years. As we said farewell with heavy hearts, we promised our friends, family and ourselves that we would be back in three short years.

CHAPTER TWENTY-TWO

WE REMEMBER

New Jersey, USA, 1977

Age thirty-nine

I never imagined how distressing it would be to leave Israel. Even though we had spent many rewarding years in America, returning to the United States was something of a culture shock and required some major adjustments, not just for me, but also my family. The instant we landed in cold, wet Newark, New Jersey, I found myself pining for the sunshine and warmth of Jerusalem, along with the light, which infused colours with a vibrancy rarely replicated in the latitudes of the north-eastern United States.

The sound of America was so different, too. Sirens, air-conditioning units, construction sites and traffic all conspired to create a wall of sound that reverberated off the skyscrapers. As the days passed, I yearned for the more human scale of Jerusalem's soundscape, where the stones seemed to absorb the bustle of its narrow, ancient streets. I craved the aromas of Middle Eastern spices and cooking and missed wearing the invisible cloak of history that came from living in one of the cradles of civilization.

Over time, I became acclimatized to the sensory changes. But I struggled with the spiritual differences. We had lived an emotionally invested life for ten years in a country created as a haven for my people. America, on the other hand, is the great melting pot.

When I try to explain the reasons for how I felt, inevitably, I fall back on the Holocaust and Auschwitz, because those experiences in my formative years forged the way for almost every thought I have and every action I take. I love and respect the United States. I believe in almost everything this nation stands for, and I will forever be grateful for the sanctuary it provided, along with my education, and the gift of my husband, Maier, and my family. But I was unable to disconnect from Israel. I ran up enormous phone bills calling my friends every day, pumping them for news. I devoured coverage of Israel's culture, politics and social issues.

We bought a small three-bedroom house in Highland Park, a pleasant town on the banks of the Raritan river near Rutgers University in New Jersey. In material terms we were comfortable, but I was overwhelmed by feelings of emptiness and uselessness.

One spring day, I was wandering with my youngest child, Shani, on the grounds of Rutgers. Crowds of enthusiastic young people were milling about the campus. I was pushing Shani in his stroller and was very much the odd person out. It was registration day, and students were signing up for classes in their first semester. My interest was piqued, and as I entered the building, a guidance counsellor assumed I had come to register and ushered me into a room. Within forty-five minutes, she had convinced me to enrol at the School of Social Work. She said my age and background virtually guaranteed a full scholarship if I studied gerontology – the effect of ageing on the individual and society. It was an epiphany; a moment of recognition that a portal to a new direction had opened.

Although I had started out with a bachelor's degree in psychology, my love of literature and interest in Richard Wright had diverted me from what I now believed was my true vocation. That day felt like both kismet and serendipity. I was receiving a gift that would enable me to work with vulnerable, fragile, elderly people – the very same segment of the population targeted by Hitler at the start of the war because he deemed them to be worthless. As a child, I had hardly known anyone over the age of fifty. My new life would introduce me to a diverse group of people weighed down by a broad range of challenges.

During my internship at a nursing home, I met a lovely eighty-nine-year-old woman who would sit wrapped up in a hat and coat next to a packed suitcase. She was waiting to be picked up by her son. She had been waiting for three years. He had died five years previously. I sat with her, we talked about the life she'd had with her son and she seemed to relax. Eventually, she stopped dressing up for the trip that never came and accepted that he was gone.

I remember another senior who was convinced she was being poisoned and, as a result, hardly ate anything. With staff approval, I brought in food which we ate together. Proving that her food had not been tampered with enabled her paranoia to gradually subside. Another elderly resident was constantly teetering on the edge of depression. Being outside in the fresh air seemed to keep the darkness at bay. We walked around the grounds together as often as we could, and the experience lifted his spirits.

The care that I was providing and the difference I was making were a revelation to me. And there was a reciprocal effect. I felt much less useless.

With Maier's moral and practical support over three years – often typing my papers and covering my household chores – I earned a master's in social work, gerontology and counselling.

A week after graduating, I began working on a home-care programme for the elderly at a Jewish Family Service – a non-profit agency which helped people regardless of their religion. It was an eye opener. I learned more from my clients than I ever thought possible. They unburdened themselves about past traumas, fear of illness, death, abandonment and destitution. Often, all I could do was sit and listen. But just being there, I believe, is a key dynamic of the healing process. A person can change their self-image once they understand that they are truly being seen, heard and valued. I encouraged my clients to think about their past achievements and to concentrate on their strengths. Recovery wasn't instant. But after several months of visits, there were noticeable signs of improvement. Those who had been listless and indifferent became more engaged, dressing up smartly for our sessions. They opened up more about their pasts and seemed to grow as people, deriving confidence and pleasure from accomplishments earlier in their lives.

One of my unforgettable clients was a ninety-two-year-old former lawyer. Immaculately dressed, tall, if a little stooped, he had been living alone and increasingly needed help to maintain his independence. Over a cup of tea, the lawyer shared his background with me. He had emigrated to America all alone after the Second World War. He retrieved a photo album full of pre-war pictures of his wife and children in his law office in Hungary. All perished in the Holocaust.

'Have you ever heard of Auschwitz?' he asked, uncovering a large tattoo on his forearm.

I didn't say anything. I simply rolled up my left sleeve.

'You are my family now,' he wept.

He clutched my hand as if he'd found a lost treasure and we cried together.

I don't often share my past with my clients, but sometimes I do when I feel it's appropriate. For the next year, I made home visits to the lawyer where we discussed not just his grief, but also his strength. He passed away in a nursing home. In his will, he left me a beautifully carved family heirloom desk that he had brought from Hungary. It came with a note: 'From my family and for my family. Keep it always and remember me.'

The desk is in my home in Highland Park. I sat there as I worked on this book. The desk will stay in my family as a reminder of the lost generations.

A few years later, during my autumn visit to Israel, I went to see another man who was alone with his memories: my father. He had lost his second wife, Sonia, three years earlier and was very lonely. I missed my return flight back to the US and, fortunately, was able to spend an unexpected additional twenty-four hours with him. We went to the bank together and then to the cemetery where he showed me his plot. With nothing else planned, we passed the rest of the time just talking and reminiscing.

At one point, he went to the bookshelf and reached for a heavy leather-bound volume. The spine was nearly 3 inches thick. Still vigorous at seventy-two, his fingers had no trouble pulling the *Yizkor* book clear, even though it weighed nearly 10 pounds. A low evening sun streamed through the window of the small apartment in Tel Aviv. Dust particles sparkled in a shaft of light, illuminating his favourite chair. Outside, the traffic hummed as always. Papa placed the book on the armrest and sat down heavily.

I sat down opposite him and smiled. Smart in a V-neck

sweater and blue shirt, he hadn't changed clothes since we'd visited the bank manager a few hours earlier.

'This is my only daughter,' he had told the man. 'Please treat her well if something should happen.'

I knew why Papa was troubled. He was six months shy of his seventy-third birthday. When he was ten years old, a gypsy, as the Roma were then known, predicted that he would die at seventy-two. The prophecy had sustained him through the war. In his darkest moments – and they were legion – Papa clung to the belief that he would survive. If he could avoid being killed, then maybe he could save the lives of Mama and me. Protecting us was his abiding motivation for staying alive and guided every decision he was forced to take.

My father opened the book and looked at me with sadness. I have Mama's eyes. I reminded him of her. She was his great love.

'Read it to me Papa,' I said.

Papa opened the cover. His fingers felt for the edges of the well-worn pages in the middle of the book. He had read this segment many times before. He still had that mellifluous tenor voice that had sung popular melodies and delivered fine speeches when he was an actor in his youth. It was no longer as powerful – age had added a brittle edge – but it was still easy on the ear.

Papa swallowed hard and his eyes moistened. I looked at him and my own eyes prickled. He had been alone with his terrible memories for so long. I was glad I was there to share them. And to remember as well.

He began to read aloud in Yiddish, His delivery and intonation were perfect. It was almost a stage reading.

'We were cut off from the outside world. Any sort of travel to a nearby town or village was strictly forbidden . . . There were rumours that the deportees were sent to labour camps in Germany. The word "concentration camps" was also heard . . . a feeling reigned that something terrible was about to happen. Something compared to which, life in the ghetto was child's play.'

Dusk was falling hard now. But Papa read on without the need for electric light. Tears trickled unchecked down the creases of his cheeks. My face was damp as well. Neither of us wanted to stem the flow. Together, we yielded to the torrent, springing from the groundwater of our past.

My father didn't finish reading the complete story. We sat in the dark for a while. Then he stood up, went to the kitchen and brewed some tea. His sadness lifted a little.

'There's a woman I rather like,' he said. 'I am thinking about asking her to marry me. I've been so lonely since Sonia died three years ago. I can't stand the loneliness, especially with you living so far away. I'm not going to ask her yet. I'm thinking of spending the holidays in a hotel with friends.'

'Papa, I'm so happy for you,' I replied. 'I wish I could spend the holidays with you, but I have to go. My plane leaves at midnight.'

The taxi came and took me to Ben Gurion airport. It was the

last time the two of us saw each other. The Roma prediction came true. Born in 1910, my father died in 1983, aged seventy-two.

Mourning my father, I threw myself into my work. Several years later, I became the director of a smaller, financially strapped Jewish Family Service providing a wide range of programmes. It was one of the most satisfying experiences of my professional life. The Board of Directors and I were constantly creating innovative ways of fund-raising to keep our programmes going, including counselling, services for the elderly, jail visitations, employment services and mentoring programmes. The Jewish Family Service's Café Europa programme, for example, enabled lonely, socially isolated Holocaust survivors to connect with each other and find companionship.

As a former refugee, I was keen to help other fugitives from tyranny. Seventy-five refugees escaping life-threatening anti-Semitism in the Soviet Union were given shelter, food, English lessons and toys for the children. We sprang into action when Albanians and Serbs fought a brief war in Kosovo. Some arrived with nothing but a plastic bag of essentials. Always at the back of my mind was the image of me as a child entering New York Harbor on the refugee ship from Europe. This new generation of asylum seekers deserved the same opportunities as I had.

In 1998, I received an urgent call from my doctor. I had stage-two breast cancer, required surgery and needed to start treatment immediately. Though I had experienced life struggles before, this was a completely new battleground for me. My own body was attacking me this time. With excellent medical care and family support, however, I was able to go into remission within a year and return to full-time work. I felt as if I'd survived again.

Days after the shocking attack on the World Trade Center on 11 September 2001, our small office was flooded with young Jewish and non-Jewish families fleeing Manhattan, trying to find shelter in New Jersey. We offered counselling and helped them figure out new lives. One young woman was clutching the hand of her three-year-old daughter. 'I was picking up my daughter from the nursery across the street from the towers as they crumbled and people were jumping to their deaths,' she said. 'I thought the US was under attack. Just in case my daughter and I would be separated, I put her name and my phone number on her back in lipstick so she could be found.' We found her temporary accommodation and psychological support, until she was ready to return to New York.

A week after the attack, together with a colleague, I went to Manhattan to ease the anguish of other survivors. We'd been asked to help fifteen male executives who were traumatized after identifying the remains of their co-workers. In common with every other American, 9/11 was an unbelievable new experience for me; warfare at its most unconventional, but warfare just the same. At first, I stood in front of the shell-shocked ensemble, not knowing what to say. But then I began to talk about my war and what had happened to me, to let them know that I understood what they were going through.

It was as if a dam had been breached. Bottled-up emotions burst forth. They wept, removed their jackets, loosened their ties and began to express shock, disbelief, pain and guilt that so many of their close colleagues had been killed, while somehow, they had escaped. I understood, and I identified quite strongly with their emotions. As we talked, I tried to provide them with the hope that in time, they would recover, just as I have.

The group counselling session was interspersed with spiritual songs, led by one of the executives who was a church minister. The communal singing also helped to ease their pain. After several hours, some came to acknowledge that gratitude at having survived was a more constructive emotion than guilt. That was progress. On the way home to New Jersey, my colleague and I discussed the strength needed to get by in life and decided to set up support groups for people affected by the terrorist attack. That project lasted for years.

I only played a small part in the aftermath of 9/11. But the experience reinforced my conviction that sharing my Holocaust story publicly could be a powerful force. Talking about it not only reminds people of the evil that took place, but can also help them to see the ability in each of us to overcome.

I began public speaking in the early 1990s when I was

fifty-four years old. My first engagement was at a school, with an audience of 200 children aged twelve to fourteen. I was outlining how my mother had sacrificed so much for me. An image of Mama floated in front of my eyes as I described her giving me her last piece of bread and saying, 'I'm not hungry'.

Suddenly, I started crying. Me. The girl who couldn't and wouldn't cry in Auschwitz. I was extraordinarily embarrassed by my tears, and to my surprise, the children began applauding. I was deeply touched by their response and by the letters that followed, especially one from a twelve-year-old girl. 'Mrs Friedman,' she wrote. 'I'm sorry your experience was difficult to share but thank you. I now know how important family is. I will be nicer to my brother.'

The reaction from the students spurred me on to share my experiences far and wide. Supported by Maier, I spoke at synagogues, churches, colleges and prisons, where even the toughest criminals could be moved, learn something about themselves and perhaps change as a result.

'I'm not Jewish and I knew nothing about the Holocaust,' wrote one inmate. 'But I never realized before just what violence and cruelty can do. I am in prison because of my own actions but you were imprisoned by blind prejudice and hatred.'

The need to remind people to be vigilant about anti-Semitism and hatred is constant. The Raritan Valley Community College near my home in New Jersey established the Institute of Holocaust and Genocide Studies in 1981. I joined the committee to bolster their mission to educate students and others about people's capacity for inhumanity and injustice, as well as the importance of nurturing compassion and resilience. I believe passionately in sharing the lessons of the Holocaust. Maybe if one can teach people to identify the danger signals, there's a chance of preventing another round of genocide.

Every year, thousands of students come to the college to hear survivors share their stories. Invariably, a flood of letters follows, with young people unburdening themselves of a multitude of personal struggles, including parental divorce, bereavement and bullying. Regardless of race, creed or sexual orientation, people have the same need for intimacy, inclusion and safety. At speaking engagements across the country, I have tried to use my story of survival to instil audiences with hope, courage and self-confidence. They often seek answers to life's fundamental questions. They've asked whether I believe in God, if I could trust people or whether I could forgive.

I answer as honestly as I can. I do believe in God but not necessarily the biblical one. Trust is essential and I never lost my faith in humanity, despite my experiences. As for forgiveness – in Judaism, only the living can forgive. I have no authority to forgive on behalf of those who have been slaughtered.

We all hope to be remembered by family, friends and colleagues. We write books, build monuments and establish institutions to attest to our existence. But the murdered millions of the Holocaust left few traces. An inferno engulfed everything about them, including their legacies. I speak to honour and remember mothers, fathers, children and grandparents who went to their deaths because of our religion. I'm always guided by the scene witnessed by my father in Tomaszów Mazowiecki, as a rabbi climbed into a cattle car to Treblinka.

'Save yourself, my sons,' the rabbi had implored. 'And remember me.'

I fervently hope my efforts have not been in vain and that my audiences will keep the memory of the Shoah alive. There has, however, been a price for committing to a life of remembrance. After my traumatic childhood, I have constantly sought inner peace. But my tranquillity has been disturbed throughout adult life by nightmares of being hungry, chased and shot. As my family grew, so did the nightmares, as I dreamed about my children facing the same terrors that eliminated their ancestors.

There were other unintended consequences that occurred as a result of my history and the path I chose. I was a complicated mother and parenting was a challenge. Having had neither a conventional childhood nor a conventional mother, I had to develop my own style. My mother's ideas of exposing me to the reality of life were always foremost in my mind. Many survivors protect their children by not exposing them, but I shared my own story with Risa, Gadi, Itaya and Shani as soon as they were mature enough and the timing was appropriate.

My emphasis, however, was never on the horrors I witnessed and experienced, but on their grandparents' bravery and ingenuity during that time. They would never meet my mother, so I wanted them to know her through me. Living in Israel – a country surrounded by enemies – was very conducive to helping them face reality. It took strength and determination for us to live fearlessly. They learned to be vigilant, self-protective and self-sufficient in both school and our home. We had very few rules for the children. They could stay up as late as they wanted to, as long as they made it to school the next morning. If their grades were good and they were home for dinner, they were pretty much free to spend their days as they chose. For us, this type of parenting fostered trust and a relaxed home atmosphere.

When we returned to the US in 1977, we announced that ours would be a no-television home, as we did not want to expose the children to America's materialism and consumerism. Our dinner-time discussions always started with recounting our days. We would invariably turn to politics and current events, but we would often end on a topic related to Judaism, Zionism and social justice. Subjects close to our heart.

The time I spent working and sharing my story meant less time for my family. They were never anything other than supportive, however, and though I never missed a graduation or recital, Maier was the one who drove the children to most soccer practices, doctor visits and parent–teacher conferences. He loved it, and especially enjoyed just playing with the children when they were young, which is something I never learned to do.

He was truly a Renaissance man. Maier not only had a Ph.D.

from Columbia in biochemical engineering and two master's from the Massachusetts Institute of Technology in nuclear engineering, but he also loved music, art, literature, politics and puzzles. To him, problems were just engineering challenges and puzzles could always be solved with the proper tool, method and sense of humour. He spent countless hours teaching, sharing and theorizing with the children about everything from their latest homework assignments to the current state of the world.

Maier's sudden passing on 31 March 2020 left an irreplaceable void for the entire family. But I draw solace from the fact that were he here today, I know he would be as proud as I am of our children and grandchildren.

Maybe our arrangement was unconventional for the time, but we made it work. Though I am biased, I believe my children have all grown into mature, responsible, kind and thoughtful adults. I consider them my four miracles, added to my own one of survival. They were born in defiance of Hitler's plan to exterminate our people and are themselves raising my eight grandchildren to uphold their values and to become stewards of Jewish culture. I am comforted in the knowledge that they will continue telling my story and remember the victims, especially the 1.5 million murdered children whose contributions to the world have been lost for ever.

When I walked out of the Gate of Death in 1945, I thought I'd never set eyes on the place again. However, I have returned to

Auschwitz on five occasions, always for compelling reasons. It required considerable fortitude to step back in time, but I felt the need to share my experiences with my children. The first time, my elder son, Gadi, flew in from Israel and having him by my side was reassuring.

As I was a former prisoner, the guards allowed us special access and I was able to actually show Gadi where the stories that I have shared in this book took place. It was extremely emotional, but it was imperative to hand down both my family and our people's history, so it could start its onward journey to lives that hadn't even started yet.

Once I had overcome my initial hesitancy, it became easier to go back. The second time, I took a group of American Jewish teenagers and acted as their guide. Then, I returned to contribute to a documentary for WGVU, a Michigan-based public television station. I brought my daughter Itaya, and we were accompanied by another survivor from Tomaszów Mazowiecki and her son. On this occasion, we visited Tomaszów and saw the ghetto apartment where I hid under the table, and the cellar where my mother and I lived after the liberation of Auschwitz.

The most memorable trip was the one on which I brought four of my grandchildren, two sets of twins, fifteen-year-old Ari and Eitan, and Noah and Aron, both eleven. In Auschwitz, we had an excellent guide who was sensitive to the children, as she described the experiments that the Angel of Death, Dr Josef Mengele, performed on twins. As I described earlier, Mengele's laboratory was separated from my barrack block by just a barbed-wire fence. My building was burned to the ground as the Germans liquidated Birkenau to cover up their crimes. All that remained were the foundations. I worked out where I had slept and showed the twins where the brick oven once stood. I showed them where I was tattooed and where I dragged the body of the girl who died of starvation in bed beside me during the night.

A lone, symbolic cattle car sits on the railway track where the platform used to be. There, I helped my grandchildren visualize how I stood swaying for thirty-six hours propped up by the women around me. We descended the steps to the waiting room of the gas chamber where I stood naked for hours, waiting to die. I showed them the towering piles of hair and baby shoes, so they could understand the enormity of the crimes committed there. We all said *Kaddish* over ashes and cried. It was hard for them, but they are now my witnesses and will tell the story of our people when my generation is gone.

Accompanied by my daughter-in-law, Sarah, my last visit in January 2020, for the seventy-fifth anniversary of liberation, was genuinely uplifting. Hundreds of survivors and their families came together from all over the world. Not to lament or cry or discuss atrocities. They came to celebrate the human spirit and the lives they had lived. Some wore blue-and-white-striped concentration-camp uniforms as a badge of honour. It seemed strange to see those uniforms clean and freshly pressed. Some of us were strong enough to walk unaided. Others, pulling oxygen tanks, on crutches and in wheelchairs, entered slowly through the infamous *Arbeit Macht Frei* gate, demonstrating the determination that had helped them survive all those years before. The stories we shared over our meals together were of triumphs and endurance, not of past suffering.

Humanity often faces extraordinarily difficult challenges that seem to be never-ending. But I believe we are all born with natural resilience. The ability to overcome is within each and every one of us.

> It matters not how strait the gate,
> How charged with punishments the scroll,
> I am the master of my fate,
> I am the captain of my soul.
>
> 'Invictus' by William Ernest Henley, 1875

TOVA'S ACKNOWLEDGMENTS

I am truly indebted to all my family and friends who have been a part of my life and who have, therefore, contributed directly or indirectly to this book.

First, I would like to thank my mother, Reizel, who, at the worst of times, instilled in me self-reliance, inner strength and the will to survive. She imbued me with love, trust and respect for others, enabling me to marry and create my own family.

To my father, who taught me to never be a bystander and to confront evil by any means. He showed me how to find the joy in life through his singing and acting and how to celebrate every Jewish occasion with beauty and love. And to his wife, Sonia, who was a wonderful partner and a terrific grandmother to my children.

To Maier, my late husband of sixty years, who was the first person to captivate me when I came from Europe, and who continued teaching me love, trust and loyalty to family and Israel throughout his life. He was a wonderful father, never missed a

Shoah presentation and was both my greatest advocate and my greatest critic. Together, we built a life filled with Judaism, family and love. I will miss you for ever.

To Maier's family in Israel and in the US, who took me in as one of their own and became my family with whom we celebrated the joys and sorrows of life. Thank you to the Ben Chorins, the Masseys and the Schneidermans. You gave me the family I never had.

To my four amazing children and my eight wonderful grandchildren.

To my eldest daughter, Risa (Ruth), and to her beautiful girls, Sarah Esther and Dvora Chana Leiba, thank you for continuing the beautiful traditional Hasidic Jewish life for which my grandparents were murdered. Your life is a testament of human strength and resilience over those who tried to destroy us.

To my son Gadi, who was my first child to return to Auschwitz with me and acted as my emotional support. And to his wife, Sarah, who accompanied me to Auschwitz on the seventy-fifth commemoration of the Liberation, as we walked together through Birkenau and the crematorium. As I watch the growth and development of your two children, Avigail and Gil, I feel a great joy and pride, as I see them becoming responsible, kind and loving adults. I know they will not be bystanders, as they already have participated in various social causes. And to Ira and Lucille, thank you for always being there for me.

To my daughter Itaya, who not only kept me sane during the

first few months following Maier's death, but also accompanied me to several child-survivor conferences over the years. Itaya travelled with me to Poland to trace my family's history with WGVU-TV and participated in several educational documentaries for colleges and high schools. Thank you for all the support with telling my story, and for helping me confront my past. Thank you also for raising and engaging your four amazing children Eitan, Ari, Aron and Noah, who are all sensitive, intelligent, loving and passionate for Israel. Extra thanks to Aron, for bringing my story to millions of TikTok viewers and for educating many young people who would otherwise not have heard about the Shoah.

To my youngest son, Shani, who has been instrumental in helping me write my memoir, and without whose dedication, patience and love this book would not have been written. And to his wife, Joanna, who has kept us both going with her support, suggestions and encouragement.

To my aunts, Ita, Elka and Helen. As my father's only siblings who survived the war, you will always be part of my soul, as will be my three cousins, Pearl, Ben, Marty and their children and grandchildren.

To Frieda, who helped clarify some ghetto details and who hosted me and our small group of Tomaszów child survivors on 27 January for many years to reminisce and celebrate our liberation from Auschwitz. And to her Aunt Sophie, who elucidated some details about my family as I was too young to remember.

To Estelle, my first close friend and confidante in America.

Our conversations have spanned seven decades and hopefully many more.

To my Hebrew-school classmates in my first few weeks in America, Simcha and Risa. Thank you for welcoming me and for seventy years of friendship.

To Rebecca, Toby and Florence – my greenhorn friends. Together, we negotiated our new American culture as teenagers and I have appreciated your friendship ever since. Rebecca, I miss you terribly.

To Bonnie, with whom I shared several years at the Girls' Club. Thank you for sharing holidays with my family.

To my very special friends Ruth and Yaakov. You have embodied Ben Gurion's dream to 'make the desert bloom' in Mitzpe Ramon, Israel. You have been by my side through all our ups and downs and I cannot imagine my life without your love, support and encouragement.

To my friends Irris, Dalia, Ruth, Netta and Gabi. Thank you for enriching my Israeli experience and for the many years of friendship.

To Julie, Vera, David, Joy and your partners in New Jersey. Thank you for sharing my joy in Israeli folk dancing and your continuous friendship through the years.

To Pat and Dan, and Ruth and Eugene. When new friends feel like old friends, it's a gift.

To my local Jewish community and the Conservative Temple. Thank you for making me feel at home for so many years.

To Jewish Family Service, I am grateful to everyone with whom

I have worked and for the opportunity to have served both as a director and as a therapist. Special thank you to Steve, Linda, Ruth, Nancy and Susan who enabled me to be an effective Director and to my special friend and colleague Beatrix who has taught me so much. To Jerry, the Director and to Joan and Jean Marie, thank you for making it possible for me to continue being productive.

To Sir Ben Kingsley, thank you for writing such a heart-warming foreword to my biography and for spending time with me. Your portrayal of Holocaust characters is unforgettable and we, the survivors, are grateful and indebted to you.

To Dr Lillian Kaplan, my psychiatrist, who was the first person with whom I felt safe enough to cry. You will never realize the great impact you had on my life. You died too early and I miss you greatly.

To Dr Michael Nissenblatt, my oncologist and healer, who promised me a long life, and kept his promise.

To Michael Walenta the General Manager of WGVU-TV Public Media, Ken Kolbe, Assistant Manager and Phil Lane, Product Manager for our amazing experience filming in Poland that enabled me to find and share with my daughter the haunts of my past, including my bunk in Auschwitz and the basement apartment where I lived with my mother after the war. Your sensitivity allowed me to relive those experiences without any trauma.

To Milton Nieuwsma – it was your guidance and support that sparked in me the will to write my memoir. The first book we wrote together started my journey.

To my tattooist in Birkenau, your kind words to a frightened six-year-old resonate even today: 'I'll give you a very neat number. If you ever survive, you can buy a blouse with a long sleeve and nobody will know what happened to you.' It has been seventy-eight years since you were murdered, but I still remember you.

I am indebted to the late Dr Michael G. Kesler for the extensive research in his book *The Remnant* on the Displaced Persons camp in Landsberg am Lech where we both resided.

To all the synagogues, churches, schools, organizations and especially the Institute for Holocaust and Genocide Studies at Raritan Valley Community College. Thank you for inviting me to share my story of the Shoah. The audience letters I received showed that my story resonated.

Malcolm and I are indebted to the publishers on both sides of the Atlantic for placing their trust in us and for helping us bring this book to fruition. It has been a joy to work with both Katy Follain of Quercus Books in London and Peter Joseph of Hanover Square in New York. Their passion for the book has been inspirational.

We could not have done this without the negotiating skills of our agent, Adam Gauntlett, at Peters Fraser and Dunlop and his colleagues in the international department, Becky Wearmouth, Lucy Barry and Antonia Kasoulidou.

To Malcolm, whose vision inspired this book. I would never have accomplished this without your determination to see it to completion.

MALCOLM'S ACKNOWLEDGMENTS

It has been a privilege to help Tova bring her incredible life story to such a potentially large international audience.

But it would have been a far more difficult task without the assistance and support of some wonderful people.

First, I must thank Milton Nieuwsma, journalist, film writer and author of *Surviving Auschwitz: Children of the Shoah* for the most vital connection of all. Milt introduced me to Tova before I travelled to Auschwitz for the PBS Newshour to cover the seventy-fifth anniversary of the liberation. Throughout the preparation of this book, Milt has been a rock of support, wisdom and a great sounding board.

I am indebted to Therkel Straede, Professor of Contemporary History at the University of Southern Denmark, and a leading Scandinavian expert on the Holocaust. Therkel pointed me towards the most pertinent literature that enabled me to place Tova's memories in a historical timeline. His attention to detail was critical in terms of fact checking and correcting my initial errors.

I am grateful for the hand of friendship offered by Professor Yoel Yaari, a neuroscientist at the Hebrew University Faculty of Medicine in Jerusalem, whose mother, Bella Hazan was a courier for the Jewish resistance in Poland during the Nazi occupation. She was tortured by the Gestapo, never gave up her secrets and survived two and a half years' incarceration in Auschwitz. Yoel has been a font of critical information and I'm glad that he applied a brain specialist's precision when analysing my prose.

Pivotal components of this narrative would been impossible without the perspective of Dr Tony Bernard of Sydney Australia, whose grandfather was a member of the *Judenrat* in Tomaszów Mazowiecki, and whose father, Dr Henry Bernard, was a member of the Jewish police force in the ghetto at the same time as Machel Grossman. Before he died, Dr Bernard sat down with Tony and recorded his life story. The resulting tussle with his conscience has been turned into a remarkable book called *The Ghost Tattoo*, published by Allen and Unwin in Australia.

Special thanks are due to Dr Justyna Biernat of the Spaces of Memory Foundation, working to chronicle the dark past of Tomaszów Mazowiecki. Justyna furnished me with some key documents, maps and photographs, which brought much of the occupation back to life. The foundation relies on donations to survive, and Justyna would welcome contributions and purchases of her excellent short history, *Black Silhouettes* at www.pasazepamieci.pl

I'm grateful to my good friend Freddie Spence who, among their diverse talents, is a trauma specialist. Freddie gave me some useful pointers about unlocking nuggets of information buried within the amygdala, the almond-shaped part of the brain where emotions are remembered, analyzed, and attached to associations.

One of the most invaluable resources that helped us construct this memoir was the contribution to the *Yizkor* book of Machel Grossman, Tova's father. For giving us permission to quote liberally from Machel's writing, I am indebted to JewishGen, the global home of Jewish Genealogy, which owns the translation. I am also grateful for the generosity of Kirsten Gradel, widow of Morris Gradel, a distinguished Yiddish and Hebrew linguist, who translated Machel's chilling description of the liquidation of the Tomaszów Mazowiecki ghetto.

I honour the poet Henryka Łazowertówna for her poignant work, 'The Little Smuggler', which is contained in *The Song Will Go Unscathed*, an anthology of poems about Jews under German occupation, edited by Michael Borwicz. Tova and I are most grateful to the United States Holocaust Memorial Museum for giving us permission to use the English translation in Patricia Heberer's book, *Children During the Holocaust*.

Thank you also to Natalia Jeziorna of the Mordechaj Gebirtig Memorial in Kraków for allowing us to quote the lyrics of his song 'Reizel'. During the Nazi occupation of Poland, Gebirtig's songs became anthems of resistance. The Memorial is working to keep his legacy alive at https://mordechaj-gebirtig.pl/

From the PBS Newshour, I'm indebted to Executive Producer Sara Just and Foreign Editor Morgan Till, for generously allowing me the time and space to work on this important project.

Thanks to my former BBC colleagues Caroline Wyatt, Rob Watson and Mandy Stokes, for providing encouragement and insightful feedback.

Shani Friedman, Tova's youngest son, has my eternal gratitude for devoting so much time, helping us to get the book over the finishing line and for being such a fine arbitrator when creative differences occasionally arose.

I acknowledge that during the months I was engrossed in the book, my normally cheerful disposition occasionally deserted me. Let the record show my profound gratitude to my wife, Trine Villemann, and our son, Lukas, for their forbearance. I'm so fortunate to have Trine in my corner. She's one of the best journalists I've ever met, and her incisive reading, notes and suggestions were invaluable when it came to sharpening up some of my woollier thoughts.

And to Tova, thank you for trusting me. Mazel tov.